Access Visi...

Catherine Parkerson

que

Access 2 VisiRef

Copyright © 1994 by Que® Corporation.

All rights reserved. Printed in the United States of America. No part of this book may be used or reproduced in any form or by any means, or stored in a database or retrieval system, without prior written permission of the publisher except in the case of brief quotations embodied in critical articles and reviews. Making copies of any part of this book for any purpose other than your own personal use is a violation of United States copyright laws. For information, address Que Corporation, 201 W. 103rd Street, Indianapolis, IN 46290.

Library of Congress Catalog No.: 94-67035

ISBN: 1-56529-863-2

This book is sold *as is*, without warranty of any kind, either express or implied, respecting the contents of this book, including but not limited to implied warranties for the book's quality, performance, merchantability, or fitness for any particular purpose. Neither Que Corporation nor its dealers or distributors shall be liable to the purchaser or any other person or entity with respect to any liability, loss, or damage caused or alleged to have been caused directly or indirectly by this book.

96 95 94   6 5 4 3 2 1

Interpretation of the printing code: the rightmost double-digit number is the year of the book's printing; the rightmost single-digit number, the number of the book's printing. For example, a printing code of 94-1 shows that the first printing of the book occurred in 1994.

Screen reproductions in this book were created with Collage Complete from Inner Media, Inc., Hollis, NH.

Publisher: David P. Ewing

Associate Publisher: Don Roche, Jr.

Managing Editor: Michael Cunningham

Product Marketing Manager: Greg Wiegand

Associate Product Marketing Manager: Stacy Collins

Credits

Publishing Manager
Nancy Stevenson

Acquisitions Editors
Thomas F. Godfrey III
Jenny Watson

Product Directors
Joyce J. Nielsen
Robin Drake

Editor
Michael Cunningham

Technical Editor
Michael Watson

Book Designer
Amy Peppler-Adams

Cover Designers
Dan Armstrong
Amy Peppler-Adams

Production Team
Steve Adams
Claudia Bell
Cameron Booker
Steve Carlin
Teresa Forrester
Joelynn Gifford
Aren Howell
Betty Kish
Bob LaRoche
Beth Lewis
Malinda Lowder
Kaylene Riemen
Caroline Roop
Dennis Sheehan
Mike Thomas
Tina Trettin
Mary Beth Wakefield

Indexer
Michael Hughes

Composed in *Stone Serif* and *MCPdigital* by Que Corporation

About the Author

Cathy Parkerson has extensive experience in the field of computers and education. With degrees in both areas, she has spent 15 years programming, teaching, and writing documentation. She is a consultant specializing in Windows database, spreadsheet, and word processing applications. She is based in the Indianapolis area. She has written numerous manuals and courseware for national corporations and is a technical editor and author for Que Corporation. With her wide range of programming experience and 7,500 hours of classroom instruction experience, Cathy is uniquely qualified to assist clients in needs analysis, systems training, consulting, and support.

Dedication

To my father, Charles A. Peters, who teaches that learning is a life-long process. Thanks, Dad!

Trademark Acknowledgments

All terms mentioned in this book that are known to be trademarks or service marks have been appropriately capitalized. Que Corporation cannot attest to the accuracy of this information. Use of a term in this book should not be regarded as affecting the validity of any trademark or service mark.

Credits

Publishing Manager
Nancy Stevenson

Acquisitions Editors
Thomas F. Godfrey III
Jenny Watson

Product Directors
Joyce J. Nielsen
Robin Drake

Editor
Michael Cunningham

Technical Editor
Michael Watson

Book Designer
Amy Peppler-Adams

Cover Designers
Dan Armstrong
Amy Peppler-Adams

Production Team
Steve Adams
Claudia Bell
Cameron Booker
Steve Carlin
Teresa Forrester
Joelynn Gifford
Aren Howell
Betty Kish
Bob LaRoche
Beth Lewis
Malinda Lowder
Kaylene Riemen
Caroline Roop
Dennis Sheehan
Mike Thomas
Tina Trettin
Mary Beth Wakefield

Indexer
Michael Hughes

Composed in *Stone Serif* and *MCPdigital* by Que Corporation

About the Author

Cathy Parkerson has extensive experience in the field of computers and education. With degrees in both areas, she has spent 15 years programming, teaching, and writing documentation. She is a consultant specializing in Windows database, spreadsheet, and word processing applications. She is based in the Indianapolis area. She has written numerous manuals and courseware for national corporations and is a technical editor and author for Que Corporation. With her wide range of programming experience and 7,500 hours of classroom instruction experience, Cathy is uniquely qualified to assist clients in needs analysis, systems training, consulting, and support.

Dedication

To my father, Charles A. Peters, who teaches that learning is a life-long process. Thanks, Dad!

Trademark Acknowledgments

All terms mentioned in this book that are known to be trademarks or service marks have been appropriately capitalized. Que Corporation cannot attest to the accuracy of this information. Use of a term in this book should not be regarded as affecting the validity of any trademark or service mark.

Contents

Introduction	vi
Basics: Creating, Opening, Closing, Viewing Databases	1
Data Analysis: Graphs and Crosstab Queries	4
Database Management: Compacting, Repairing, Renaming	12
Finding Records: Finding, Filtering, and Sorting	16
Forms—Basics: Designing, Printing, and Editing	21
Forms—Customizing: Headers/Footers and Special Controls	28
Forms—Enhancing: Editing Controls and Special Effects	40
Help: Using On-Line Help and Cue Cards	51
Importing Data: Importing, Exporting, and Attaching	54
Macros: Creating, Running, and Attaching	62
Queries—Action Queries: Update, Make Table, Delete	69
Queries—Advanced Design: Empty Fields and Calculations	83
Queries—Select Query: Creating and Editing	97
Relationships: Defining, Using in Queries and Subforms	110
Reports—Creating: Editing, Previewing, and Printing	119
Reports—Enhancing: Graphics and Mailing Labels	129
Tables—Basics: Creating, Maintaining, and Printing	136
Tables—Designing: Adding Fields and Data Types	145
Tables—Field Properties: Sizes, Formats, and Keys	152
Index	156

How To Use This Book

Welcome to a revolutionary concept in quick references! Unlike traditional pocket references, which usually pack a lot of text on the page but few, if any, illustrations, the *VisiRef* series presents nearly all of its "how to" information v*isually*. You'll find all the essential tasks here, color-coded and organized alphabetically by larger task category. Use the color-coded sections to locate quickly the task you need to find, follow the full-color screen shots to see each step in the process, and then do it yourself. If you're someone who prefers to learn or recall information by being *shown* how a task is accomplished, Que's *VisiRef* series is well matched to your needs. The *VisiRef* books are the perfect complement to today's graphical software. You don't have to read a lot of text to find the reference information you need.

Each page provides the following information:

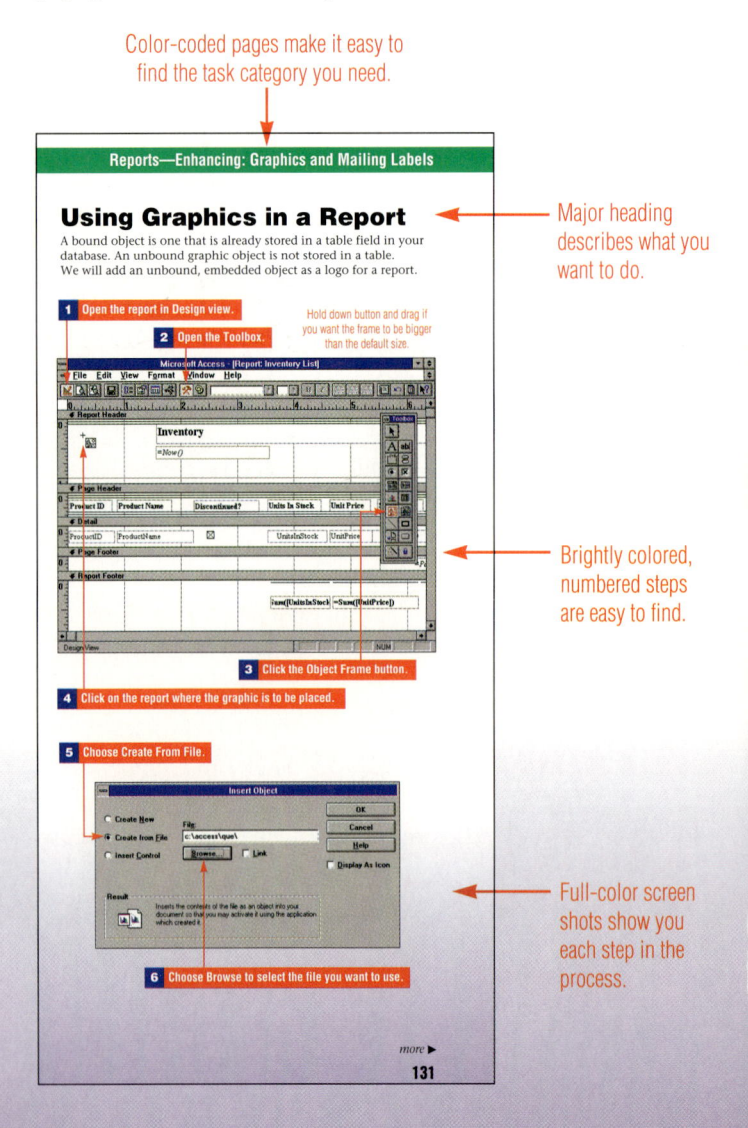

Color-coded pages make it easy to find the task category you need.

Major heading describes what you want to do.

Brightly colored, numbered steps are easy to find.

Full-color screen shots show you each step in the process.

Basics: Creating, Opening, Closing, Viewing Databases

Creating a Database

A database is the container for tables, forms, and reports. These objects store and display data that is related to a particular use, such as information about the products you sell. This could include what the product is and where you get it; also, who your customers are and what they bought.

1 Click on the New Database button.

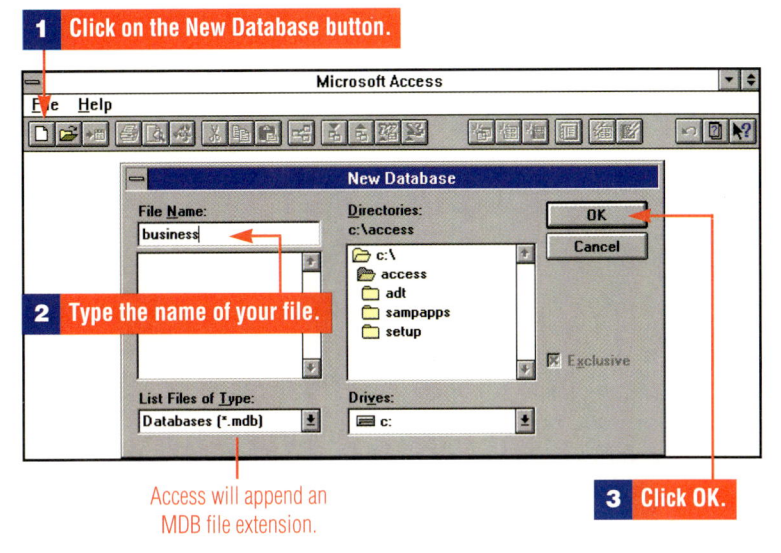

2 Type the name of your file.

Access will append an MDB file extension.

3 Click OK.

Opening and Closing Databases and Objects

Opening a database file retrieves a copy of the file into a database window so that you can work with it. Access allows only one database file open at a time, but you can have multiples of other objects open, such as forms, queries, tables, and reports.

To open a database

1 Click on the Open Database button.

2 Select the Drive containing your database file.

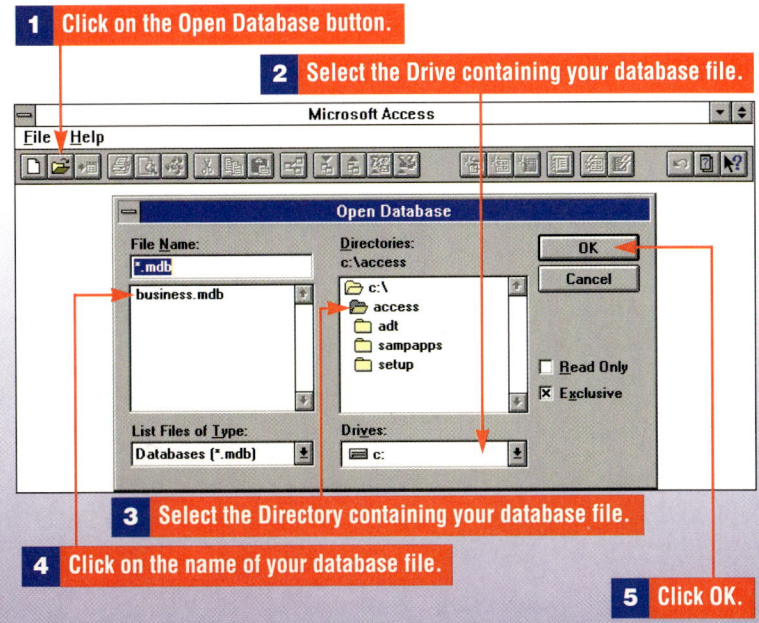

3 Select the Directory containing your database file.

4 Click on the name of your database file.

5 Click OK.

Basics: Creating, Opening, Closing, Viewing Databases

To open a database used recently

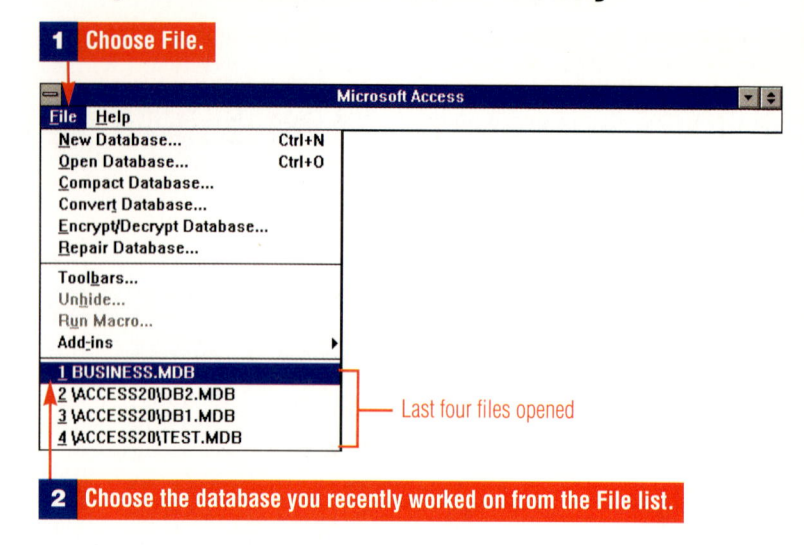

1 Choose File.

```
                    Microsoft Access
File  Help
  New Database...        Ctrl+N
  Open Database...       Ctrl+O
  Compact Database...
  Convert Database...
  Encrypt/Decrypt Database...
  Repair Database...
  Toolbars...
  Unhide...
  Run Macro...
  Add-ins                      ▶
  1 BUSINESS.MDB
  2 \ACCESS20\DB2.MDB
  3 \ACCESS20\DB1.MDB
  4 \ACCESS20\TEST.MDB
```

— Last four files opened

2 Choose the database you recently worked on from the File list.

To close a database

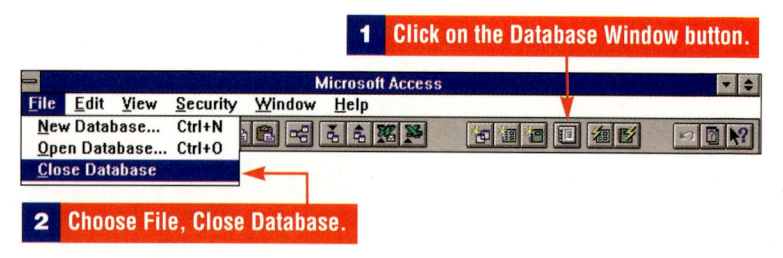

1 Click on the Database Window button.

```
                    Microsoft Access
File  Edit  View  Security  Window  Help
  New Database...  Ctrl+N
  Open Database... Ctrl+O
  Close Database
```

2 Choose File, Close Database.

To open objects in a database

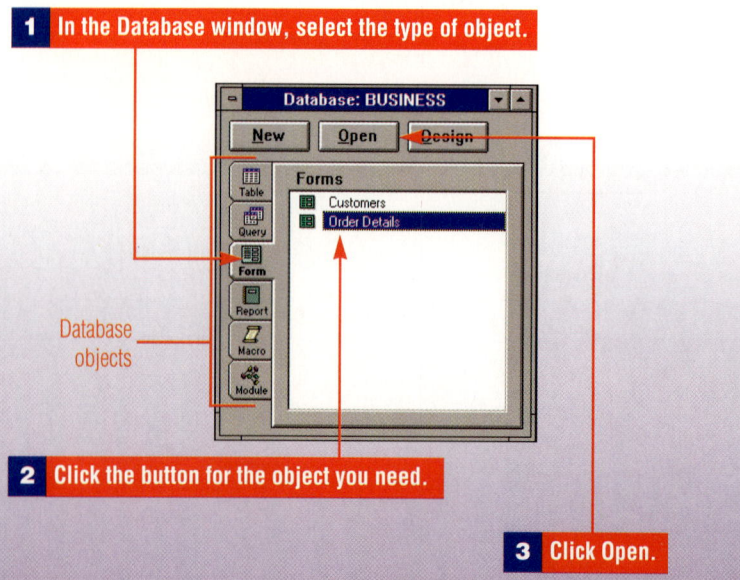

1 In the Database window, select the type of object.

```
        Database: BUSINESS
    New     Open    Design

    Table    Forms
    Query    ▣ Customers
    Form     ▣ Order Details
    Report
    Macro
    Module
```

Database objects

2 Click the button for the object you need.

3 Click Open.

You can also double-click name to open.

Basics: Creating, Opening, Closing, Viewing Databases

To close object windows

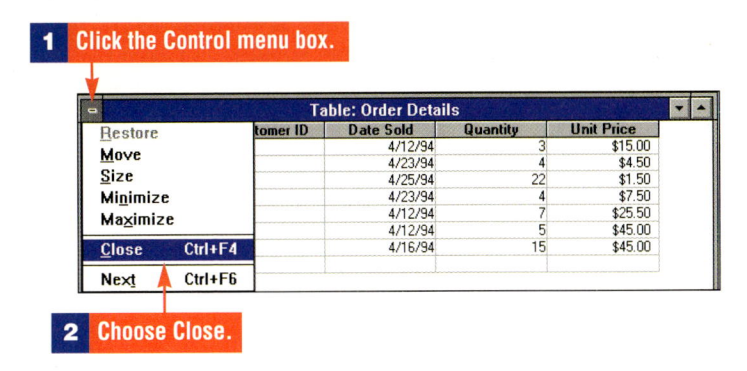

1 Click the Control menu box.

2 Choose Close.

Switching Between Objects and Views

Frequently in Access, you will have multiple windows open because you are working with several objects. All objects can be displayed in different ways. The four views are Design View, Datasheet View, Form View, and Print Preview. Not all objects use all four views.

To move between object windows

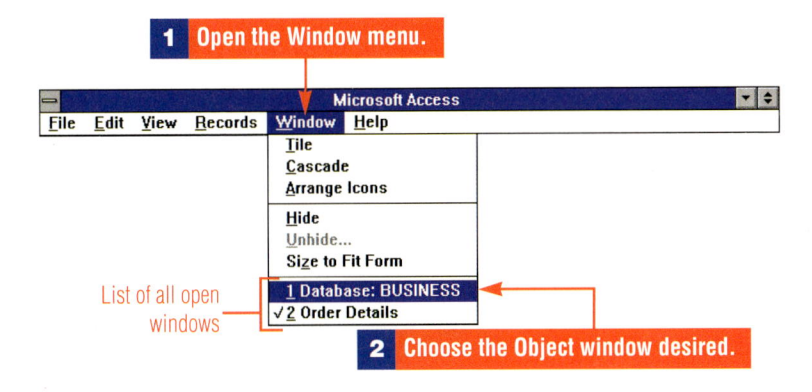

1 Open the Window menu.

List of all open windows

2 Choose the Object window desired.

To switch between views

Design View
Datasheet View
Form View
Print Preview

1 Click on the button for the desired view.

3

Data Analysis: Graphs and Crosstab Queries

Creating Graphs on Forms

You can add a graph to any report or form. Many types of graphs are available: bar and column graphs, line graphs, and even pie graphs. Access can add the numbers, average them, or count the number of records by group.

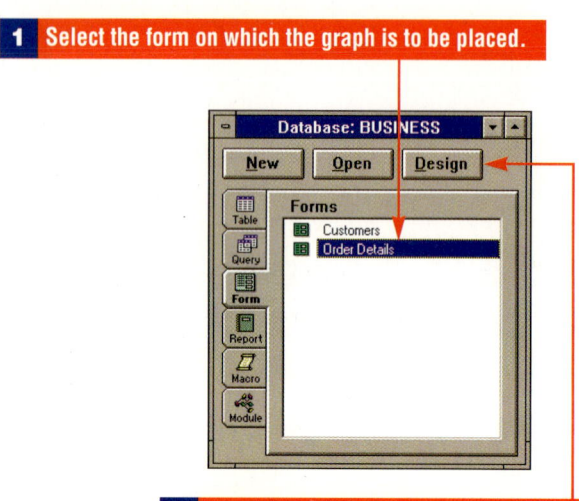

1 Select the form on which the graph is to be placed.

2 Click on Design button to open form in Design view.

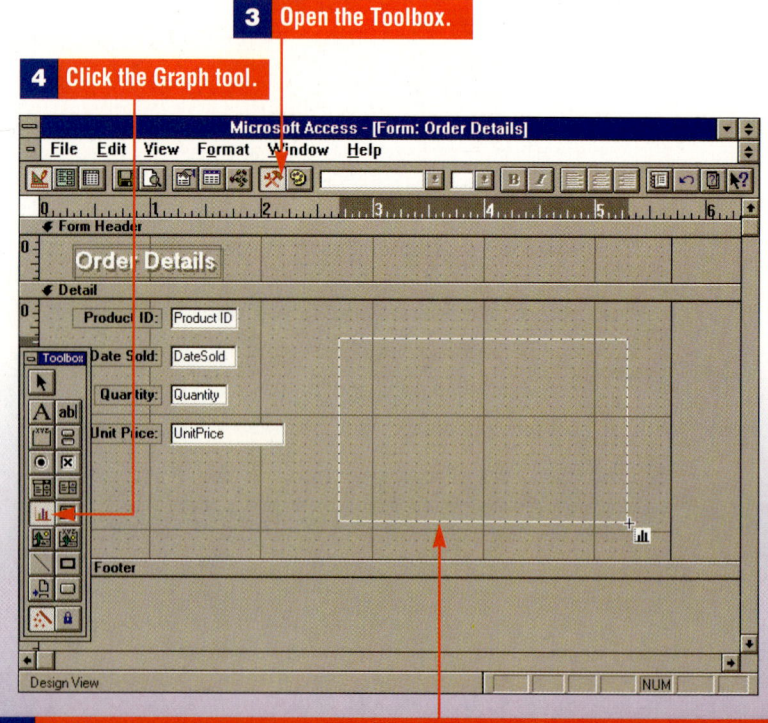

3 Open the Toolbox.

4 Click the Graph tool.

5 Click at upper left corner and drag diagonally to create a place for your graph.

4

Data Analysis: Graphs and Crosstab Queries

6 Click the table or query that has the information you want to graph.

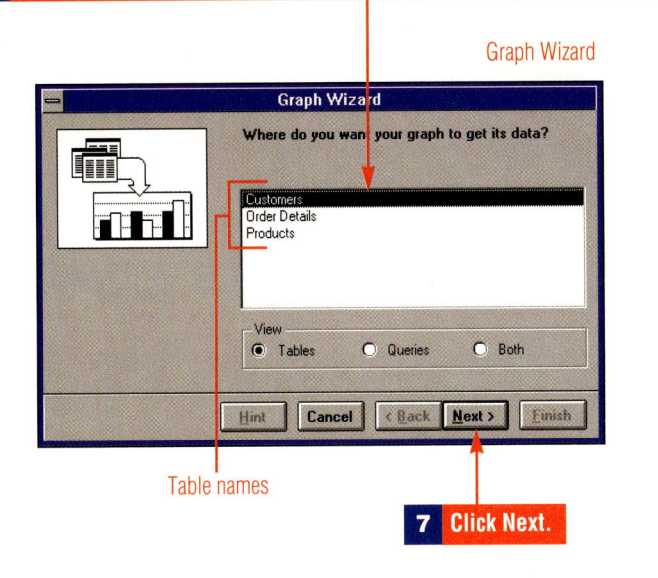

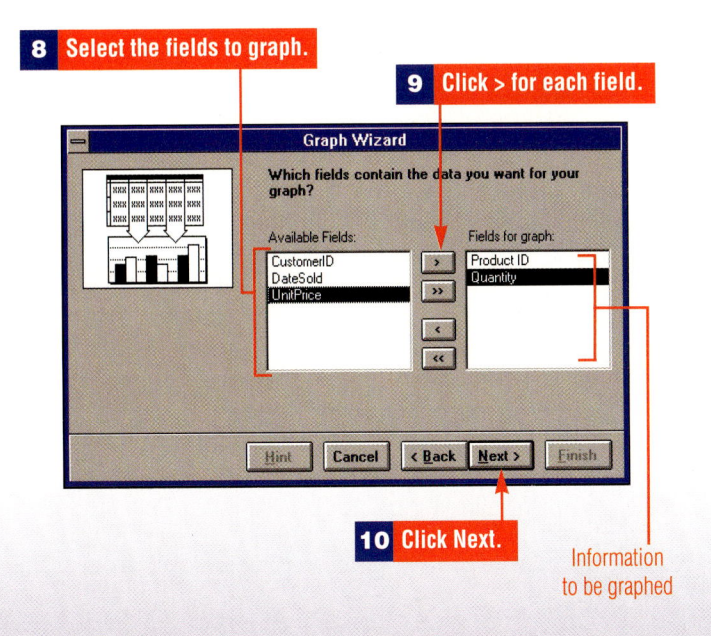

Graph Wizard

Where do you want your graph to get its data?

- Customers
- Order Details
- Products

View: Tables / Queries / Both

Table names

7 Click Next.

8 Select the fields to graph.

9 Click > for each field.

Graph Wizard

Which fields contain the data you want for your graph?

Available Fields:
- CustomerID
- DateSold
- UnitPrice

Fields for graph:
- Product ID
- Quantity

10 Click Next.

Information to be graphed

more ▶

5

Data Analysis: Graphs and Crosstab Queries

11 Tell Access how you want to group the data in your number field.

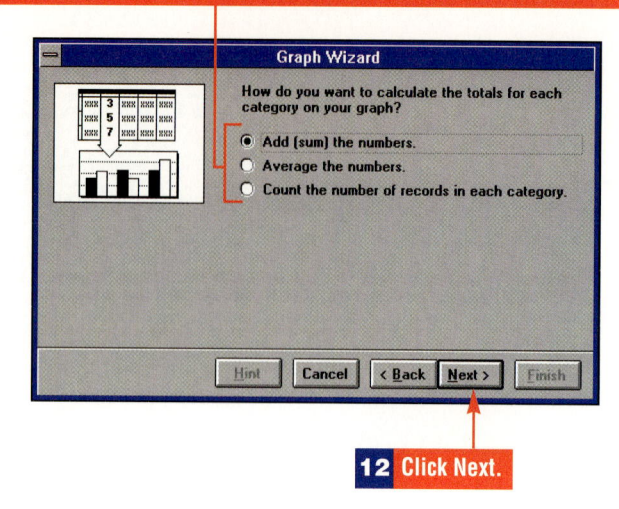

Graph Wizard

How do you want to calculate the totals for each category on your graph?

- ● Add (sum) the numbers.
- ○ Average the numbers.
- ○ Count the number of records in each category.

12 Click Next.

13 Click No to show all the records in the graph.

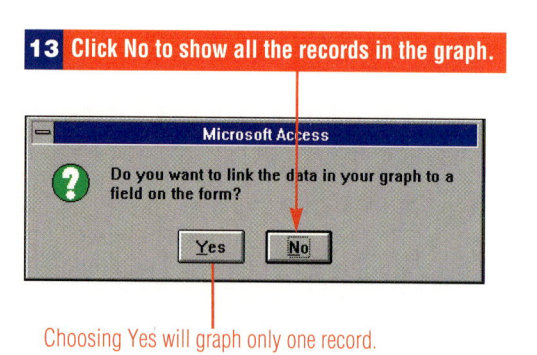

Microsoft Access

Do you want to link the data in your graph to a field on the form?

Yes No

Choosing Yes will graph only one record.

14 Click the button for the type of graph you want.

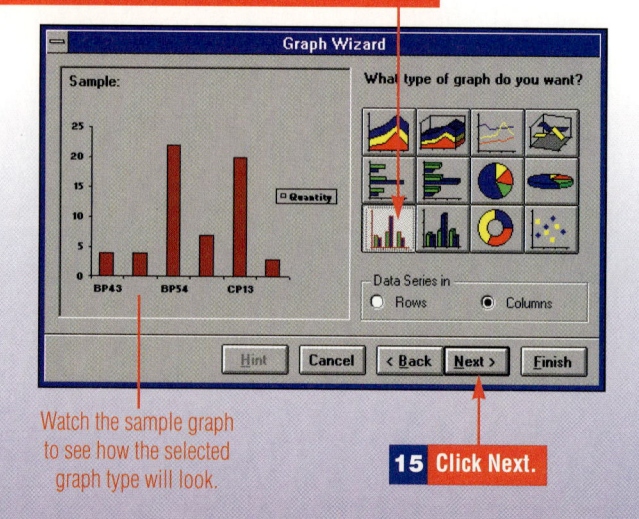

Graph Wizard

Sample:

What type of graph do you want?

Data Series in
○ Rows   ● Columns

Watch the sample graph to see how the selected graph type will look.

15 Click Next.

6

Data Analysis: Graphs and Crosstab Queries

16 Type in a title for the chart.

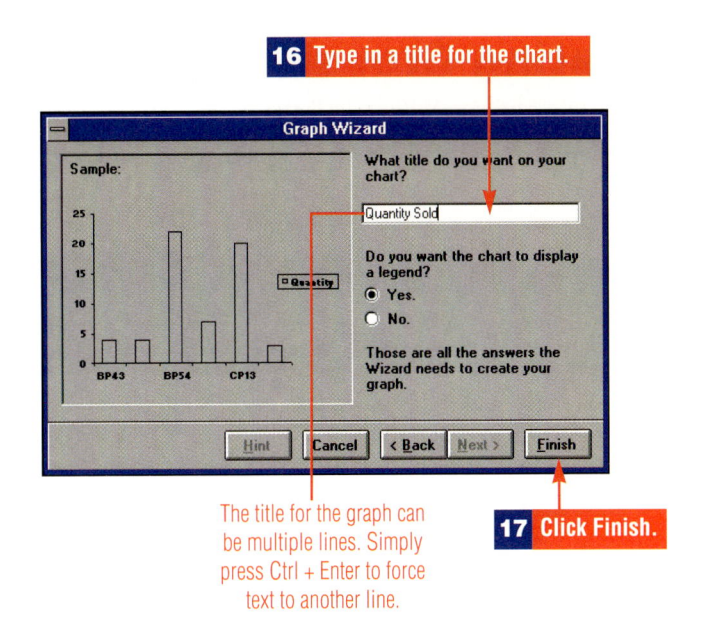

The title for the graph can be multiple lines. Simply press Ctrl + Enter to force text to another line.

17 Click Finish.

Title   Legend

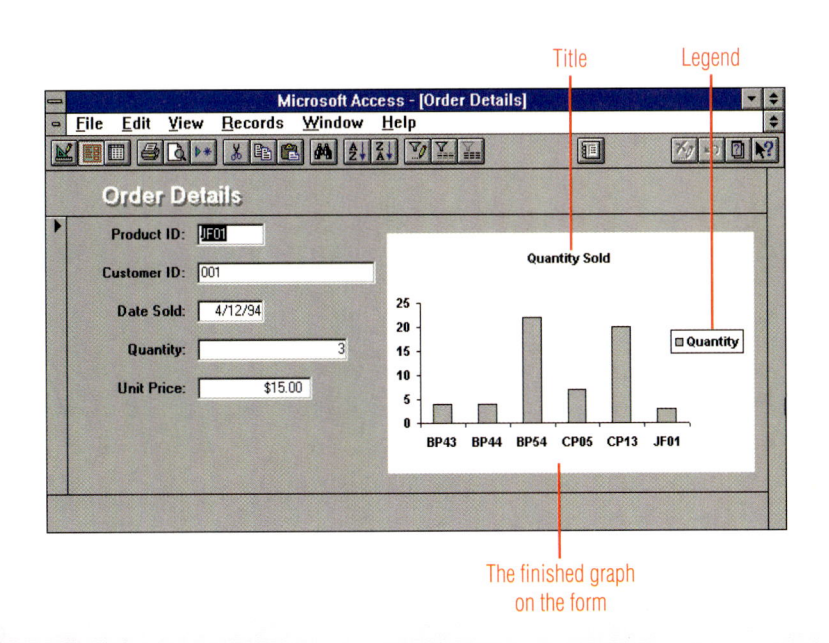

The finished graph on the form

7

Data Analysis: Graphs and Crosstab Queries

Creating Crosstab Queries

Crosstab queries show summarized answers in a format like a spreadsheet. One field's values will be the column headings and another field's values will be the row headings.

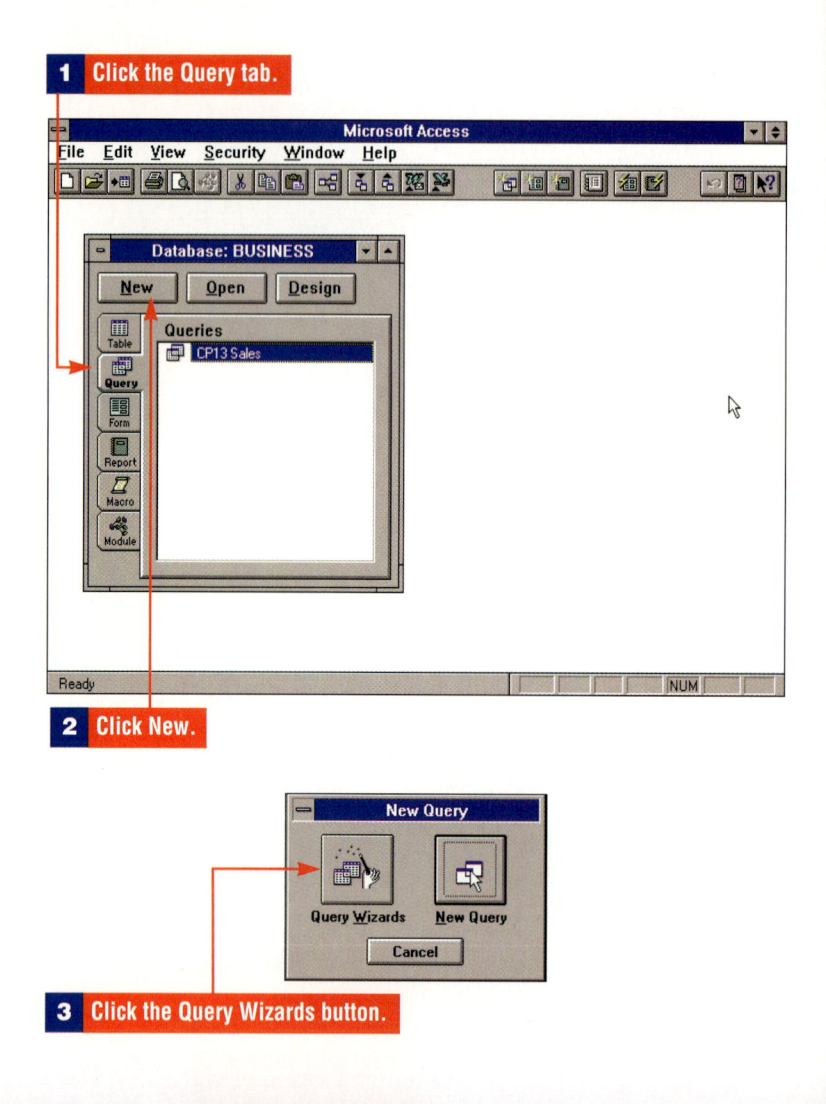

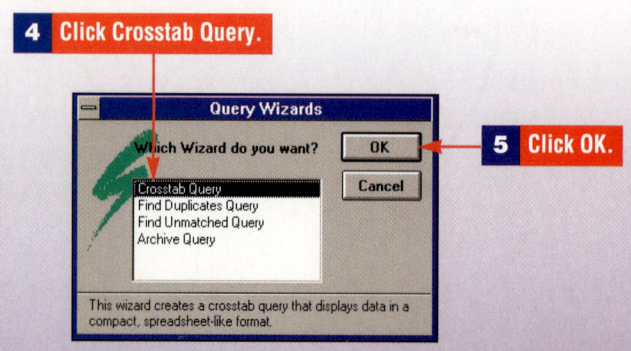

1 Click the Query tab.

2 Click New.

3 Click the Query Wizards button.

4 Click Crosstab Query.

5 Click OK.

Data Analysis: Graphs and Crosstab Queries

6 Choose the table or query name.

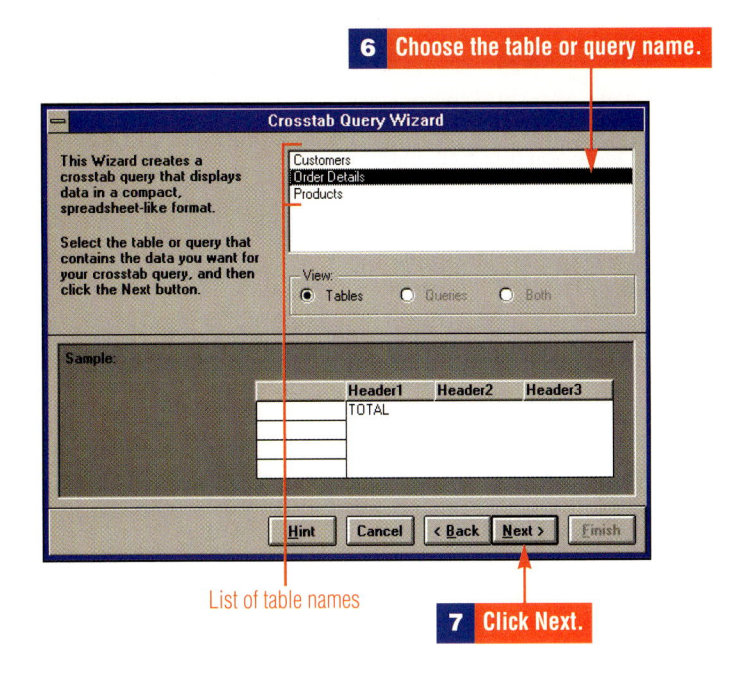

Crosstab Query Wizard

This Wizard creates a crosstab query that displays data in a compact, spreadsheet-like format.

Select the table or query that contains the data you want for your crosstab query, and then click the Next button.

- Customers
- **Order Details**
- Products

View:
- ● Tables
- ○ Queries
- ○ Both

Sample:

	Header1	Header2	Header3
	TOTAL		

[Hint] [Cancel] [< Back] [**Next >**] [Finish]

List of table names

7 Click Next.

---

8 Select a field for row headings.

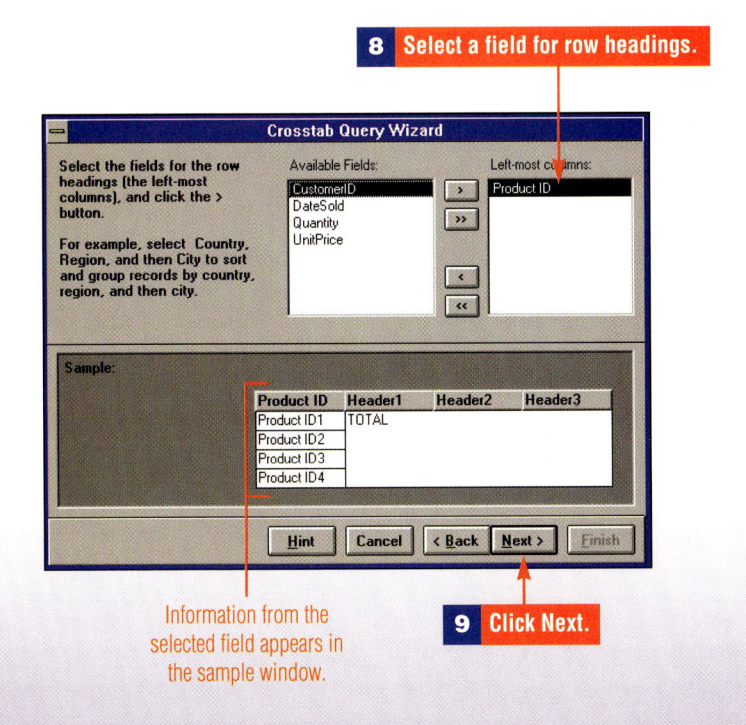

Crosstab Query Wizard

Select the fields for the row headings (the left-most columns), and click the > button.

For example, select Country, Region, and then City to sort and group records by country, region, and then city.

Available Fields:
- CustomerID
- DateSold
- Quantity
- UnitPrice

Left-most columns:
- Product ID

Sample:

Product ID	Header1	Header2	Header3
Product ID1	TOTAL		
Product ID2			
Product ID3			
Product ID4			

[Hint] [Cancel] [< Back] [**Next >**] [Finish]

Information from the selected field appears in the sample window.

9 Click Next.

more ▶

Data Analysis: Graphs and Crosstab Queries

10 Select a field for column headings.

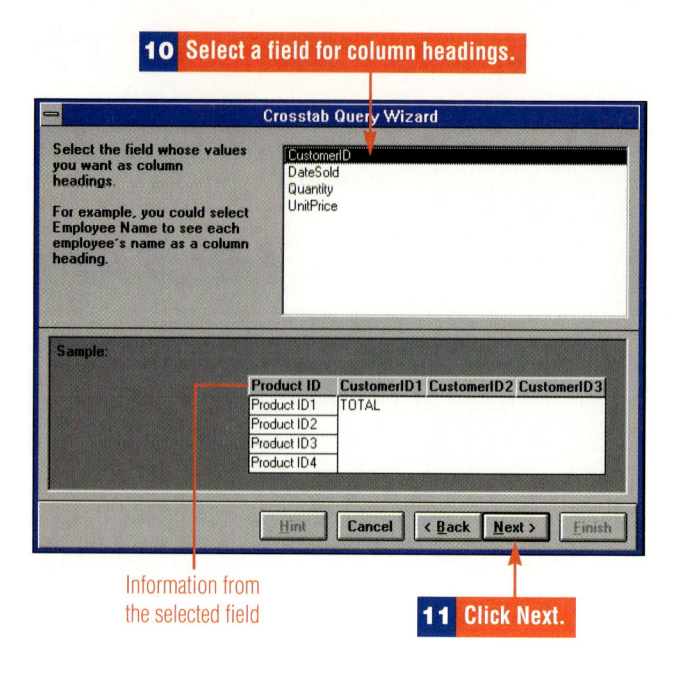

Crosstab Query Wizard

Select the field whose values you want as column headings.

For example, you could select Employee Name to see each employee's name as a column heading.

- CustomerID
- DateSold
- Quantity
- UnitPrice

Sample:

Product ID	CustomerID1	CustomerID2	CustomerID3
Product ID1	TOTAL		
Product ID2			
Product ID3			
Product ID4			

[Hint] [Cancel] [< Back] [Next >] [Finish]

Information from the selected field

11 Click Next.

---

12 Select which field has the numbers to calculate.

13 Select the type of calculation you want.

Crosstab Query Wizard

What numbers do you want in the middle?

Select the field and type of calculation you want. For example, you could calculate the Sum of Order Amount.

If you want, you can:
☒ Calcuate Summary for Each Row

Available fields:
- CustomerID
- DateSold
- **Quantity**
- UnitPrice

Functions:
- Avg
- Count
- **Sum**
- Min
- Max
- StDev
- Var
- First

Sample:

Product ID	CustomerID1	CustomerID2	CustomerID3
Product ID1	Sum(Quantity)		
Product ID2			
Product ID3			
Product ID4			

[Hint] [Cancel] [< Back] [Next >] [Finish]

Number field

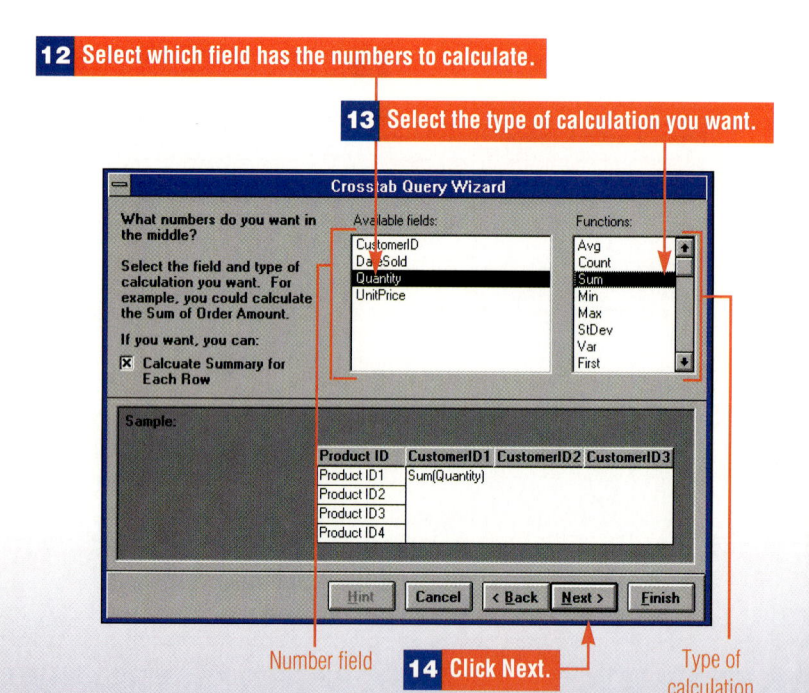

14 Click Next.

Type of calculation

Data Analysis: Graphs and Crosstab Queries

Name query is saved with

15 Type a name for the query.

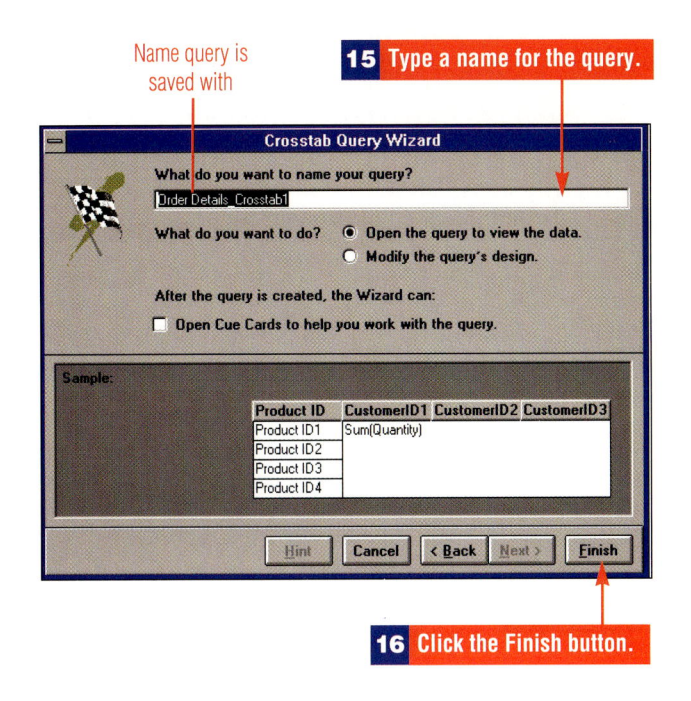

Crosstab Query Wizard

What do you want to name your query?
[Order Details_Crosstab1]

What do you want to do?
- ● Open the query to view the data.
- ○ Modify the query's design.

After the query is created, the Wizard can:
☐ Open Cue Cards to help you work with the query.

Sample:

Product ID	CustomerID1	CustomerID2	CustomerID3
Product ID1	Sum(Quantity)		
Product ID2			
Product ID3			
Product ID4			

[Hint] [Cancel] [< Back] [Next >] [Finish]

16 Click the Finish button.

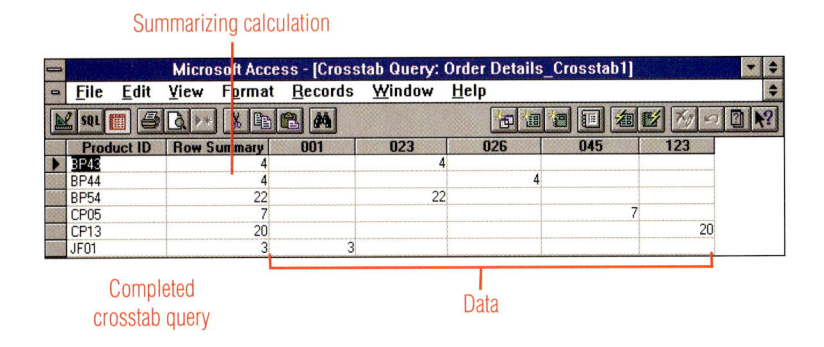

Summarizing calculation

Microsoft Access - [Crosstab Query: Order Details_Crosstab1]
File Edit View Format Records Window Help

Product ID	Row Summary	001	023	026	045	123
BP43	4		4			
BP44	4				4	
BP54	22		22			
CP05	7				7	
CP13	20					20
JF01	3	3				

Completed crosstab query

Data

11

Database Management: Compacting, Repairing, Renaming

An important part of database management is to back up your database to tape or disk often in case of power outage or equipment damage. With a backup available, you can recover lost data quickly with minimum downtime. For detailed information on backing up your database files, consult Using Access 2 for Windows, *Special Edition.*

Compacting a Database

Over time, deleting records or changing the definitions of objects can leave unused space in your database file. To reclaim that space, you should occasionally run the compact database utility. Although compacting a database is relatively hazard-free, it is a good idea to give your compacted database a different name or to back up your database first.

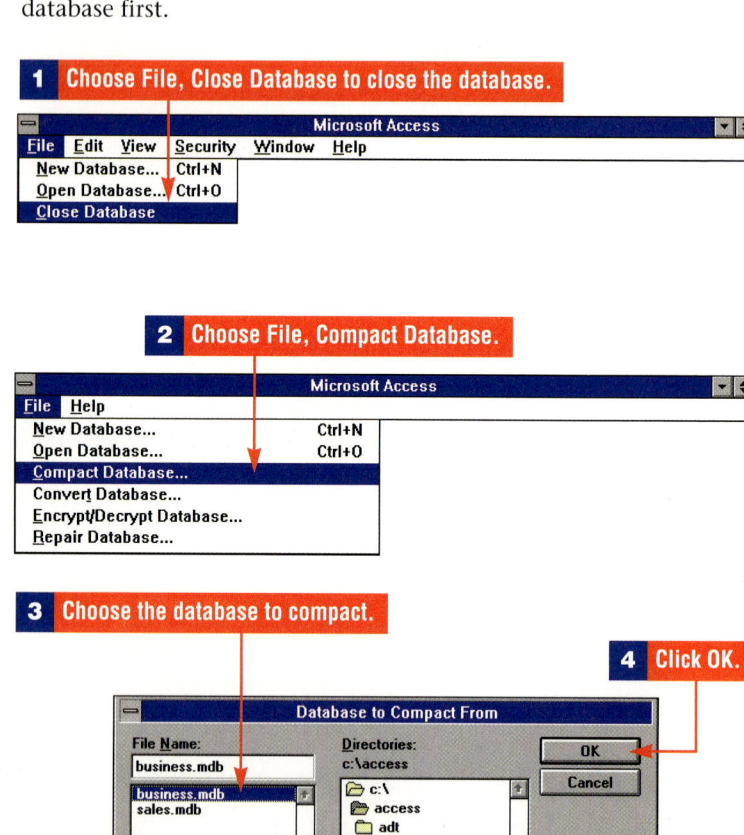

1 Choose File, Close Database to close the database.

2 Choose File, Compact Database.

3 Choose the database to compact.

4 Click OK.

Database Management: Compacting, Repairing, Renaming

5 Enter a new name for the compacted database.

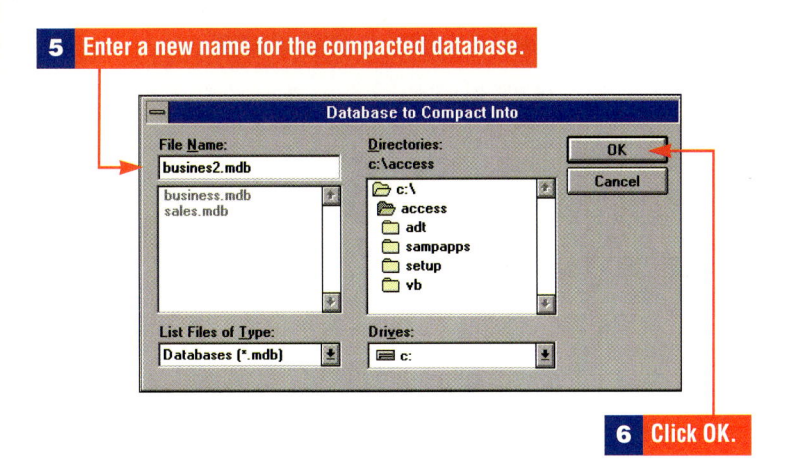

6 Click OK.

Repairing a Database

If, when you try to open an Access database file, you are told that your file is corrupted, you will have to try to repair the database to use it. (If you have a backup of the file, you can restore the backup instead of repairing the database.) This repair process is almost always successful. When the database has been successfully repaired, be sure to make a backup copy.

1 Choose File, Repair Database.

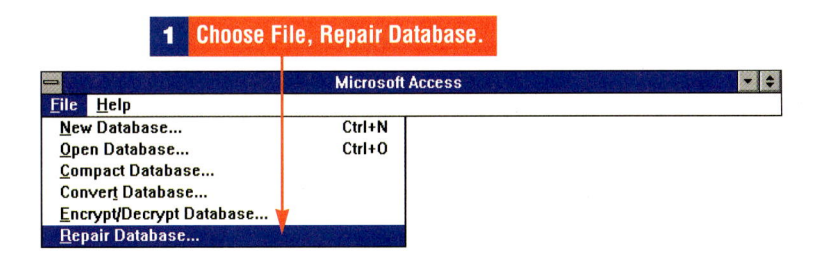

2 Choose the database to repair.

3 Click OK.

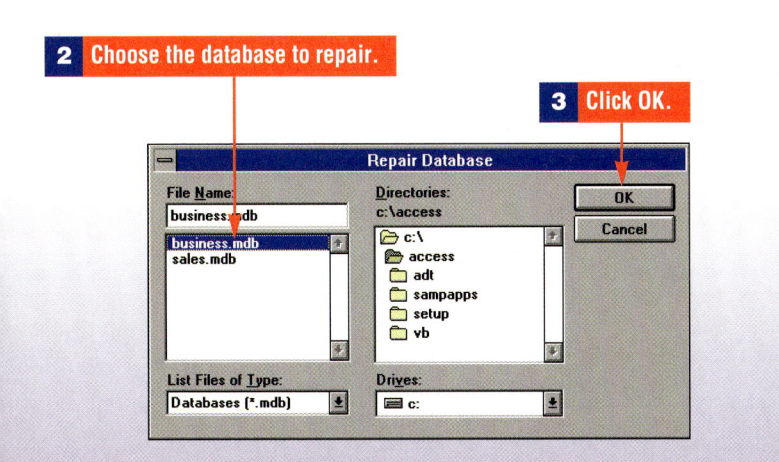

more ▶

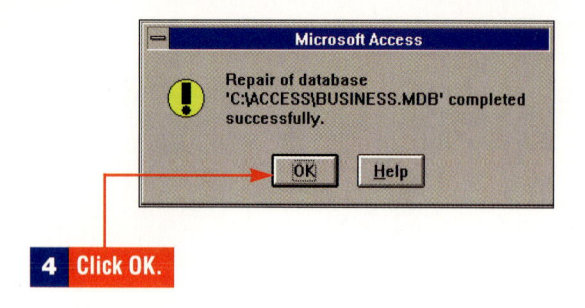

Database Management: Compacting, Repairing, Renaming

4 Click OK.

Renaming Objects

When you need to give the selected object a different name, you will use the Rename feature. This could be used because the name you originally used isn't specific enough. Be careful that you do not rename a table or a query that is being used by another object—a table that is the basis of a query, for example. If the table is renamed, the query will not be able to find it. You can't rename an open object.

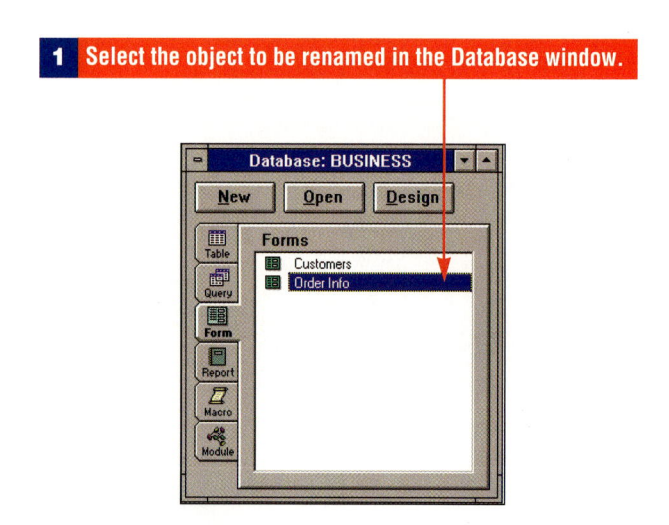

1 Select the object to be renamed in the Database window.

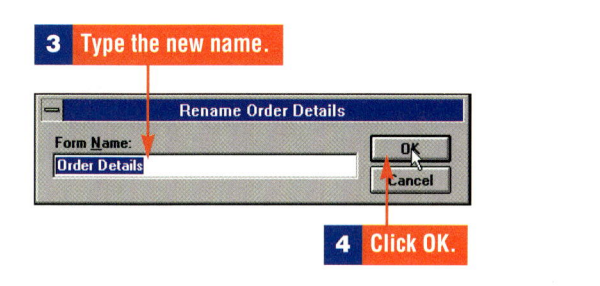

Database Management: Compacting, Repairing, Renaming

2 Choose File, Rename.

```
File  Edit  View  Security  Window  Help
 New Database...   Ctrl+N
 Open Database...  Ctrl+O
 Close Database
 New                         ▶
 Rename...
 Output To...
```

3 Type the new name.

Rename Order Details
Form Name: Order Details
[OK] [Cancel]

4 Click OK.

If you give the object a name already being used, Access asks if you want to replace it.

Microsoft Access
? Replace existing Table 'employee'?
[Yes] [No] [Help]

5 Choose Yes to replace, or No to retype table name.

15

Finding Records: Finding, Filtering, and Sorting

Finding Records

Often all you want to do is to find one specific record in your database. The easiest way to do this is to use the Find command, which allows you to find a specific value in a specific field. If you are not sure of how the text appears, type only the part you know and select the Any Part of Field option.

To find records using tables

1 Click at the top of the field to be searched.

2 Click the Find button.

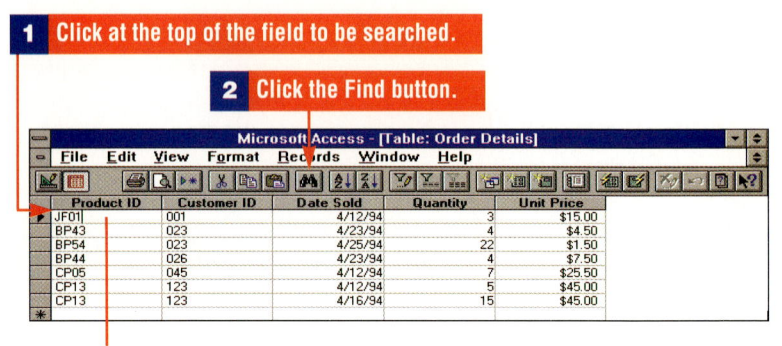

Click in the first record.

3 Enter the exact data that you are searching for.

4 Click Find First.

You might have to move the dialog box to see the results.

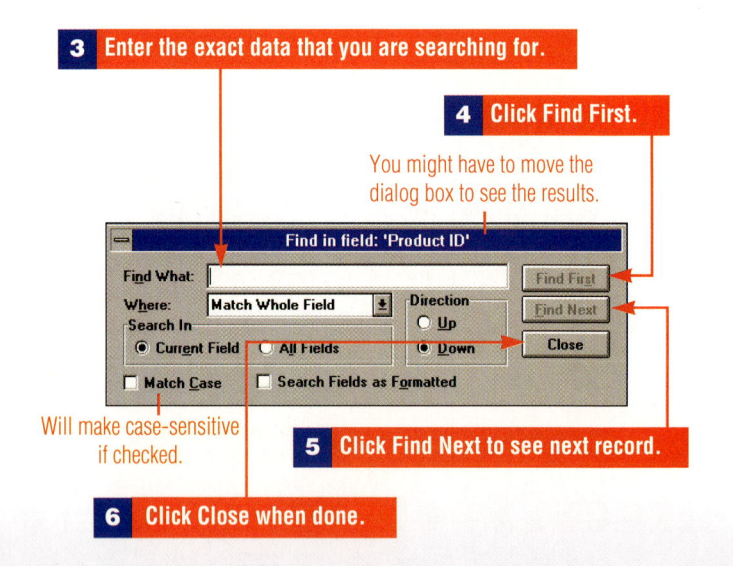

Will make case-sensitive if checked.

5 Click Find Next to see next record.

6 Click Close when done.

This dialog box appears if you began search in middle of table.

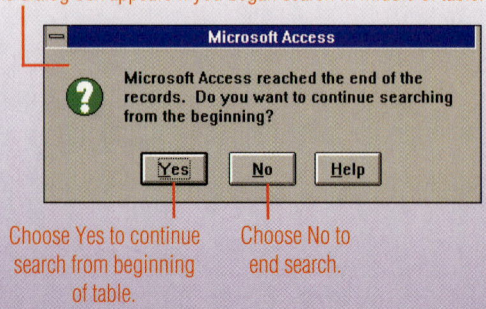

Choose Yes to continue search from beginning of table.

Choose No to end search.

16

Finding Records: Finding, Filtering, and Sorting

To find records using forms

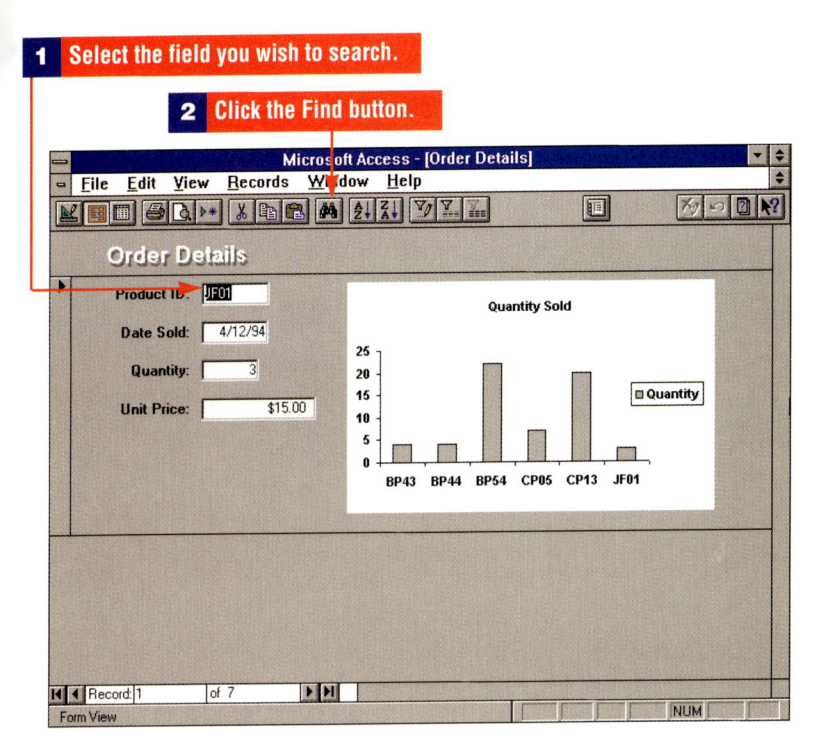

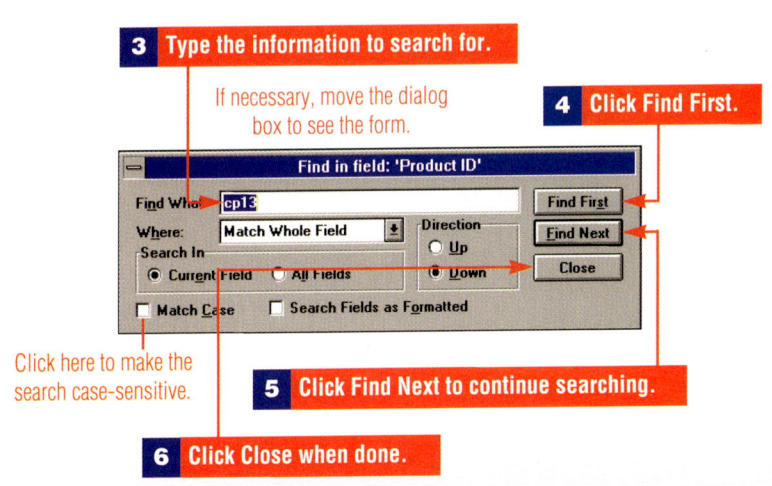

1 Select the field you wish to search.

2 Click the Find button.

3 Type the information to search for.

If necessary, move the dialog box to see the form.

4 Click Find First.

Click here to make the search case-sensitive.

5 Click Find Next to continue searching.

6 Click Close when done.

This dialog box appears if you began Search in middle of table.

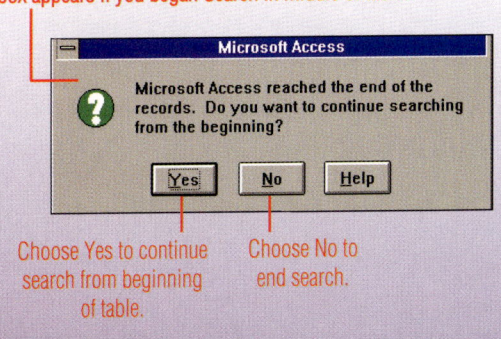

Choose Yes to continue search from beginning of table.

Choose No to end search.

17

Finding Records: Finding, Filtering, and Sorting

Filtering Records

When you have a large table and you only want to display certain records, you can use filters to show only the records you need. Filters cannot be saved.

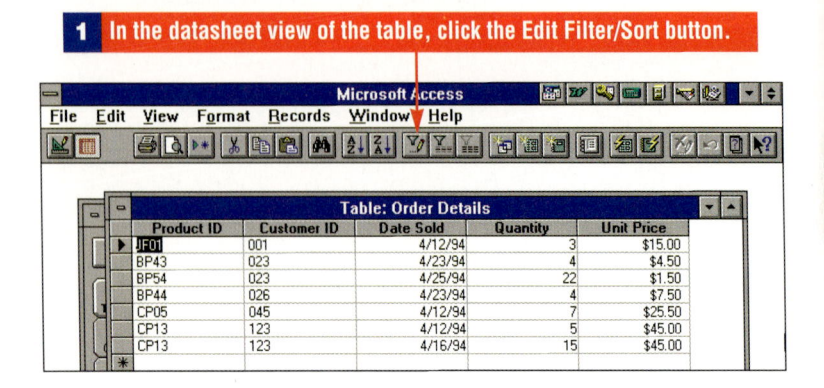

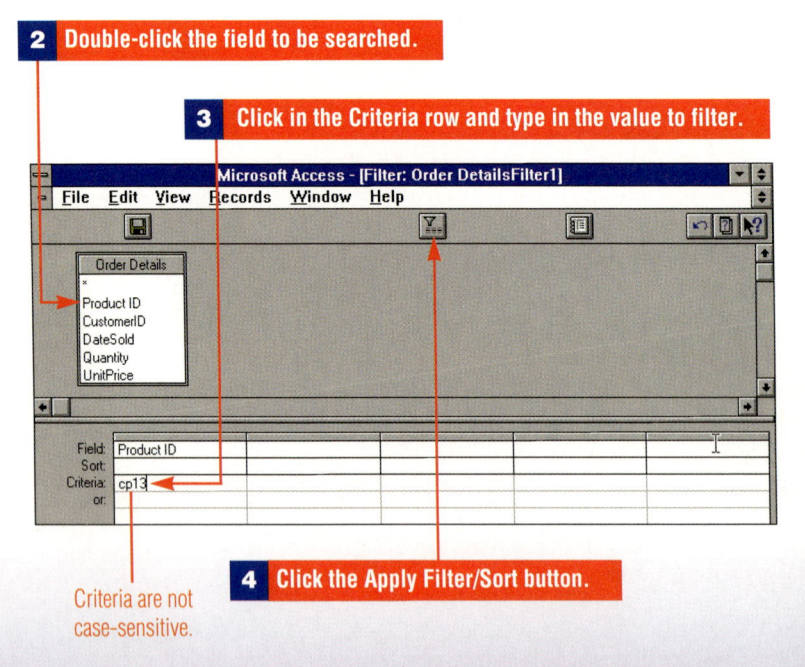

1 In the datasheet view of the table, click the Edit Filter/Sort button.

2 Double-click the field to be searched.

3 Click in the Criteria row and type in the value to filter.

4 Click the Apply Filter/Sort button.

Criteria are not case-sensitive.

You can filter on more than one field at a time and can use expressions like >100.

18

Finding Records: Finding, Filtering, and Sorting

5 Double-click the Control menu icon to close the dynaset.

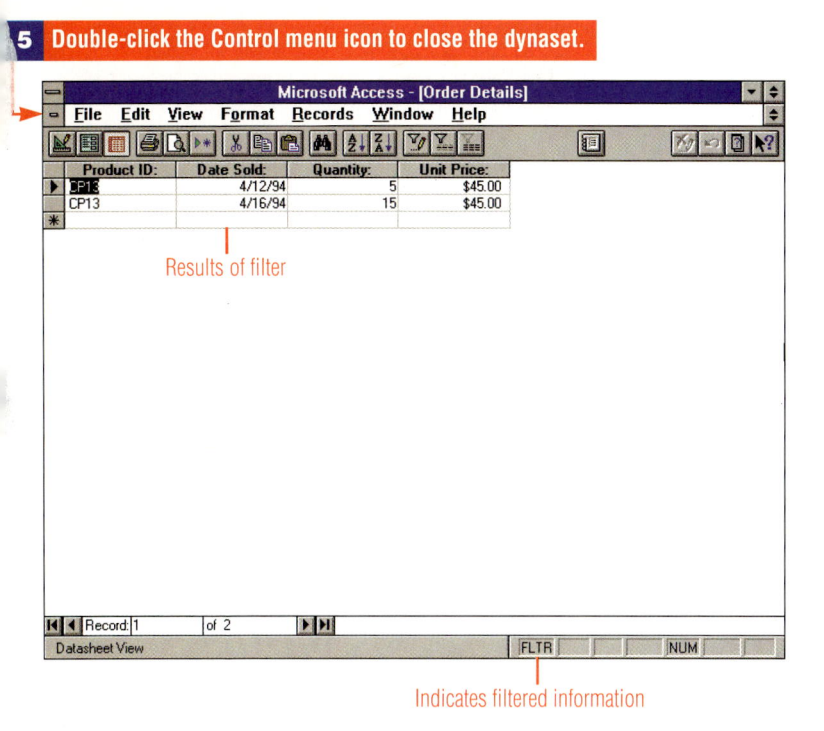

Results of filter

Indicates filtered information

Sorting Records

To create a simple sort to put records in order by one field, use the Ascending Sort button or the Descending Sort button. Ascending sorts put information in A to Z order. Descending sorts put records in Z to A order.

1 Click in the field to sort.

2 Click on one of the sort buttons.

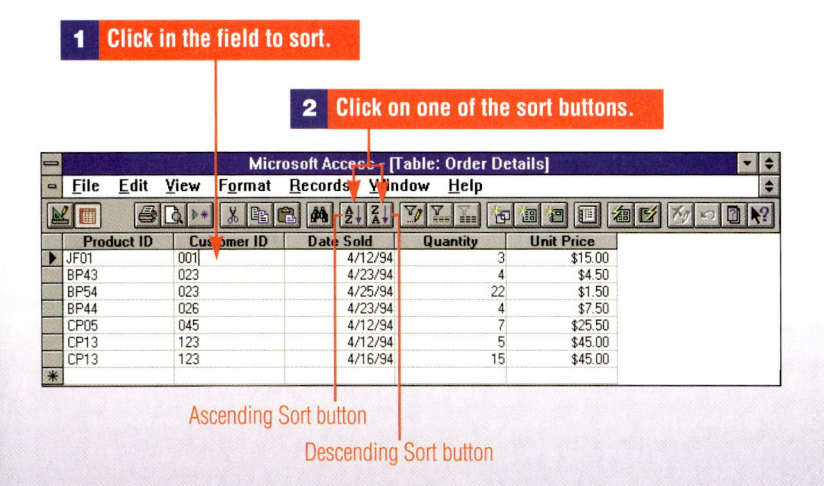

Ascending Sort button
Descending Sort button

more ▶

Finding Records: Finding, Filtering, and Sorting

Product ID	Customer ID	Date Sold	Quantity	Unit Price
JF01	001	4/12/94	3	$15.00
BP43	023	4/23/94	4	$4.50
BP54	023	4/25/94	22	$1.50
BP44	026	4/23/94	4	$7.50
CP05	045	4/12/94	7	$25.50
CP13	123	4/12/94	5	$45.00
CP13	123	4/16/94	15	$45.00

Sorted records

20

Forms—Basics: Designing, Printing, and Editing

Designing Forms

Forms are another way to enter and view data in your database. With a form you can see only one record at a time and you see all the fields at once. Before you completely close a new or redesigned form, you must save and name the form.

To use the Form Wizard to create a basic form

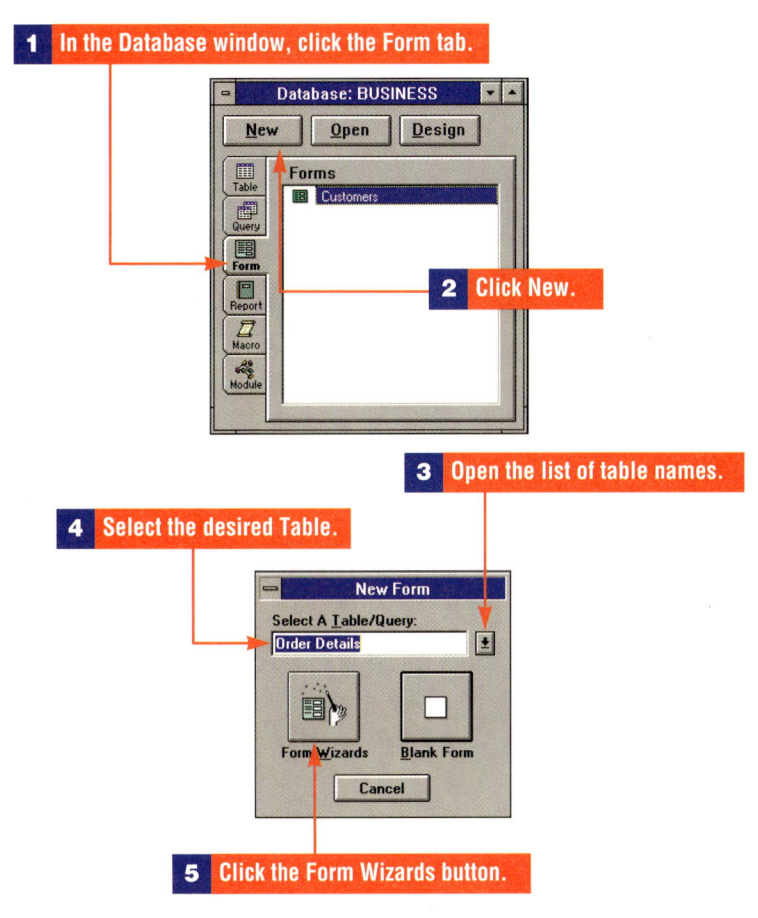

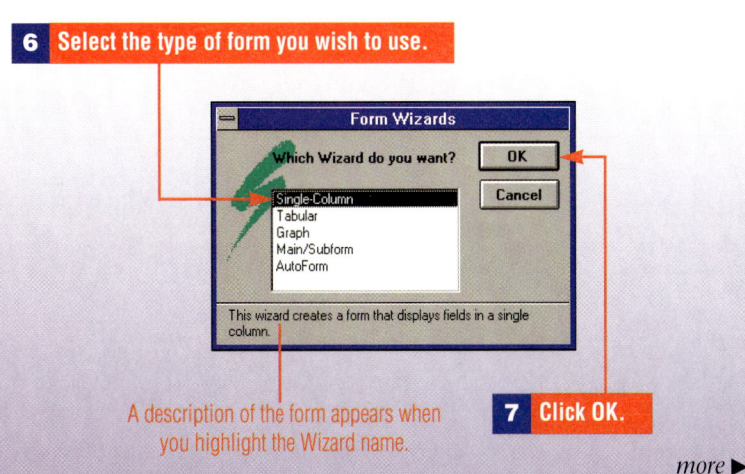

1 In the Database window, click the Form tab.

2 Click New.

3 Open the list of table names.

4 Select the desired Table.

5 Click the Form Wizards button.

6 Select the type of form you wish to use.

A description of the form appears when you highlight the Wizard name.

7 Click OK.

more ▶

21

Forms—Basics: Designing, Printing, and Editing

8 Select the fields to be displayed in the form.

Sample of form

Order of fields on form

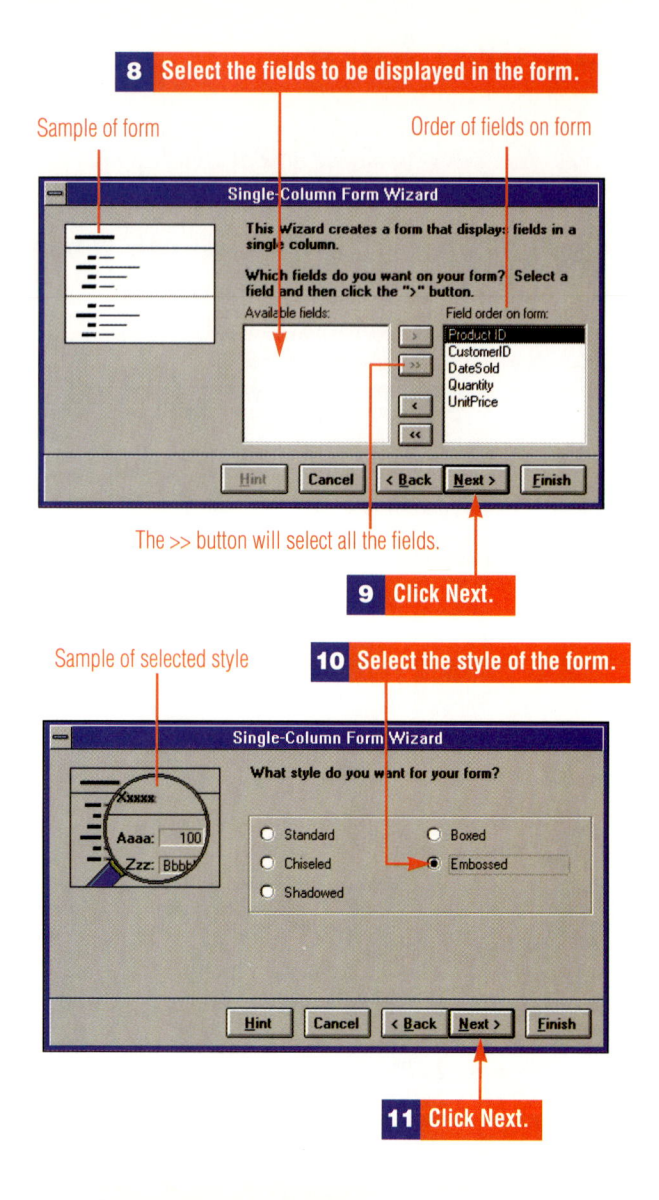

Single-Column Form Wizard

This Wizard creates a form that displays fields in a single column.

Which fields do you want on your form? Select a field and then click the ">" button.

Available fields:

Field order on form:
- ProductID
- CustomerID
- DateSold
- Quantity
- UnitPrice

The >> button will select all the fields.

9 Click Next.

Sample of selected style

10 Select the style of the form.

Single-Column Form Wizard

What style do you want for your form?

- ○ Standard
- ○ Chiseled
- ○ Shadowed
- ○ Boxed
- ● Embossed

11 Click Next.

12 Type a title for the form.

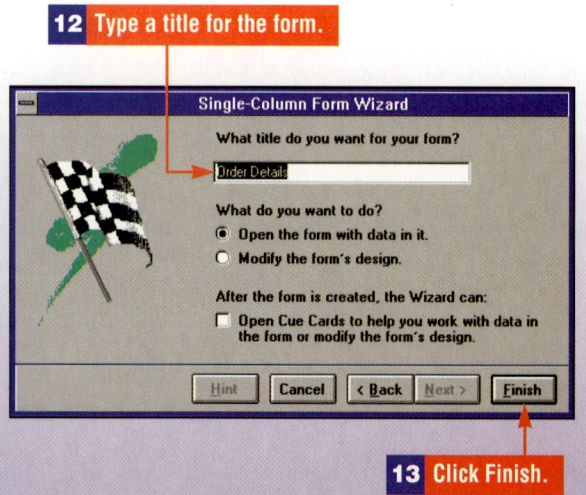

Single-Column Form Wizard

What title do you want for your form?

Order Details

What do you want to do?
- ● Open the form with data in it.
- ○ Modify the form's design.

After the form is created, the Wizard can:
- ☐ Open Cue Cards to help you work with data in the form or modify the form's design.

13 Click Finish.

22

Forms—Basics: Designing, Printing, and Editing

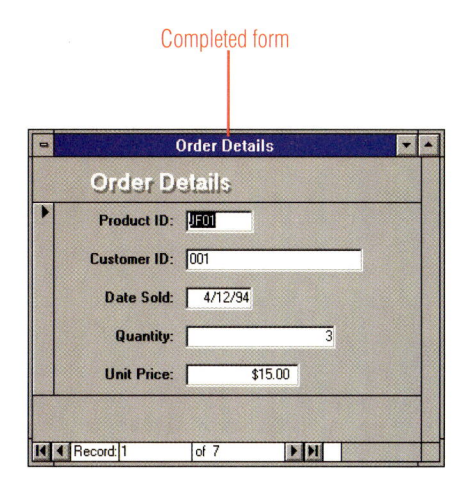

Completed form

To close and save a form

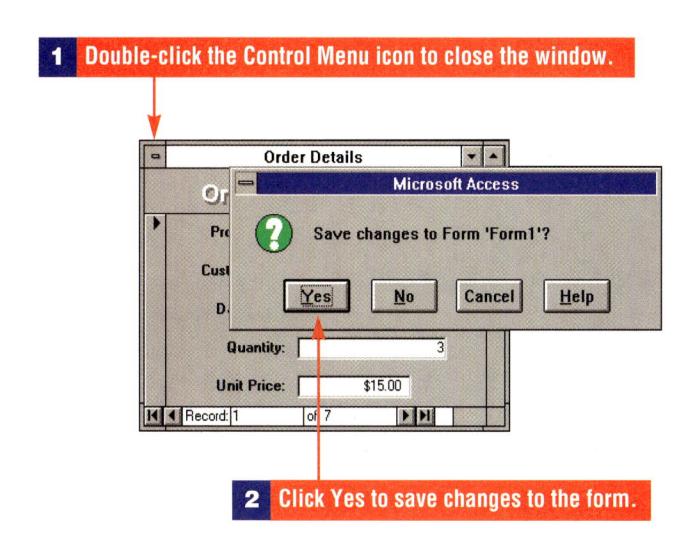

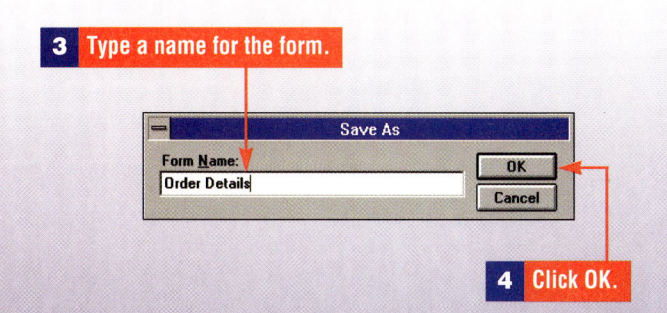

1 Double-click the Control Menu icon to close the window.

2 Click Yes to save changes to the form.

3 Type a name for the form.

4 Click OK.

23

Forms—Basics: Designing, Printing, and Editing

To open a form

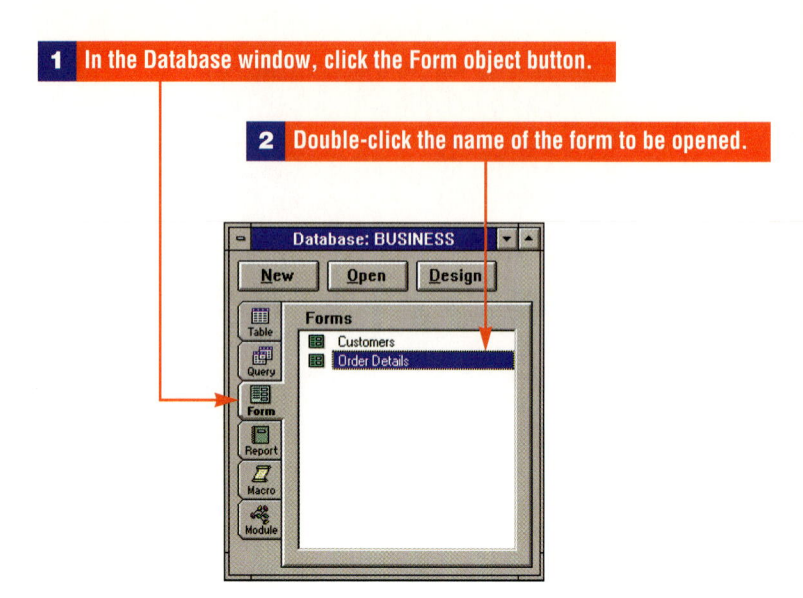

1 In the Database window, click the Form object button.

2 Double-click the name of the form to be opened.

Printing Forms

You can print a form from Form view or from Datasheet view. If you only want to print a few pages, tell Access which pages to print in the Pages Range area of the Print dialog box.

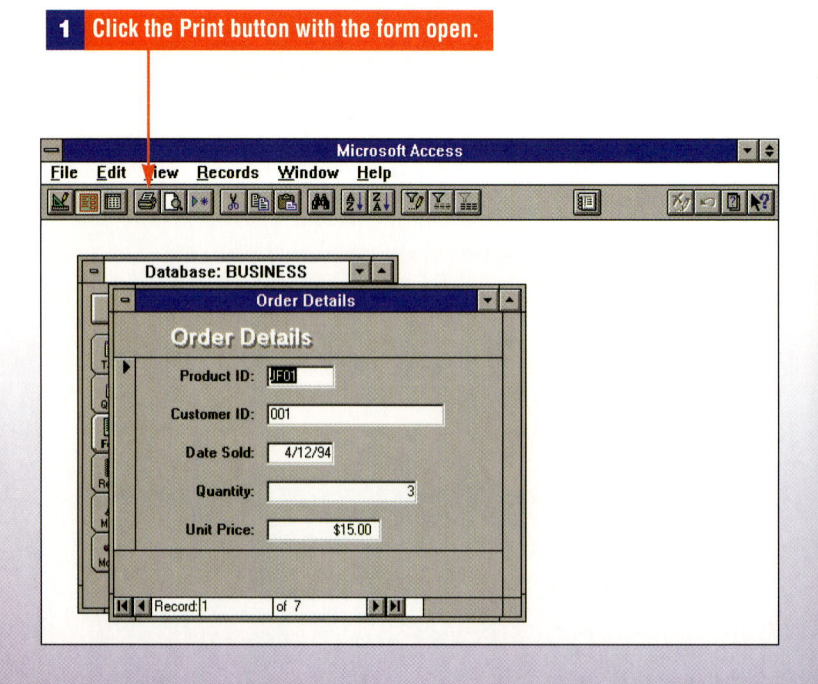

1 Click the Print button with the form open.

Forms—Basics: Designing, Printing, and Editing

2 Click OK.

Change the default settings, if desired

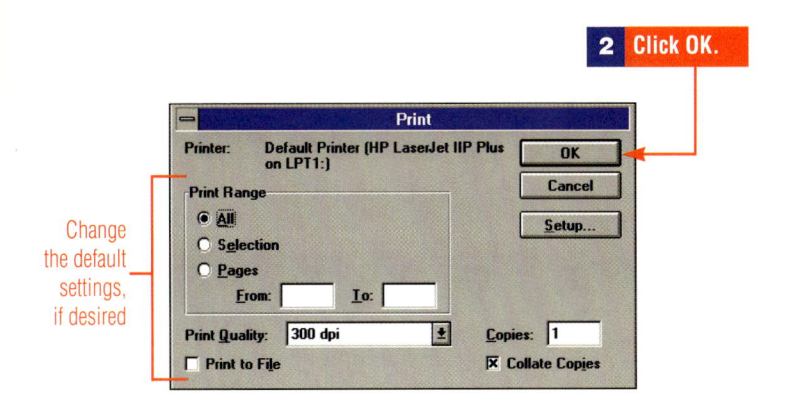

Editing Records in a Form

Because you can usually see only one record at a time, Access allows you to move quickly from record to record. Entering data with a form is very easy.

To move between records

1 Click one of the arrow buttons.

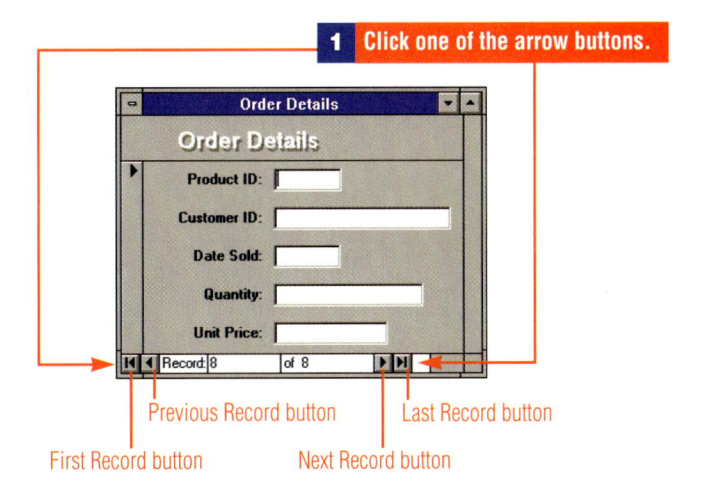

Previous Record button
Last Record button
First Record button
Next Record button

To add records using a form

1 With the form open, choose Records, Go To, New.

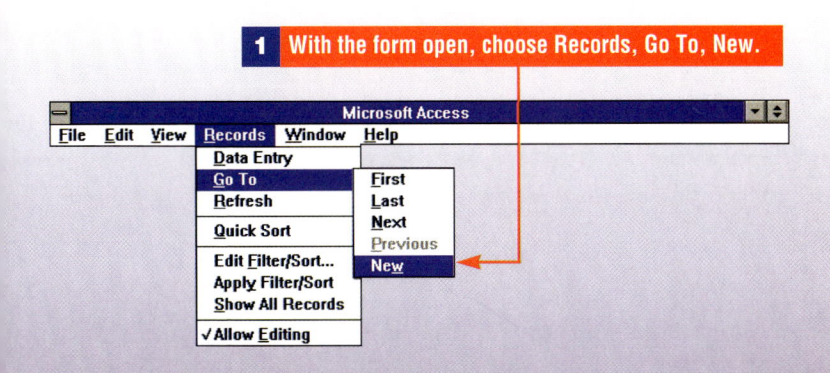

more ▶

25

Forms—Basics: Designing, Printing, and Editing

2 Enter the data in the fields.

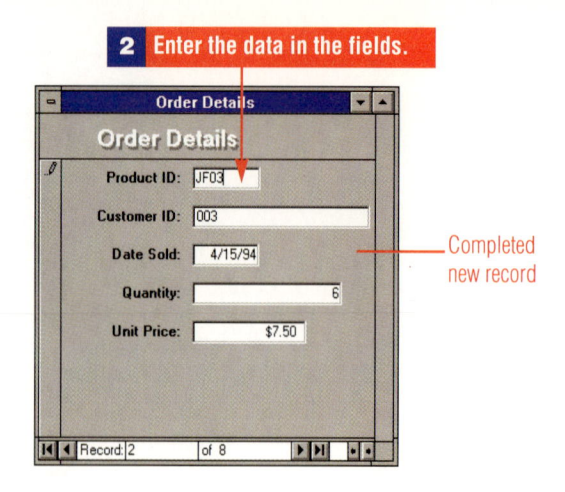

— Completed new record

To delete records using a form

1 Choose Edit, Select Record.

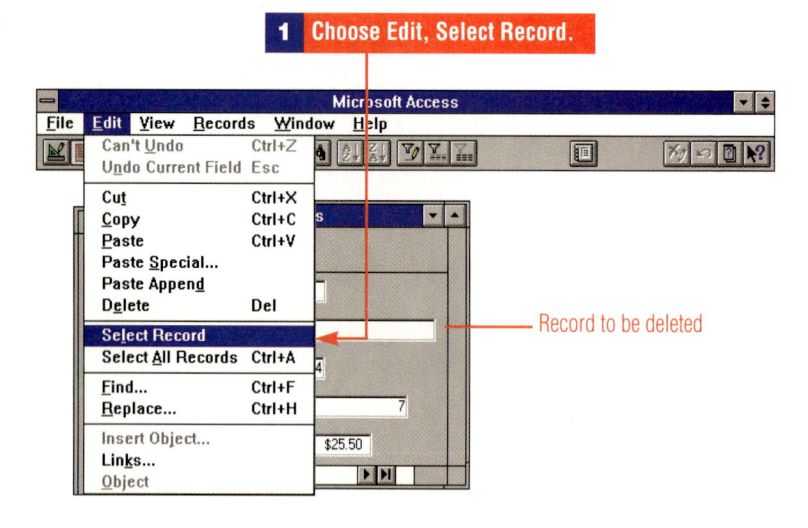

— Record to be deleted

2 Choose Edit, Delete.

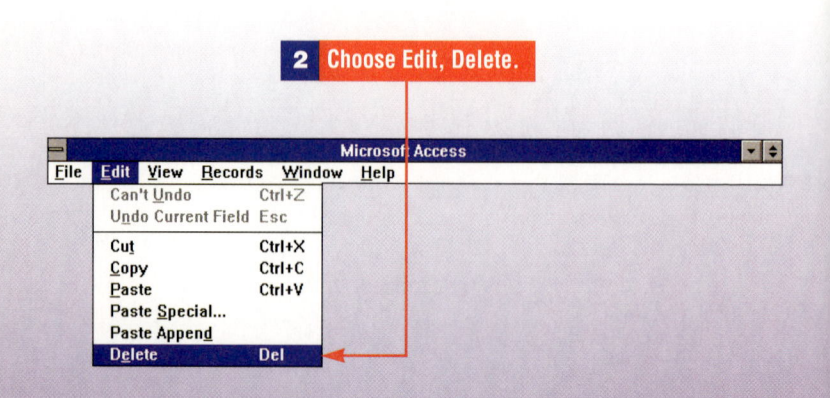

Forms—Basics: Designing, Printing, and Editing

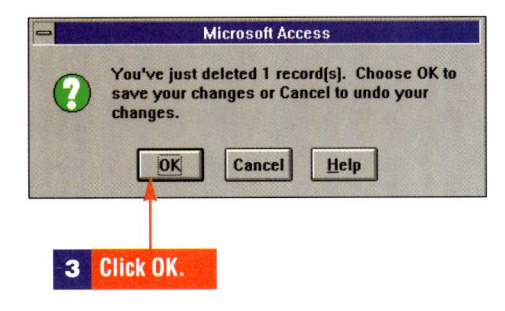

3 Click OK.

To edit existing data using a form

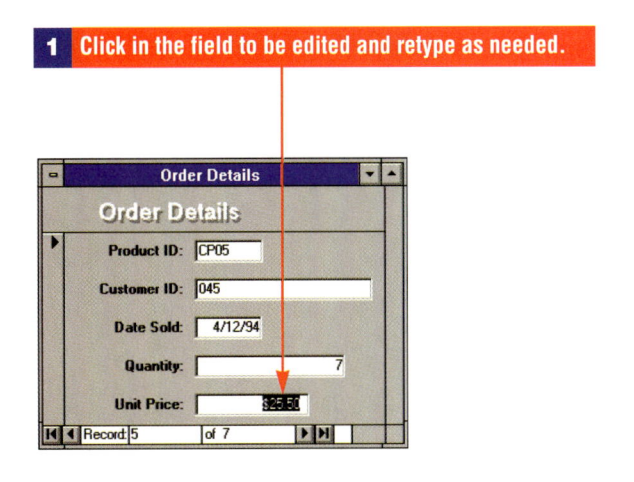

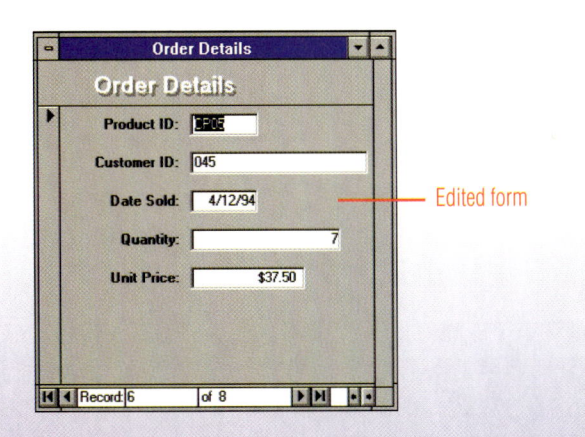

1 Click in the field to be edited and retype as needed.

Edited form

27

Forms—Customizing: Headers/Footers and Special Controls

Adding Headers and Footers

Access has five section types for forms. You add them to place information and to control appearance on-screen or in a printout. All sections are adjustable in size. Headers and footers are placed in special sections. You must add or remove a header and a footer as a pair.

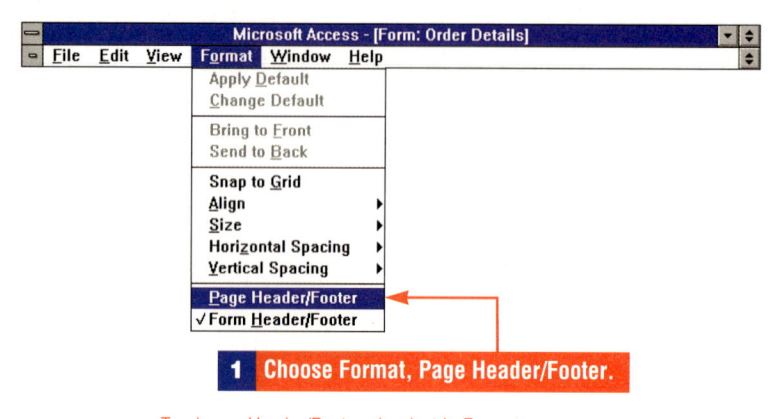

1 Choose Format, Page Header/Footer.

To close a Header/Footer, deselect in Format menu.

Form Header—displays at top of screen and at the top of the first page of a printout

Page Header—displays only at top of printed form

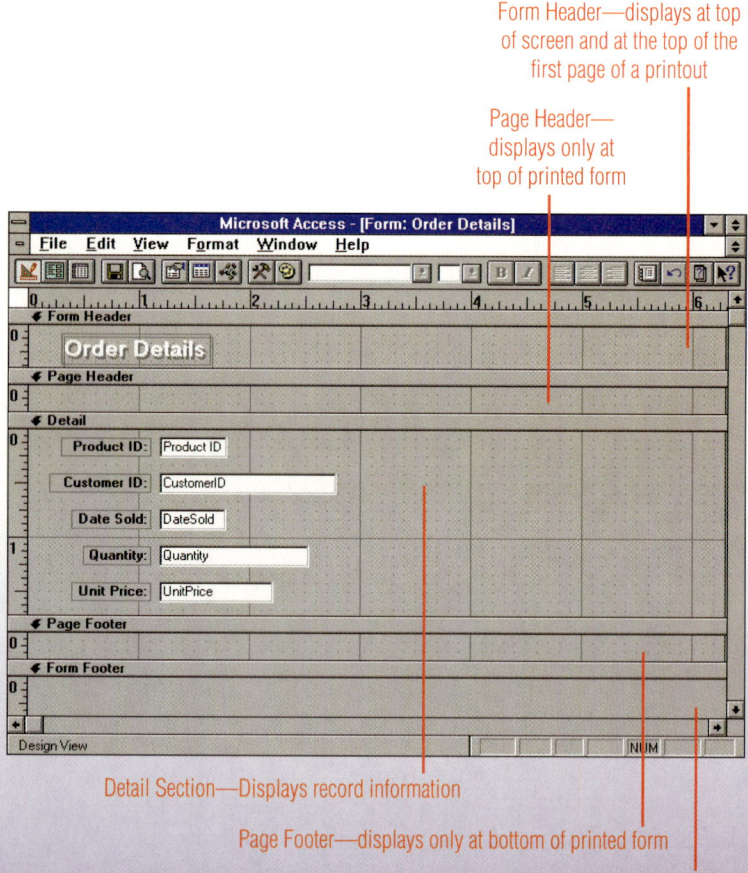

Detail Section—Displays record information

Page Footer—displays only at bottom of printed form

Form Footer—displays at bottom of screen and at the bottom of the first page of a printout

28

Forms—Customizing: Headers/Footers and Special Controls

Creating Special Controls in a Form

By creating customized controls in a form, you can restrict the information entered to predetermined choices and speed up data entry.

To create a list box with predefined values

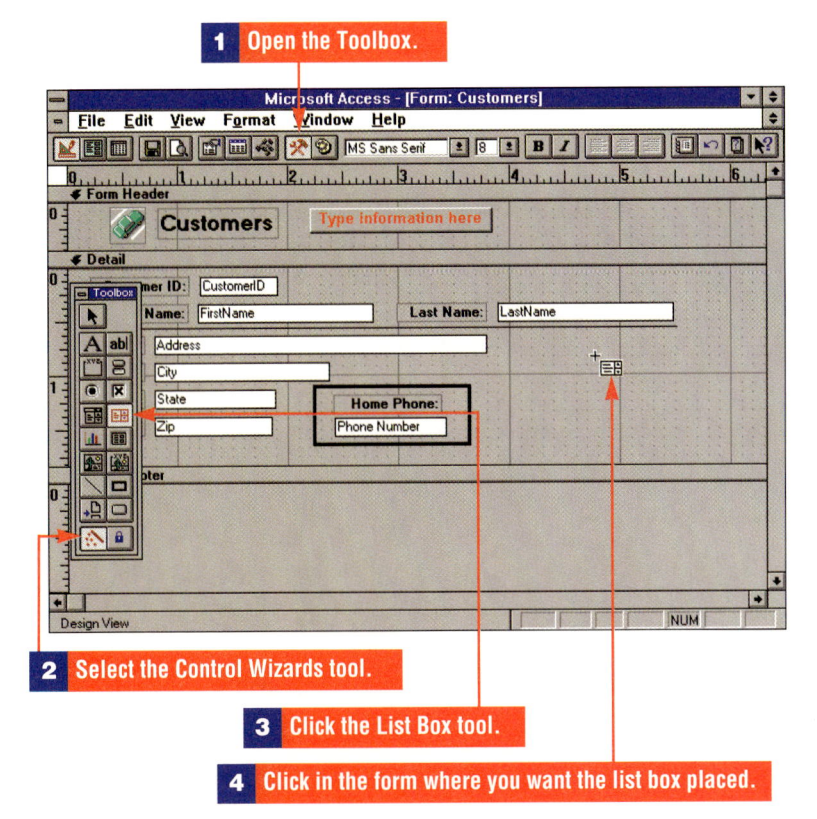

1 Open the Toolbox.

2 Select the Control Wizards tool.

3 Click the List Box tool.

4 Click in the form where you want the list box placed.

List boxes limit the available choices.

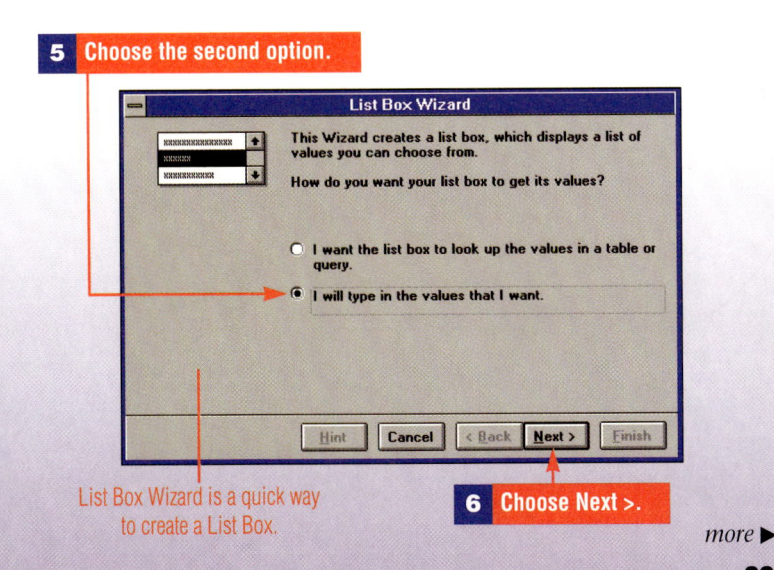

5 Choose the second option.

List Box Wizard is a quick way to create a List Box.

6 Choose Next >.

more ▶

29

Forms—Customizing: Headers/Footers and Special Controls

7 Change the number of columns to 1.

8 Type in list desired.

9 Choose Next >.

10 Choose Store that value in this field.

11 Choose Credit Rating.

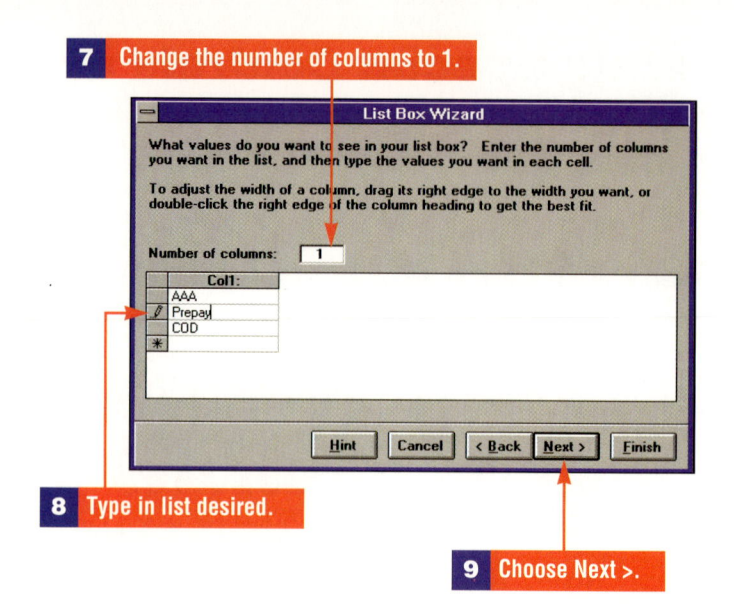

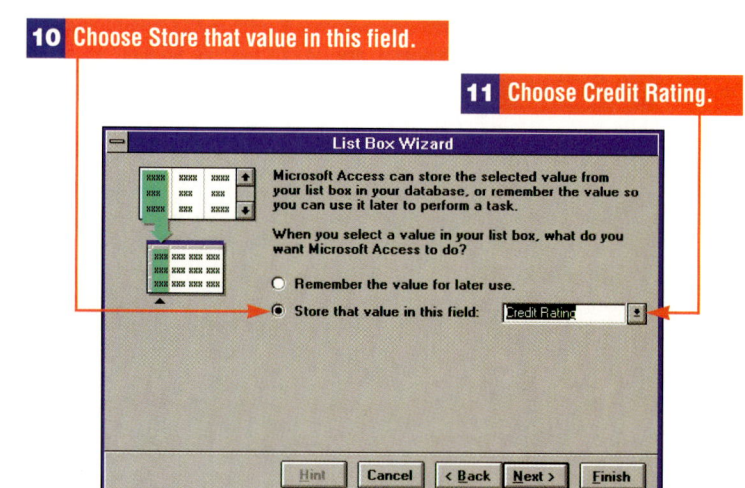

12 Choose Next >.

13 Type Credit Rating for label on list box.

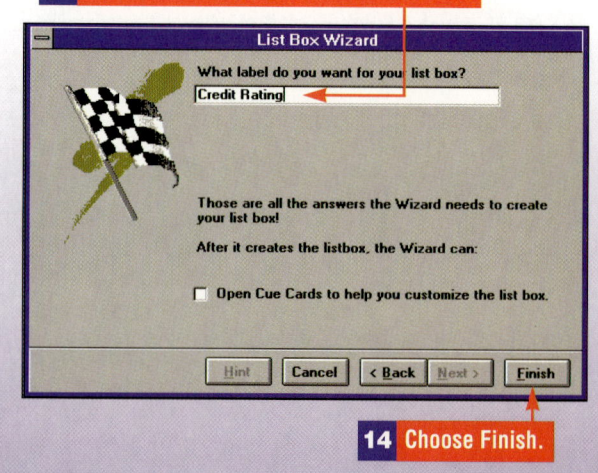

14 Choose Finish.

30

Forms—Customizing: Headers/Footers and Special Controls

15 Move and size as necessary by selecting and dragging borders.

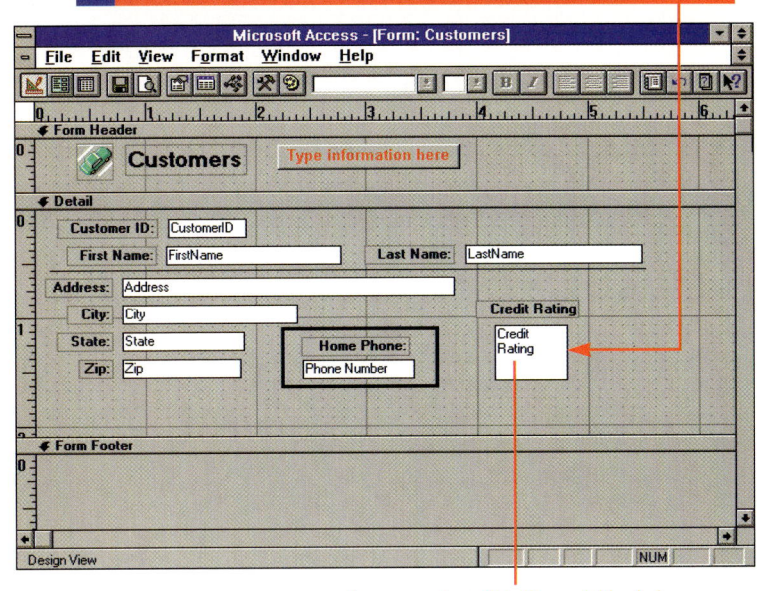

Access creates a list of acceptable choices.

To create a combo box for data entry

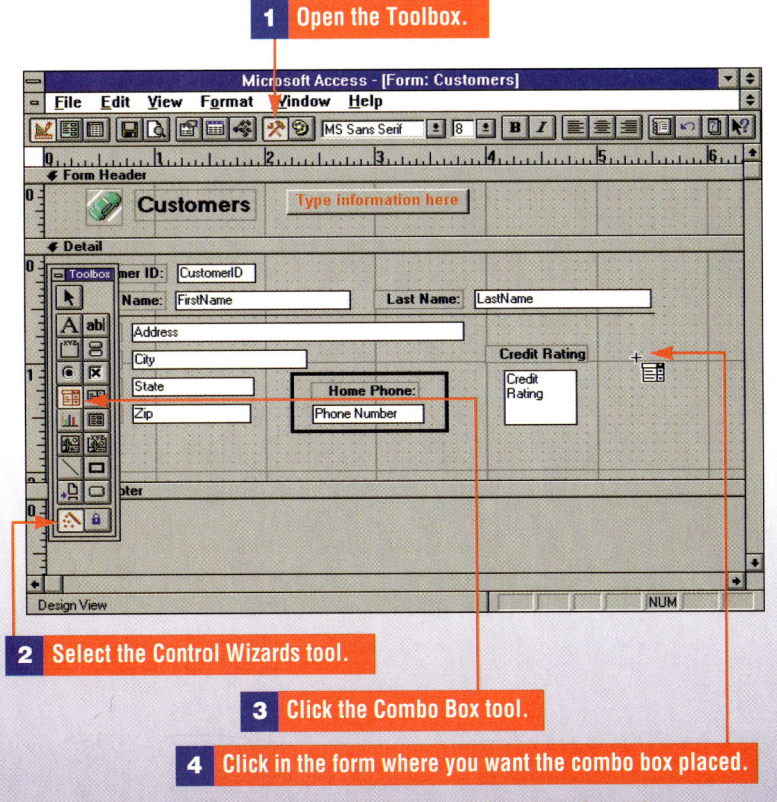

1 Open the Toolbox.

2 Select the Control Wizards tool.

3 Click the Combo Box tool.

4 Click in the form where you want the combo box placed.

Combo boxes are smaller than list boxes and allow alternative entries.

more ▶

31

Forms—Customizing: Headers/Footers and Special Controls

5 Choose the second option.

Combo Box Wizard

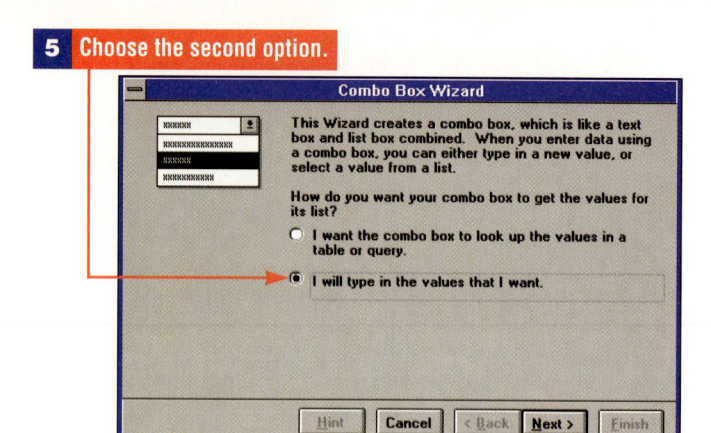

This Wizard creates a combo box, which is like a text box and list box combined. When you enter data using a combo box, you can either type in a new value, or select a value from a list.

How do you want your combo box to get the values for its list?

○ I want the combo box to look up the values in a table or query.

● I will type in the values that I want.

The Combo Box Wizard is a convenient way to automate creation of a Combo

6 Choose Next >.

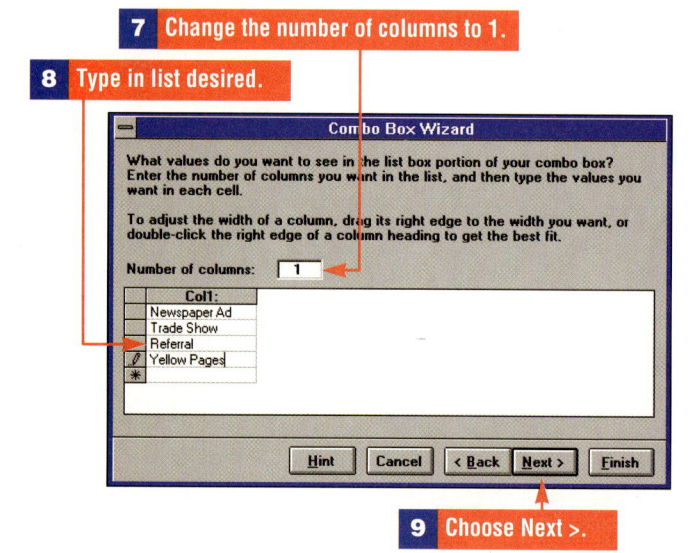

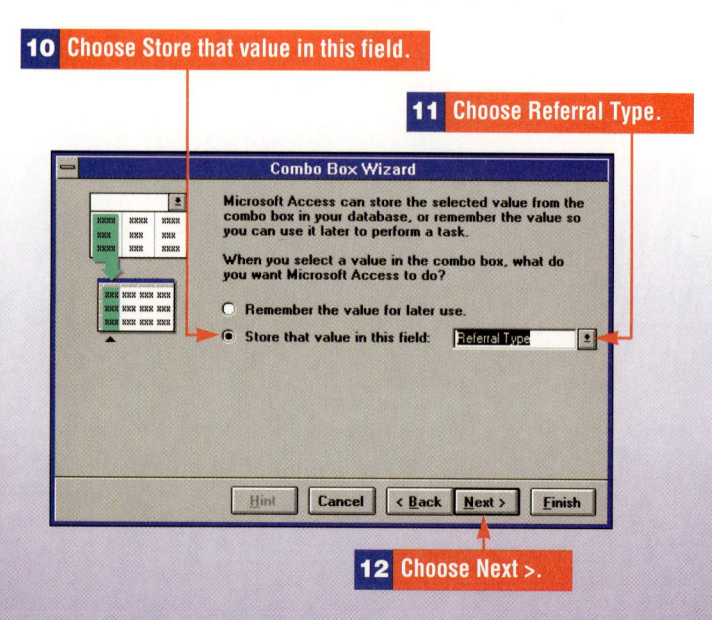

7 Change the number of columns to 1.

8 Type in list desired.

Combo Box Wizard

What values do you want to see in the list box portion of your combo box? Enter the number of columns you want in the list, and then type the values you want in each cell.

To adjust the width of a column, drag its right edge to the width you want, or double-click the right edge of a column heading to get the best fit.

Number of columns: 1

Col1:
Newspaper Ad
Trade Show
Referral
Yellow Pages

9 Choose Next >.

10 Choose Store that value in this field.

11 Choose Referral Type.

Combo Box Wizard

Microsoft Access can store the selected value from the combo box in your database, or remember the value so you can use it later to perform a task.

When you select a value in the combo box, what do you want Microsoft Access to do?

○ Remember the value for later use.

● Store that value in this field: Referral Type

12 Choose Next >.

32

Forms—Customizing: Headers/Footers and Special Controls

13 Type Customer Referral Type for label.

Combo Box Wizard

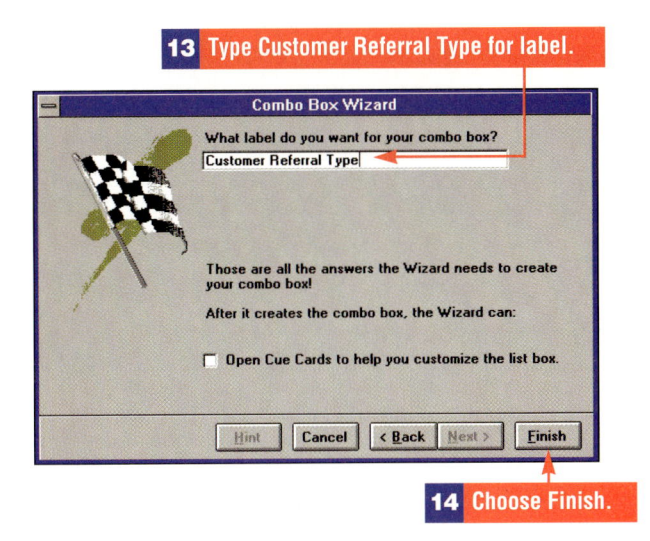

What label do you want for your combo box?

Customer Referral Type

Those are all the answers the Wizard needs to create your combo box!

After it creates the combo box, the Wizard can:

☐ Open Cue Cards to help you customize the list box.

[Hint] [Cancel] [< Back] [Next >] [**Finish**]

14 Choose Finish.

15 Size and move as necessary by selecting Combo Box and dragging borders.

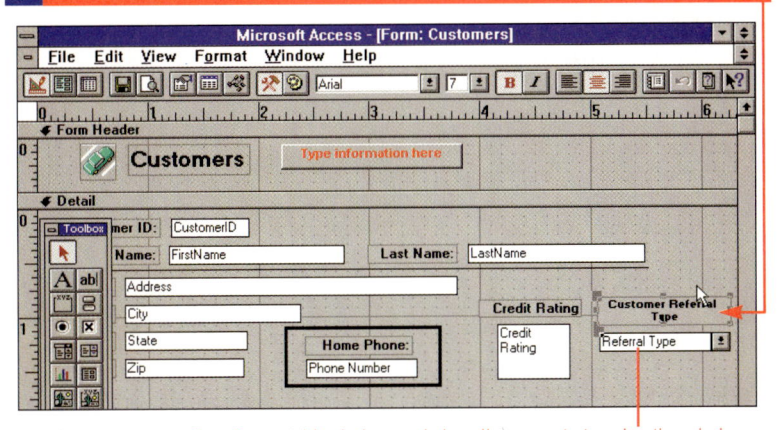

Access creates a list of acceptable choices and also allows you to type in other choices.

To create a check box

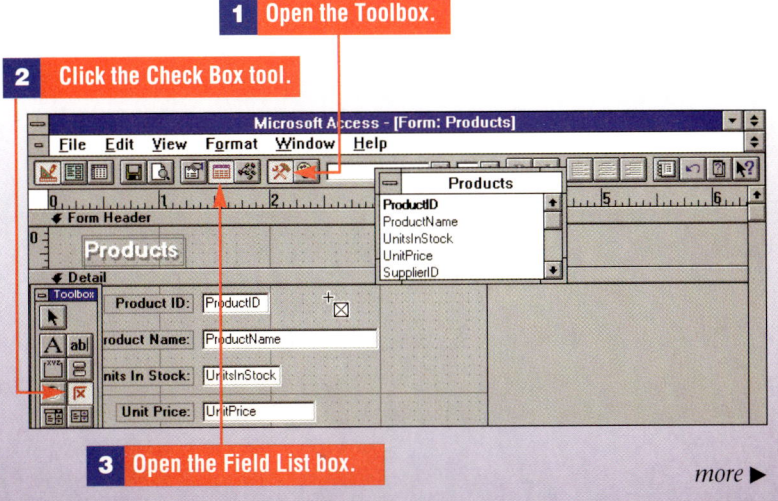

1 Open the Toolbox.

2 Click the Check Box tool.

3 Open the Field List box.

more ▶

33

Forms—Customizing: Headers/Footers and Special Controls

4 Drag the Discontinued field to the form.

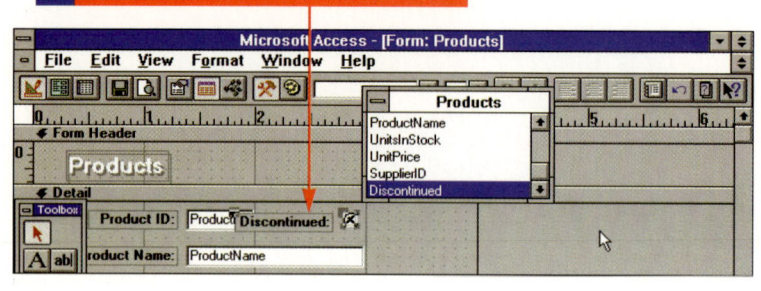

5 Change the attached label.

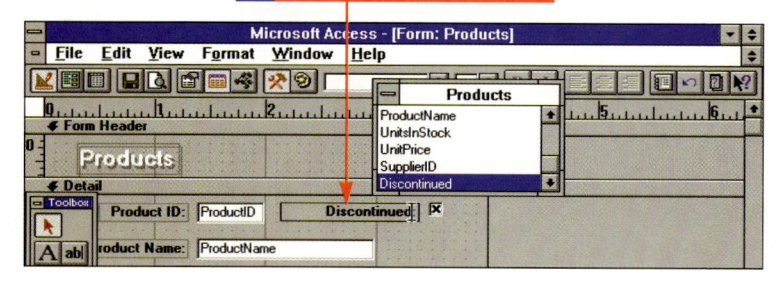

6 Size and move as necessary by selecting and dragging borders.

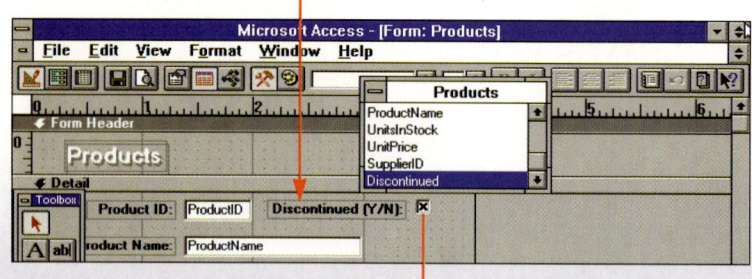

Access creates a check box in the form.

34

Forms—Customizing: Headers/Footers and Special Controls

To add option buttons

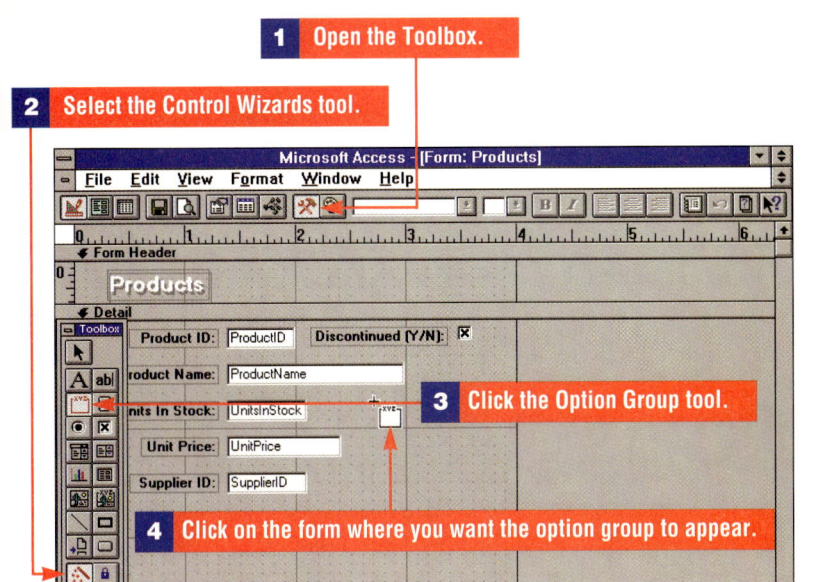

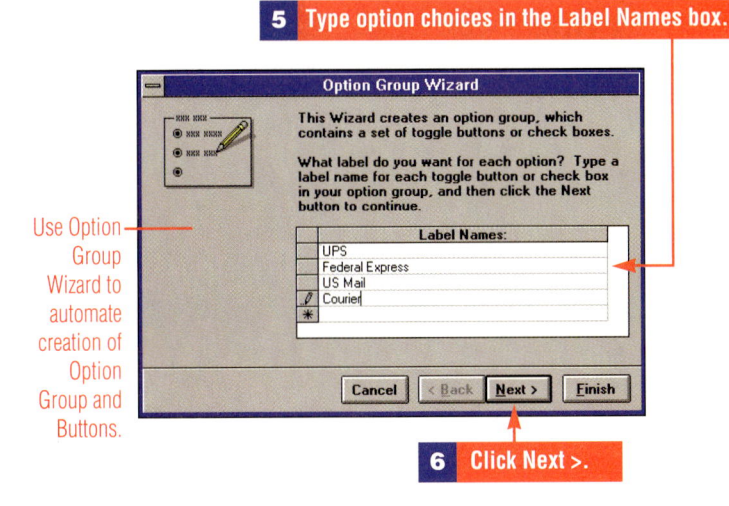

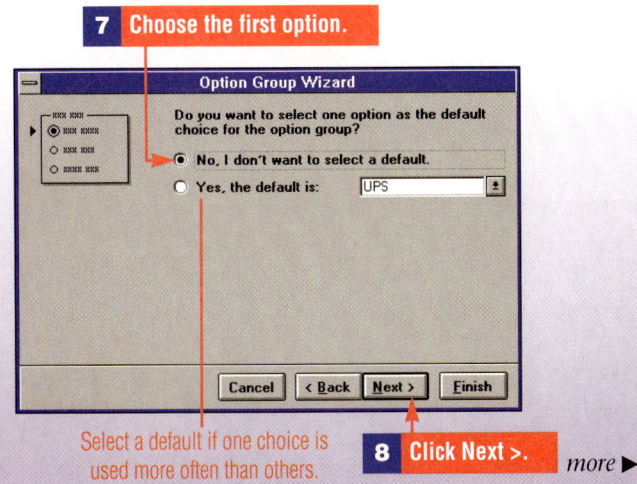

1 Open the Toolbox.

2 Select the Control Wizards tool.

3 Click the Option Group tool.

4 Click on the form where you want the option group to appear.

5 Type option choices in the Label Names box.

Use Option Group Wizard to automate creation of Option Group and Buttons.

6 Click Next >.

7 Choose the first option.

Select a default if one choice is used more often than others.

8 Click Next >.

more ▶

35

Forms—Customizing: Headers/Footers and Special Controls

9 Allow Access to automatically assign values.

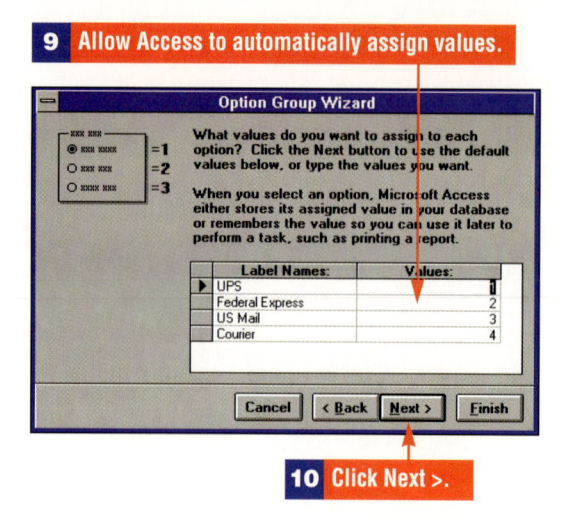

10 Click Next >.

11 Choose Store that value in this field.

12 Choose Shipped Via.

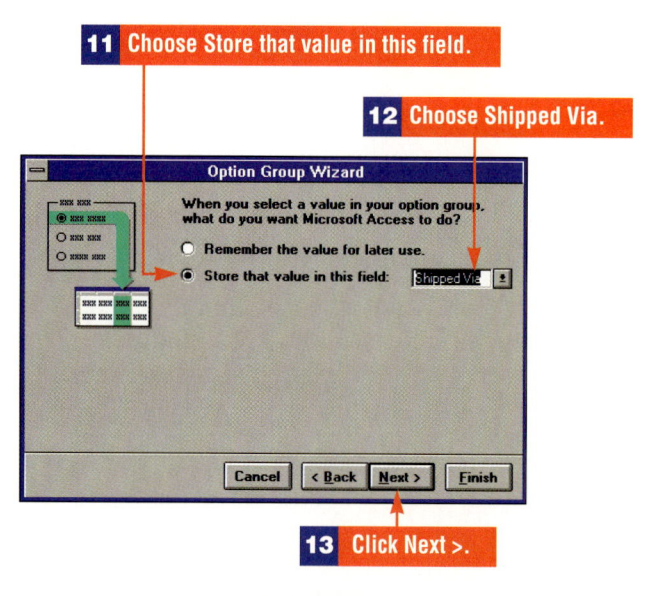

13 Click Next >.

14 Choose the style.

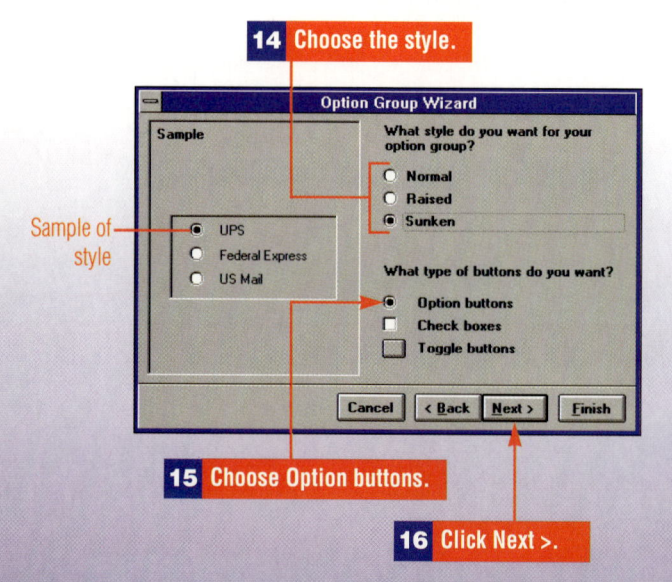

Sample of style

15 Choose Option buttons.

16 Click Next >.

Forms—Customizing: Headers/Footers and Special Controls

17 Type Shipped Via? for label.

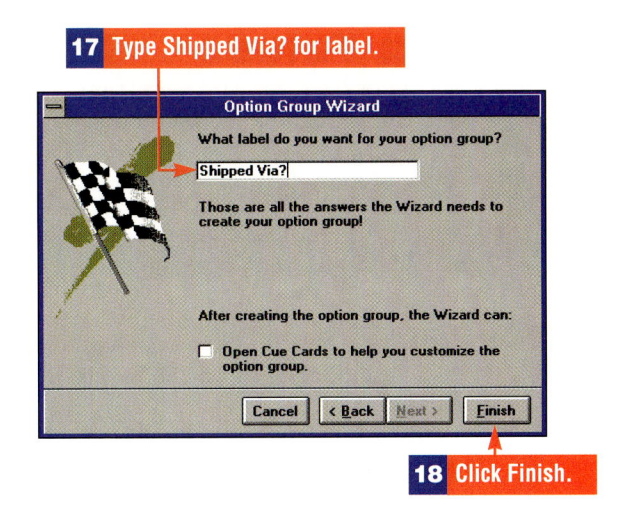

Option Group Wizard

What label do you want for your option group?

Shipped Via?

Those are all the answers the Wizard needs to create your option group!

After creating the option group, the Wizard can:

☐ Open Cue Cards to help you customize the option group.

[Cancel] [< Back] [Next >] [Finish]

18 Click Finish.

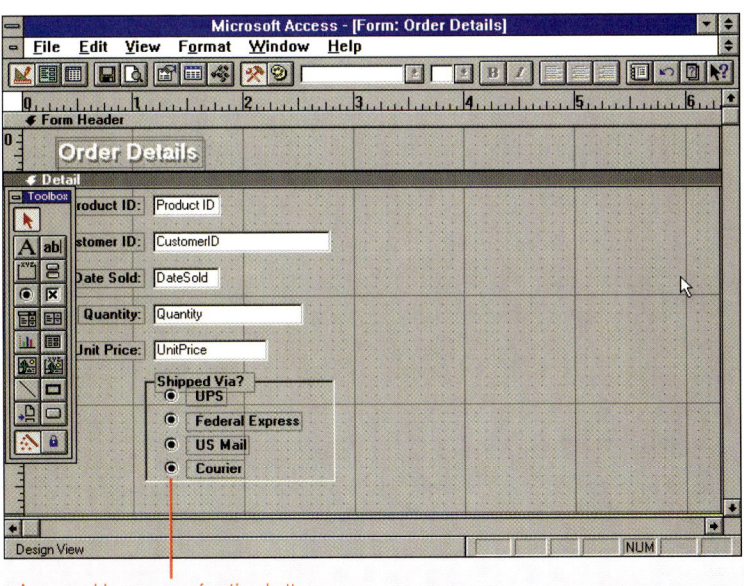

Access adds a group of option buttons.

37

Forms—Customizing: Headers/Footers and Special Controls

Formatting Values

Access can display values in many formats, with a dollar sign, for example. Setting the Format Property only changes how the value looks in a form, not how the value is stored in a table. All values are in General Format until changed and will display as they are typed.

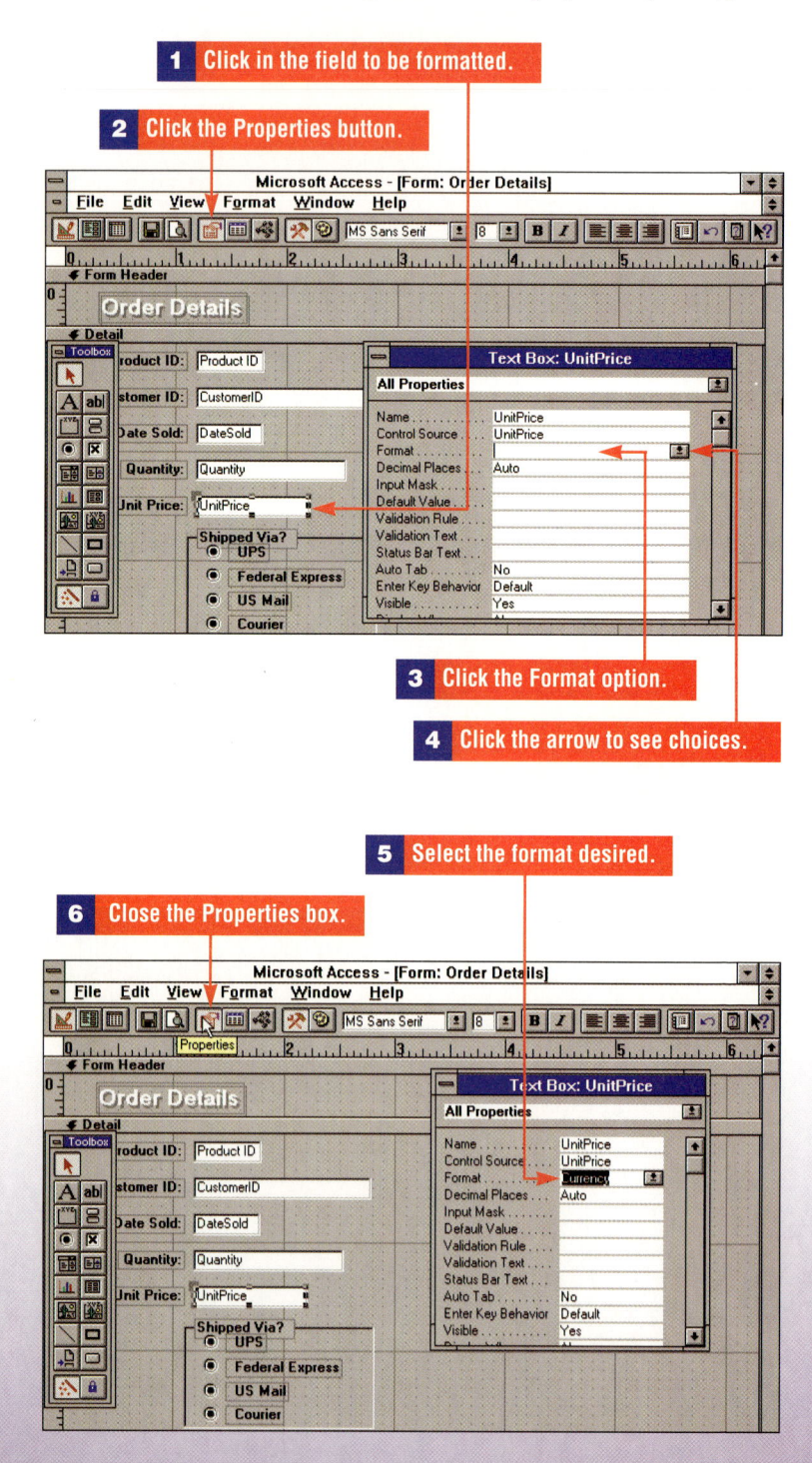

1 Click in the field to be formatted.

2 Click the Properties button.

3 Click the Format option.

4 Click the arrow to see choices.

5 Select the format desired.

6 Close the Properties box.

Forms—Customizing: Headers/Footers and Special Controls

Using Expressions in a Form

Expressions are a good way to add a calculated field to a form. You can enter the calculation directly in the text box.

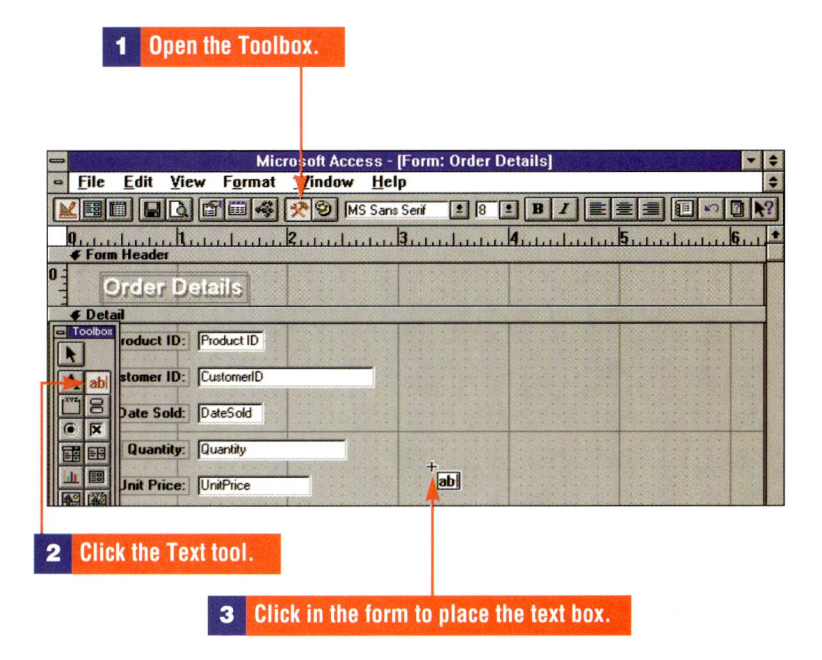

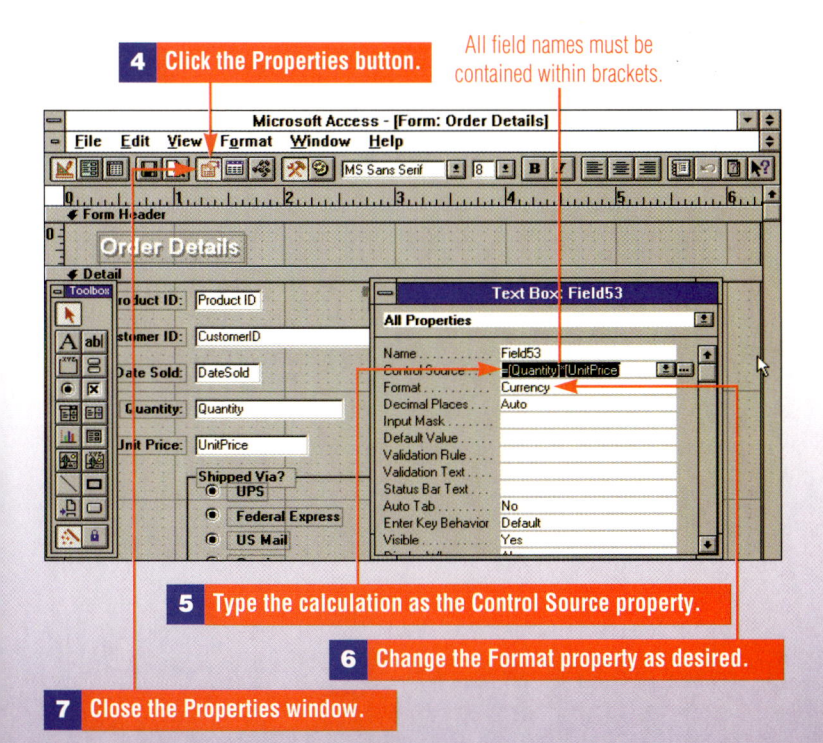

1 Open the Toolbox.

2 Click the Text tool.

3 Click in the form to place the text box.

4 Click the Properties button.

All field names must be contained within brackets.

5 Type the calculation as the Control Source property.

6 Change the Format property as desired.

7 Close the Properties window.

39

Forms—Enhancing: Editing Controls and Special Effects

Editing Controls in a Form

Objects in a form, such as fields, are called *controls*. Each control is made up of two parts. The box on the left is the label and the box on the right is the field itself. In order to make a change to a control you must first select it and the form must be in Design view.

To select and deselect controls

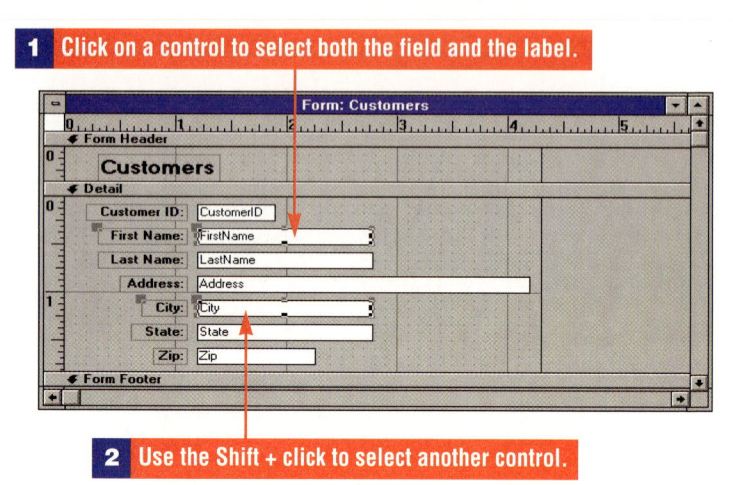

1 Click on a control to select both the field and the label.

2 Use the Shift + click to select another control.

Use the Shift + click to deselect only one control.

3 Drag around a group of controls to select all of them.

Click away from any control to deselect all.

40

Forms—Enhancing: Editing Controls and Special Effects

To move a control

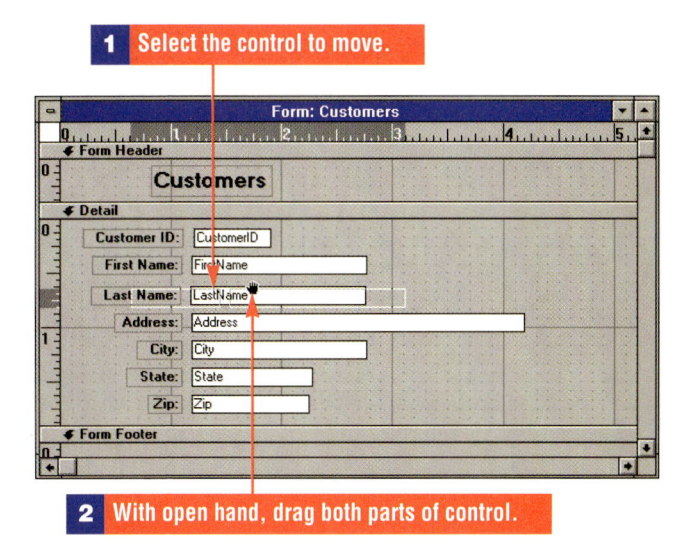

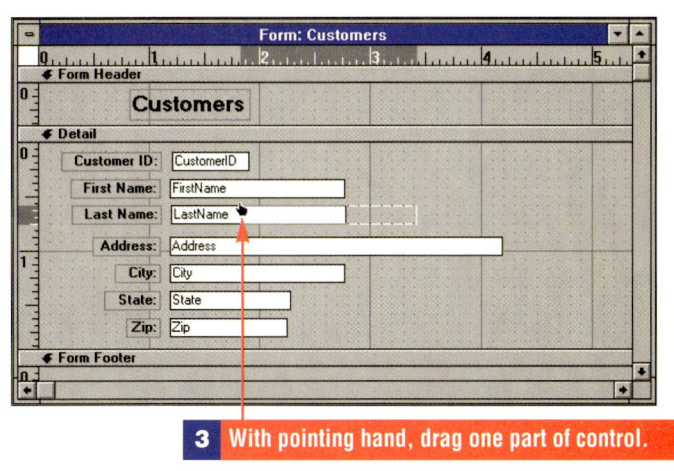

1 Select the control to move.

2 With open hand, drag both parts of control.

3 With pointing hand, drag one part of control.

To adjust the size of a form field

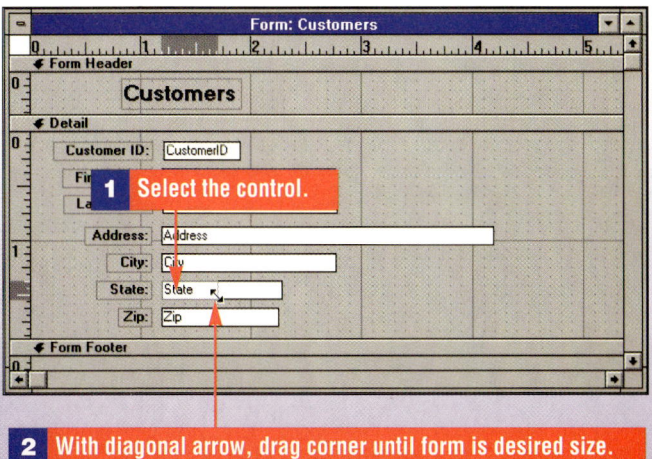

1 Select the control.

2 With diagonal arrow, drag corner until form is desired size.

Forms—Enhancing: Editing Controls and Special Effects

To change a label

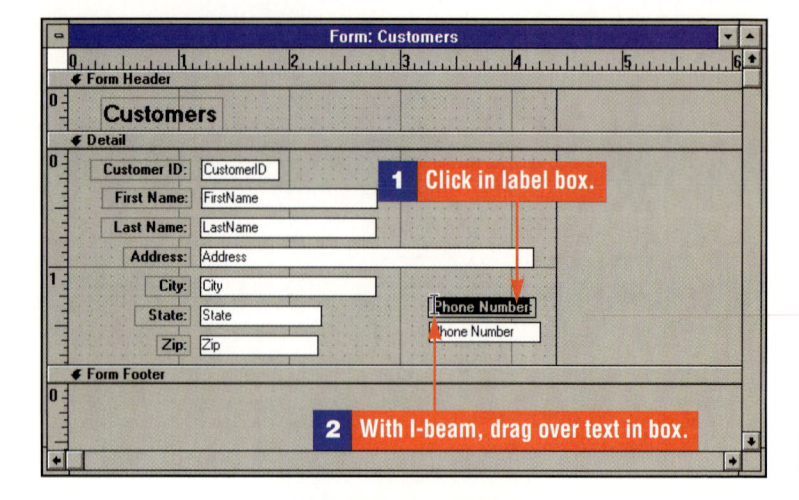

1. Click in label box.
2. With I-beam, drag over text in box.
3. Retype as needed.

Applying Special Effects to a Form

While designing a form, you can include a wide variety of features to enhance the form's appearance and usefulness. All steps are done in Design View of the form.

To add a label

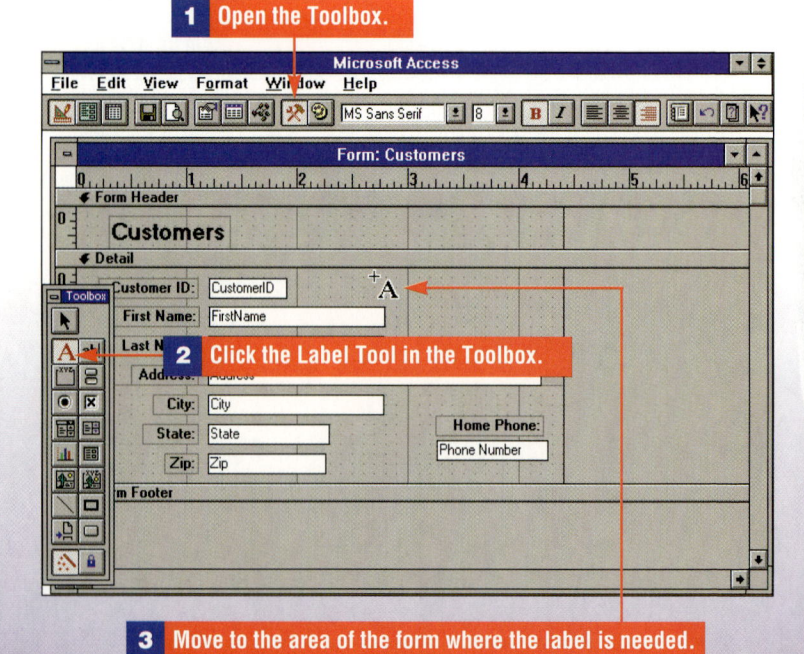

1. Open the Toolbox.
2. Click the Label Tool in the Toolbox.
3. Move to the area of the form where the label is needed.

42

Forms—Enhancing: Editing Controls and Special Effects

4 Drag mouse diagonally until label box is desired size.

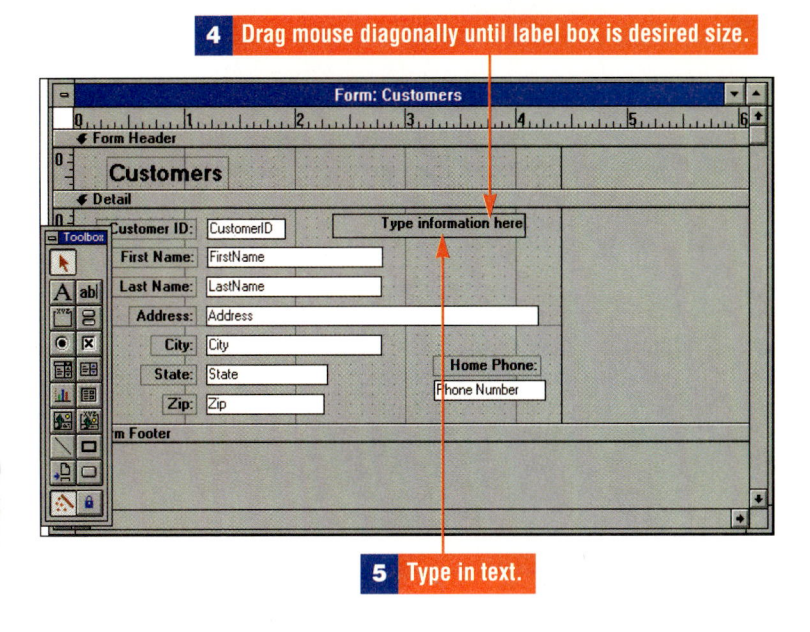

5 Type in text.

To change size, font, and alignment of text

1 Open the Toolbox.

2 Select the control(s) to change.

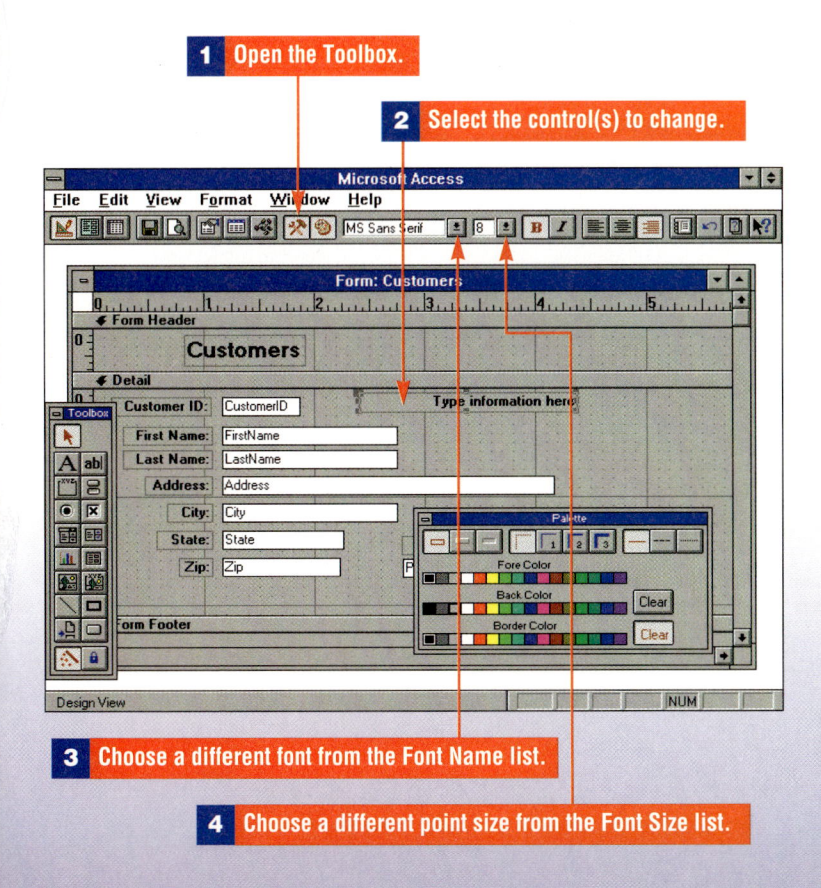

3 Choose a different font from the Font Name list.

4 Choose a different point size from the Font Size list.

more ▶

43

Forms—Enhancing: Editing Controls and Special Effects

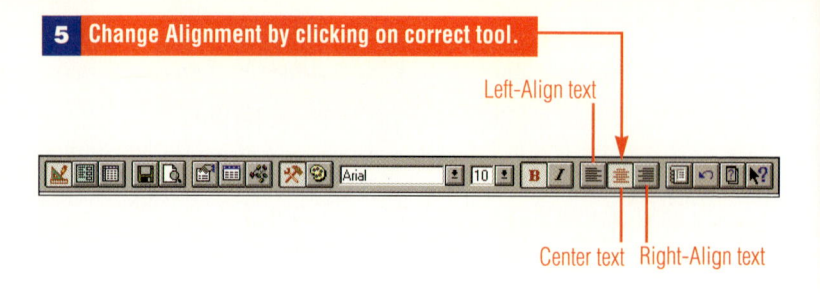

5 Change Alignment by clicking on correct tool.

Left-Align text

Center text   Right-Align text

To change the color of text

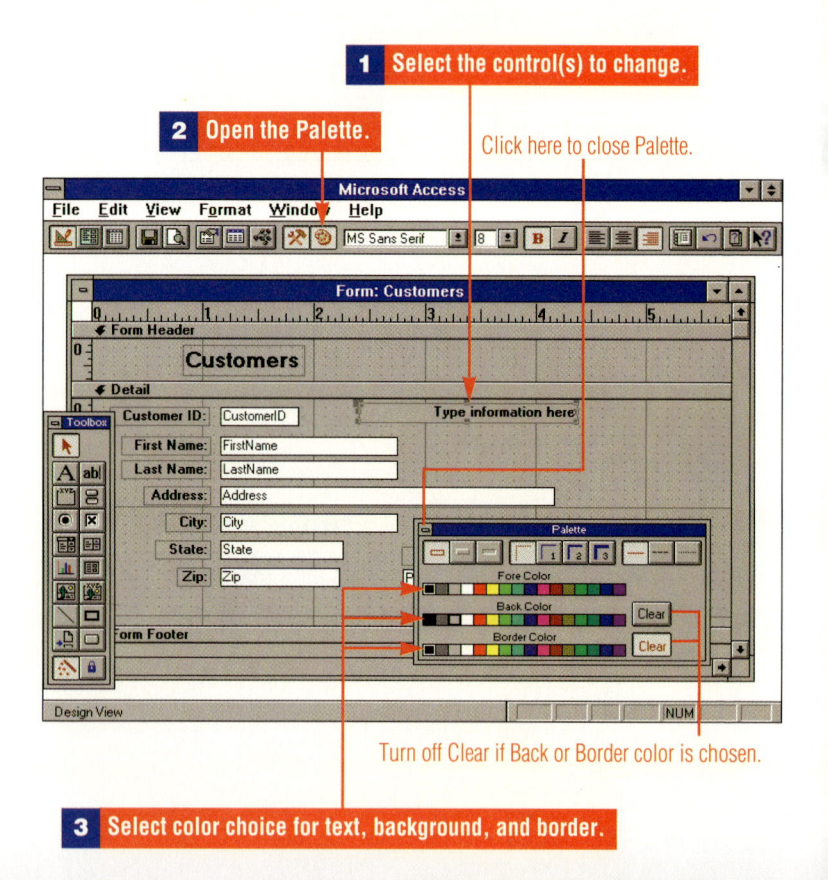

1 Select the control(s) to change.

2 Open the Palette.

Click here to close Palette.

Turn off Clear if Back or Border color is chosen.

3 Select color choice for text, background, and border.

Forms—Enhancing: Editing Controls and Special Effects

To add borders and other special effects to a control

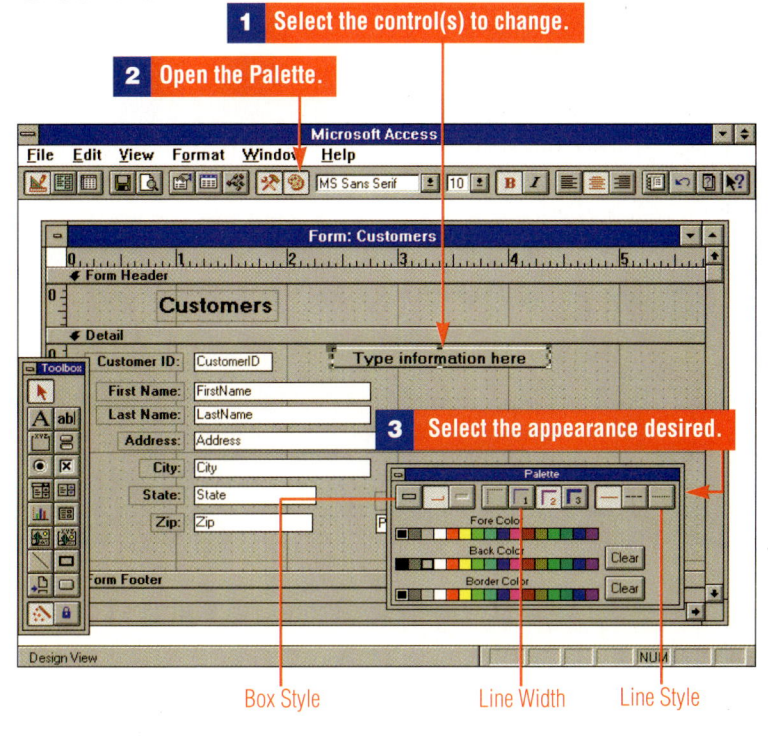

1 Select the control(s) to change.

2 Open the Palette.

Box Style   Line Width   Line Style

To add lines to a form

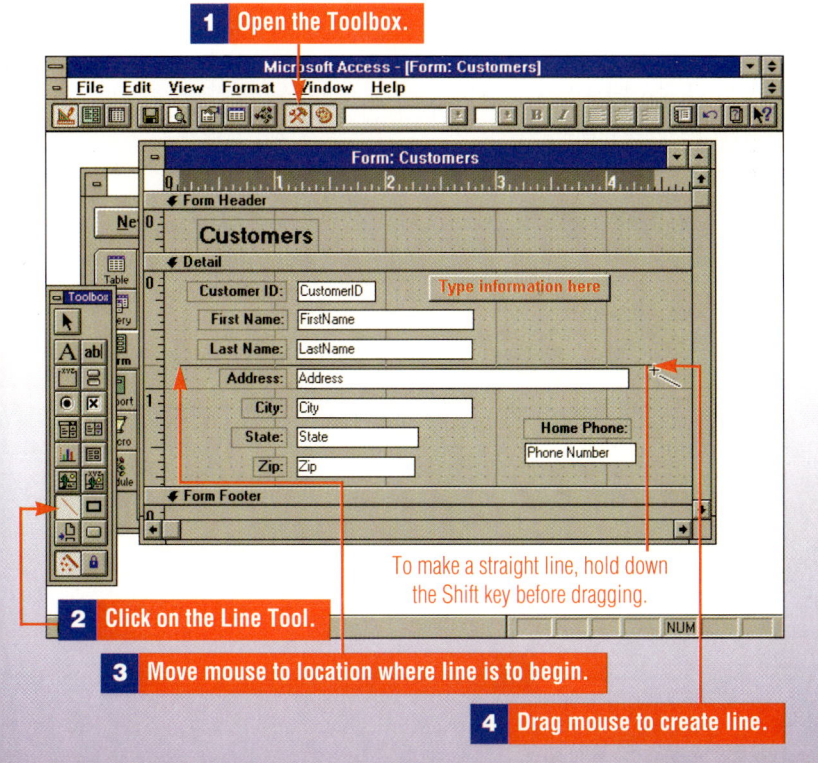

1 Open the Toolbox.

2 Click on the Line Tool.

3 Move mouse to location where line is to begin.

4 Drag mouse to create line.

To make a straight line, hold down the Shift key before dragging.

45

Forms—Enhancing: Editing Controls and Special Effects

To add boxes to a form

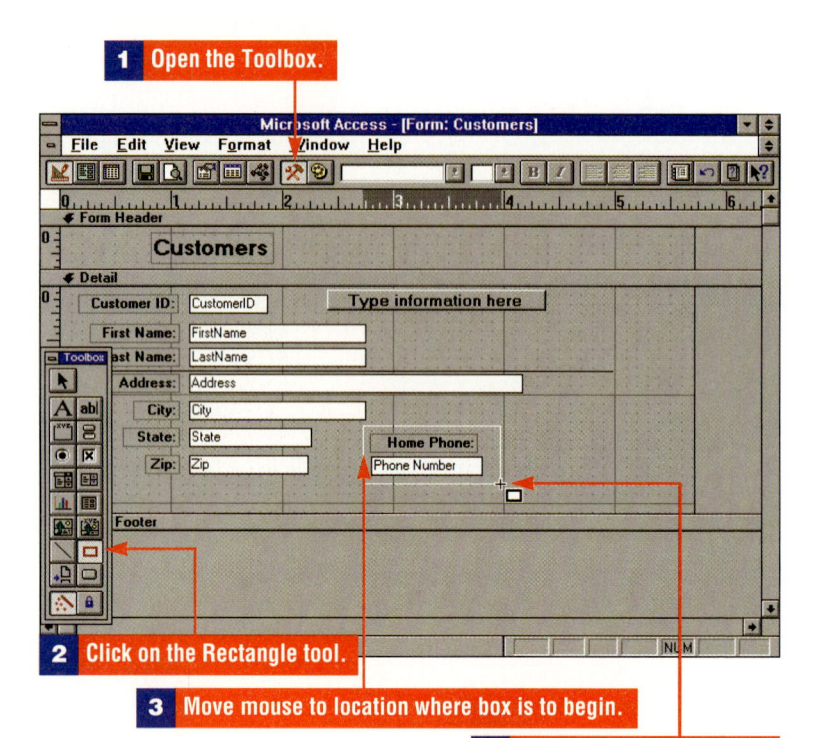

1 Open the Toolbox.

2 Click on the Rectangle tool.

3 Move mouse to location where box is to begin.

4 Drag mouse to create box.

5 If box is filled with color, open Palette.

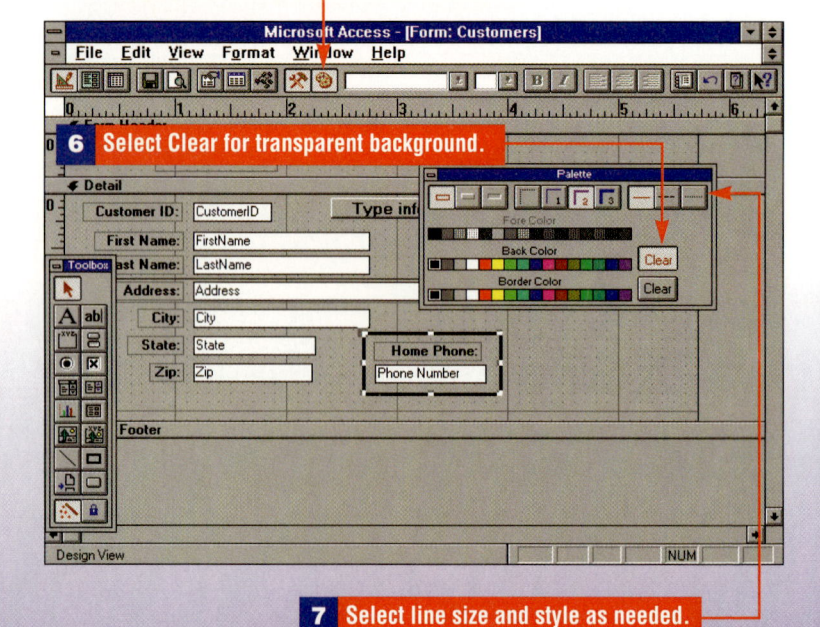

6 Select Clear for transparent background.

7 Select line size and style as needed.

46

Forms—Enhancing: Editing Controls and Special Effects

To change the size of the form

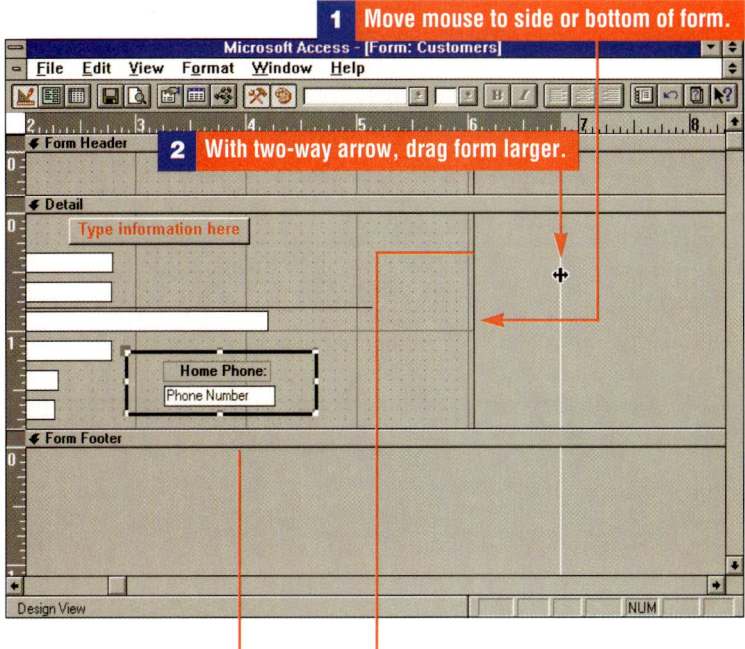

1 Move mouse to side or bottom of form.

2 With two-way arrow, drag form larger.

Drag from here to make form longer.   Drag from here to make form wider.

To align controls to a grid

1 If grid is not showing on-screen, choose View, Grid.

2 Select the control(s) to align.

3 Choose Format, Align, To Grid.

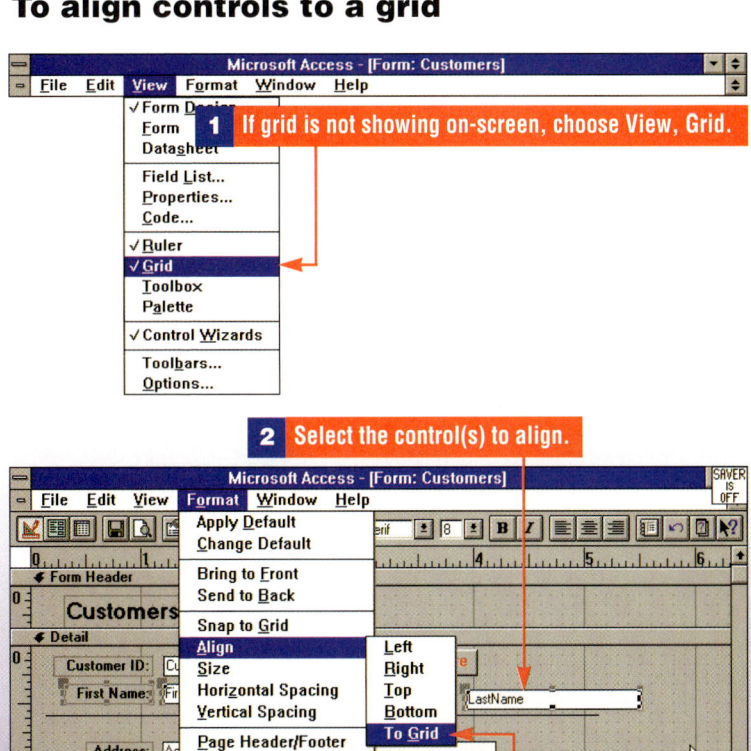

To have this done automatically, choose Format, Snap to Grid.

47

Forms—Enhancing: Editing Controls and Special Effects

Adding a Bound Field

Maybe when you created the form you didn't include one of the fields from the table or perhaps you have added a field to the table since designing the form. You need to add a bound field—one that is connected to a field in the underlying table.

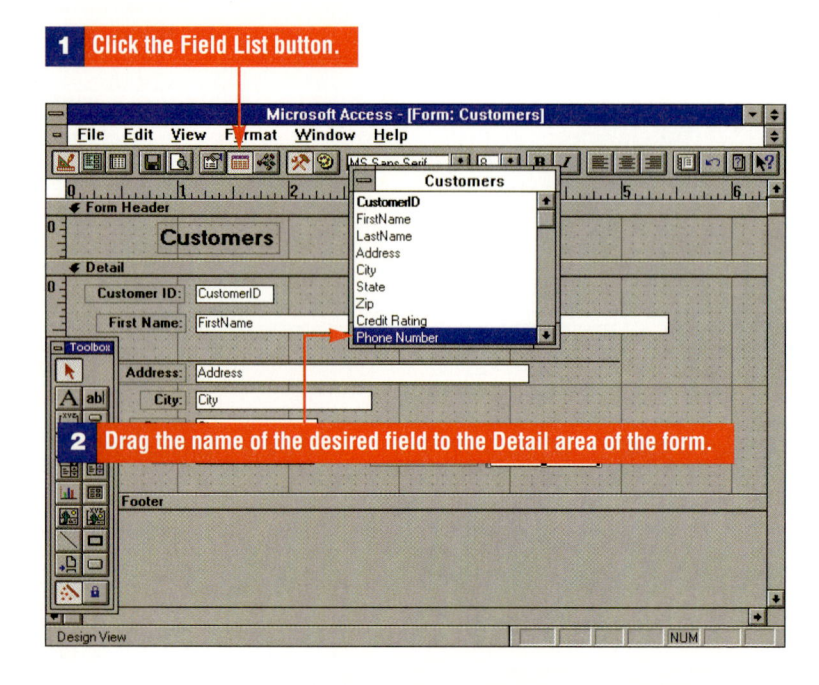

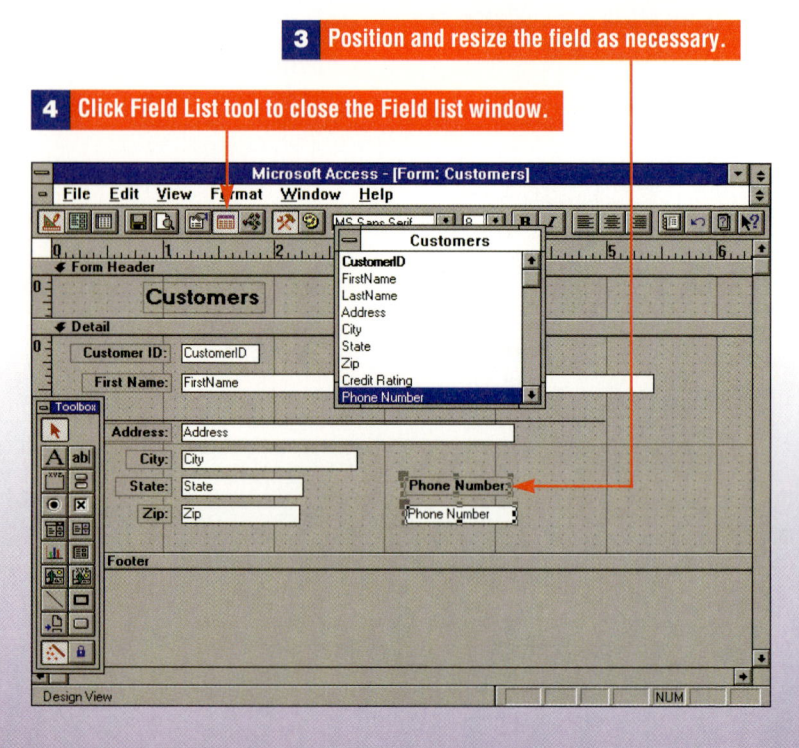

1 Click the Field List button.

2 Drag the name of the desired field to the Detail area of the form.

3 Position and resize the field as necessary.

4 Click Field List tool to close the Field list window.

48

Forms—Enhancing: Editing Controls and Special Effects

Using Graphics

Creating an unbound object picture frame allows you to embed an object into a form. You can use the ClipArt already available in Word for Windows or PowerPoint. Or you can embed an Excel worksheet to show the detail of yearly sales figures.

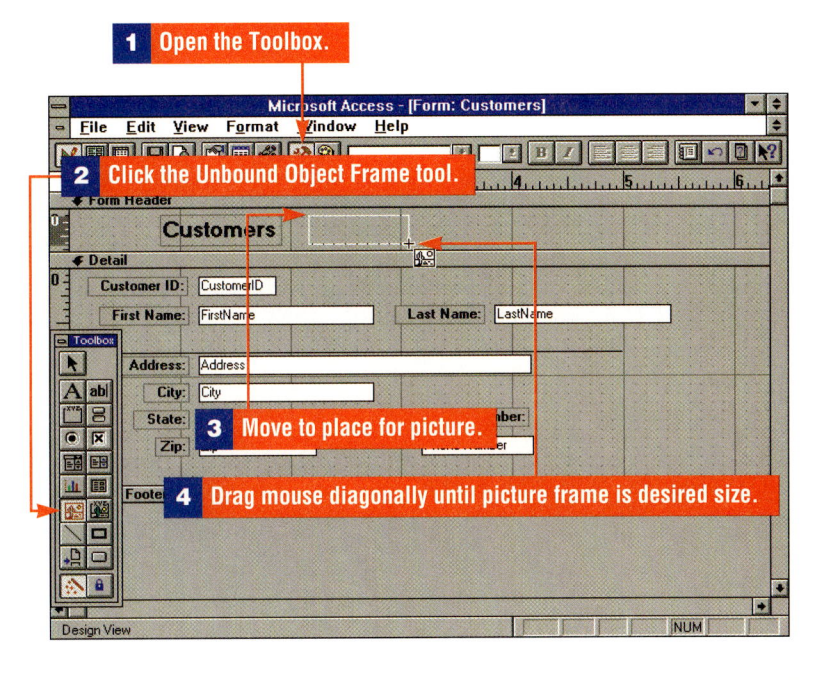

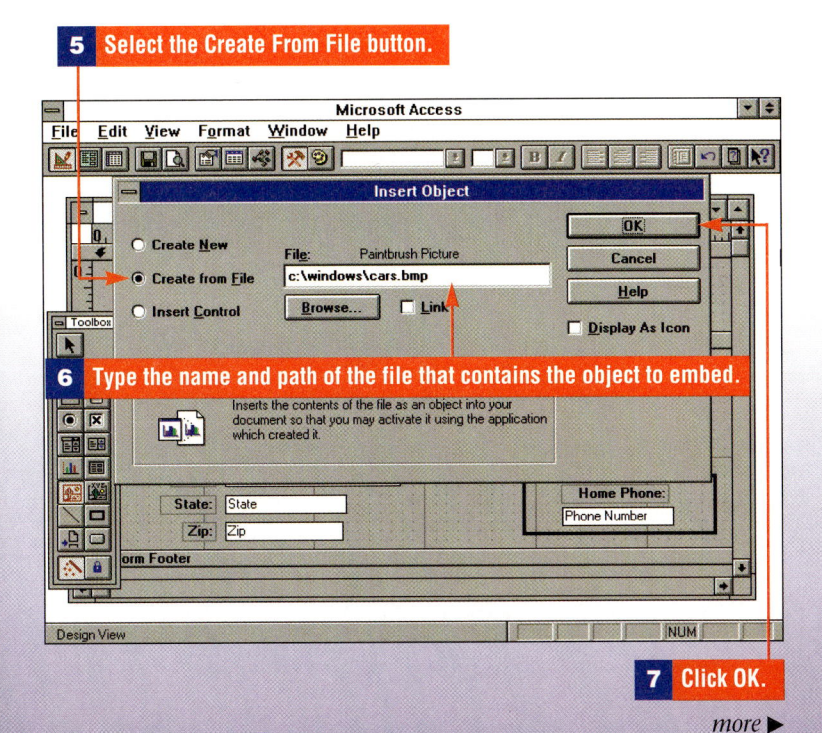

1 Open the Toolbox.

2 Click the Unbound Object Frame tool.

3 Move to place for picture.

4 Drag mouse diagonally until picture frame is desired size.

5 Select the Create From File button.

6 Type the name and path of the file that contains the object to embed.

7 Click OK.

more ▶

49

Forms—Enhancing: Editing Controls and Special Effects

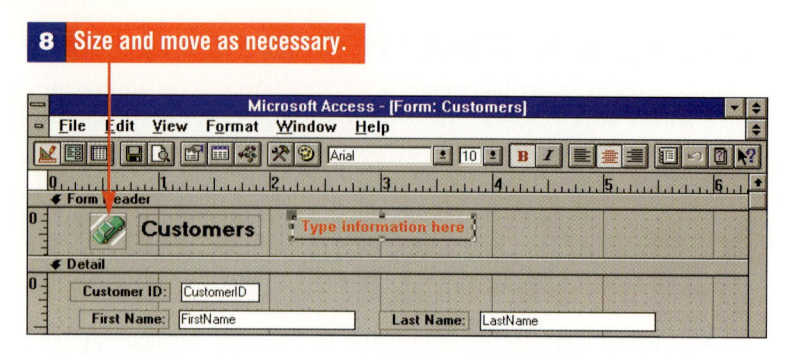

8 Size and move as necessary.

Access creates an unbound object frame and displays the object.

Setting Tab Entry Order

The tab order is the movement of the focus when you press the Tab key in Form view. Unless you change the order, Access assigns a place in the tab order for every control. When you add new controls, Access puts them at the end of the tab order.

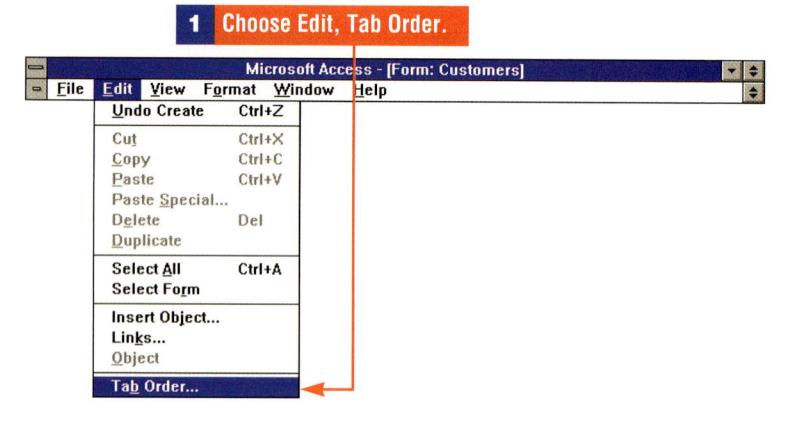

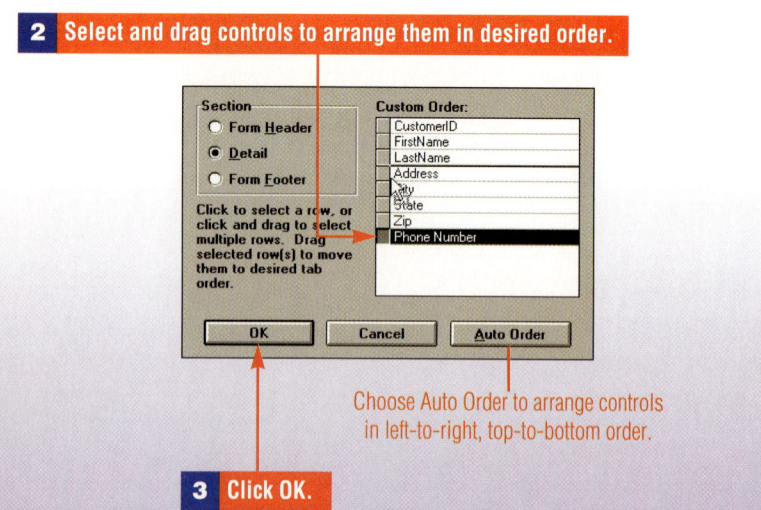

1 Choose Edit, Tab Order.

2 Select and drag controls to arrange them in desired order.

Choose Auto Order to arrange controls in left-to-right, top-to-bottom order.

3 Click OK.

Help: Using On-Line Help and Cue Cards

Using On-Line Help

There are several ways to get Help from within Access: searching for general topics using the Table of Contents in Access, getting context-sensitive help about what you are working on, or looking at Cue Cards as you accomplish a task (discussed in next section).

To search using on-line Help

1 Choose Help, Contents.

2 Click on any text that is green and has a solid underline.

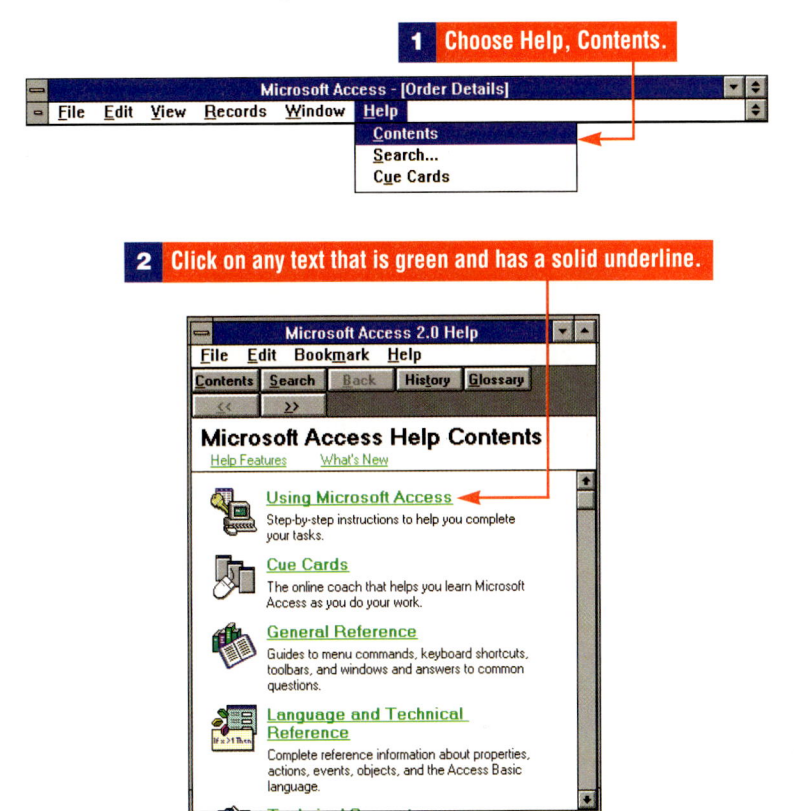

3 Continue to click on green text until the screen you need appears.

Click the Contents button to go back to Table of Contents.

Green text with dotted underline will give a definition.

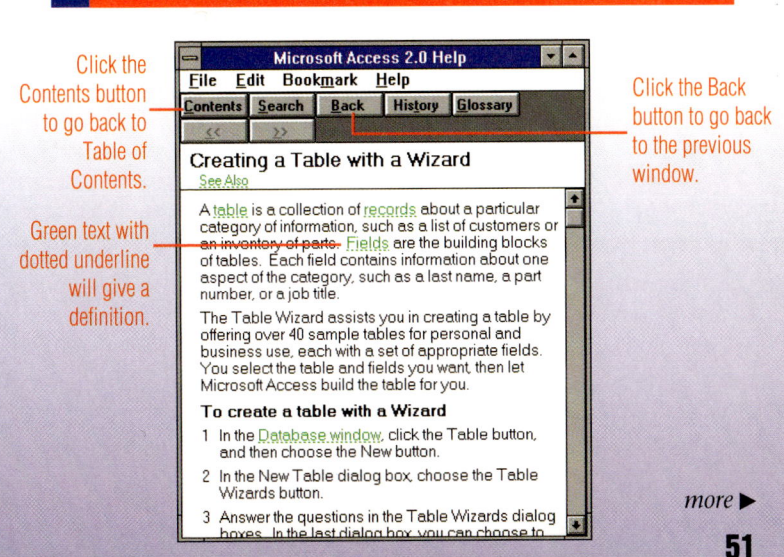

Click the Back button to go back to the previous window.

more ▶

51

Help: Using On-Line Help and Cue Cards

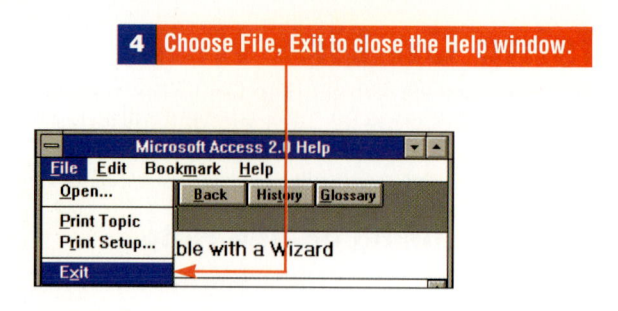

4 Choose File, Exit to close the Help window.

To get context-sensitive Help

1 With any dialog box open, press the F1 key.

2 Access provides information specific to that dialog box.

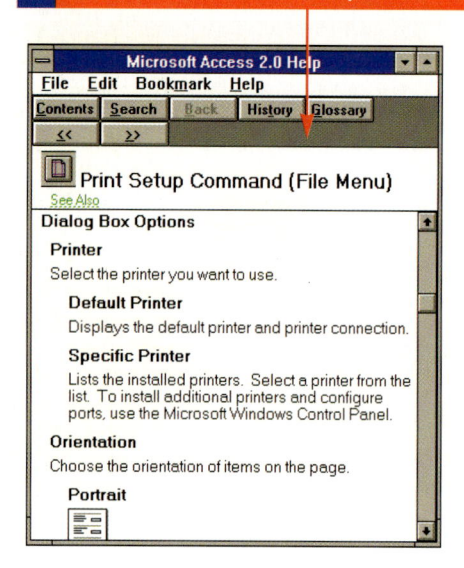

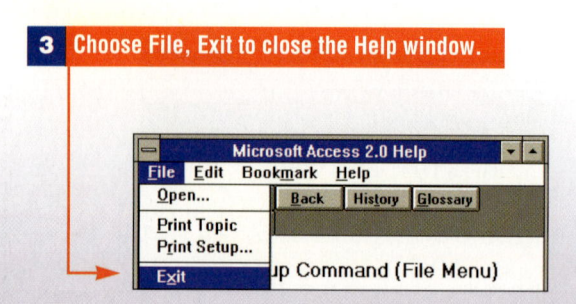

Print Setup Command (File Menu)

Dialog Box Options

Printer
Select the printer you want to use.

Default Printer
Displays the default printer and printer connection.

Specific Printer
Lists the installed printers. Select a printer from the list. To install additional printers and configure ports, use the Microsoft Windows Control Panel.

Orientation
Choose the orientation of items on the page.

Portrait

3 Choose File, Exit to close the Help window.

Help: Using On-Line Help and Cue Cards

Using Cue Cards

If you would like Access to give you step-by-step instructions as you are performing a particular task, use Cue Cards. They stay on the screen while you are working to "walk" you through the task.

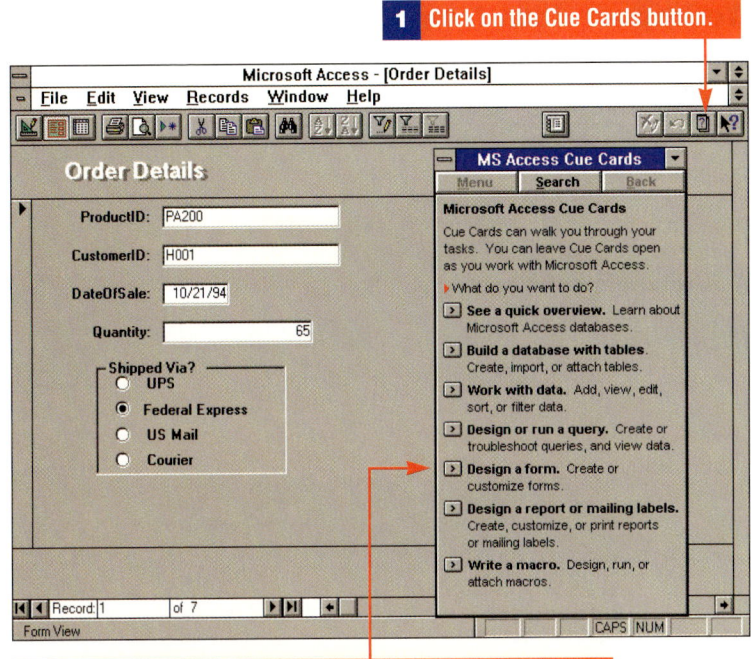

1 Click on the Cue Cards button.

2 Click the arrow button beside the desired Cue Card topic.

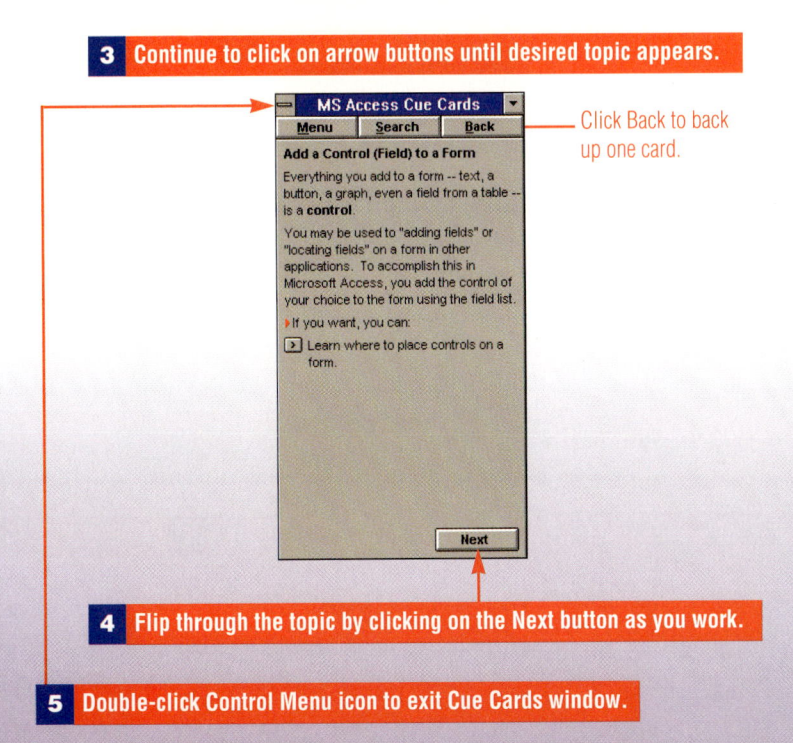

3 Continue to click on arrow buttons until desired topic appears.

Click Back to back up one card.

4 Flip through the topic by clicking on the Next button as you work.

5 Double-click Control Menu icon to exit Cue Cards window.

Importing Data: Importing, Exporting, and Attaching

Importing Data

To copy data from another Access database or another database program into your current database, use the Import feature to convert the data into Access-readable tables. These commands must be done from the Database window of an open database.

To import data from another database

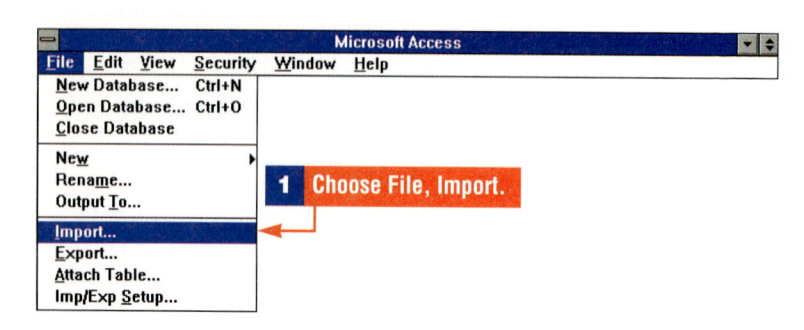

1 Choose File, Import.

2 Select the Data Source type.

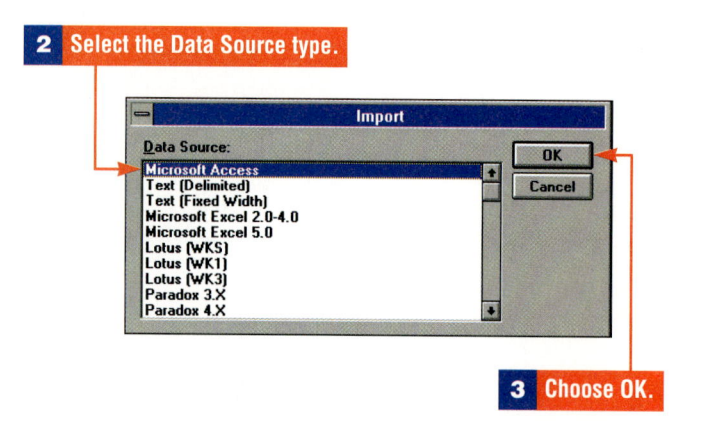

3 Choose OK.

4 Select the database to copy.

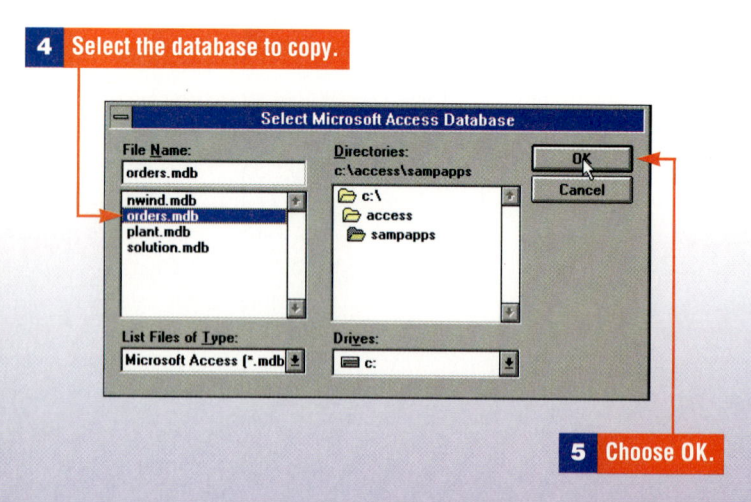

5 Choose OK.

Importing Data: Importing, Exporting, and Attaching

6 Select the type of object to be imported.

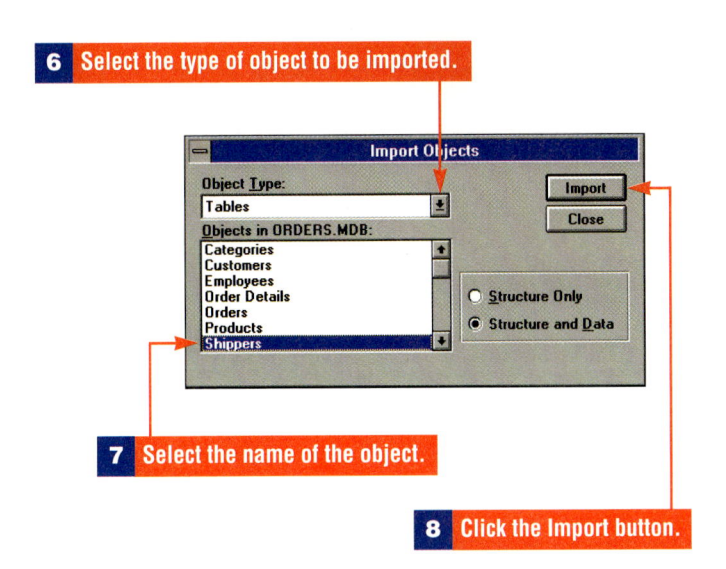

7 Select the name of the object.

8 Click the Import button.

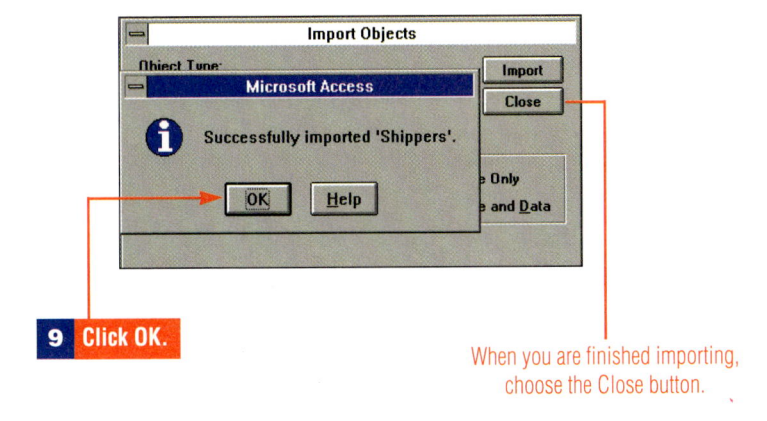

9 Click OK.

When you are finished importing, choose the Close button.

more ▶

55

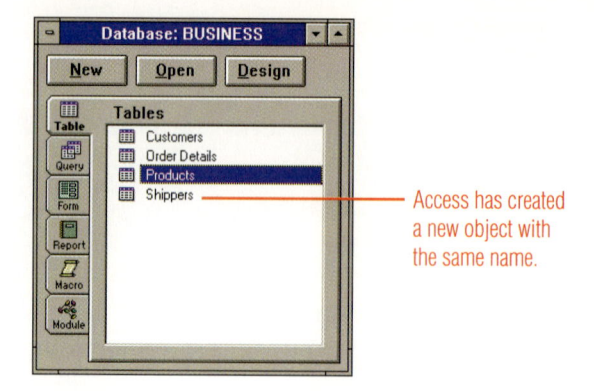

Importing Data: Importing, Exporting, and Attaching

Access has created a new object with the same name.

To import data from a spreadsheet file

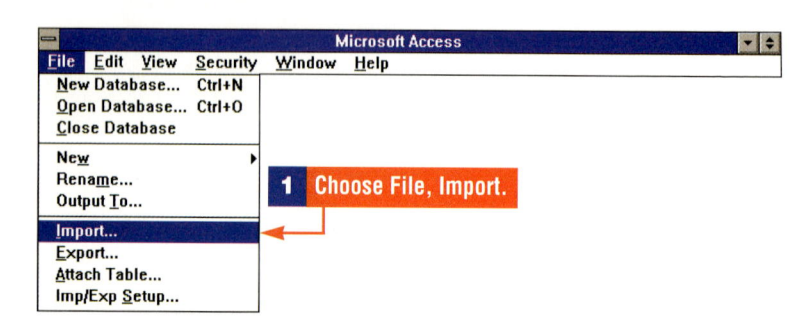

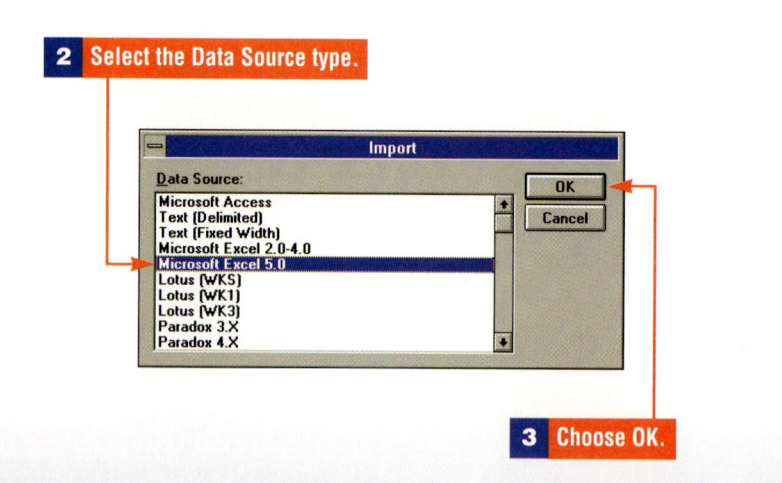

1 Choose File, Import.

2 Select the Data Source type.

3 Choose OK.

Importing Data: Importing, Exporting, and Attaching

4 Select the spreadsheet to import.

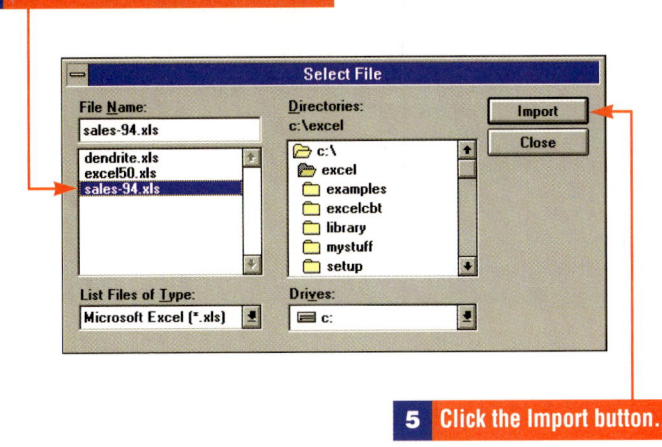

5 Click the Import button.

6 If your spreadsheet is set up this way, choose First Row Contains Field Names.

7 Choose Create New Table.

8 Click OK.

9 Click OK.

When you are finished importing, choose the Close button.

more ▶

57

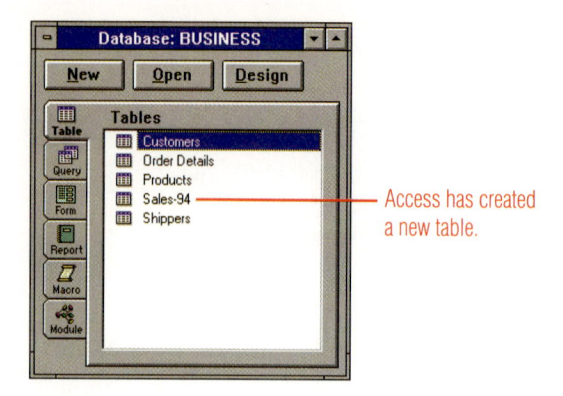

Importing Data: Importing, Exporting, and Attaching

Access has created a new table.

Exporting Data

You can export or copy data to another Microsoft Access file or to another software program. For example, you may want to export Access data to be used in a Word for Windows mail merge.

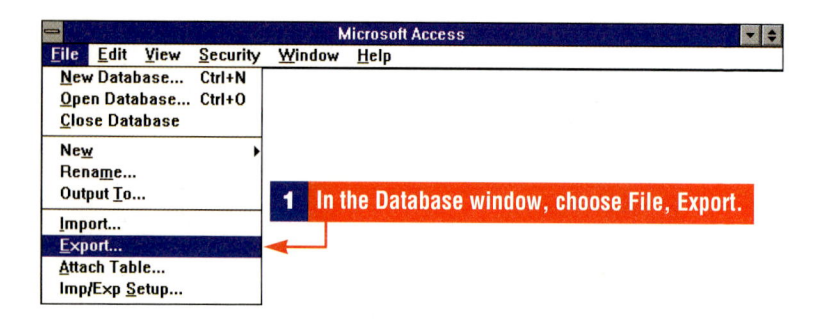

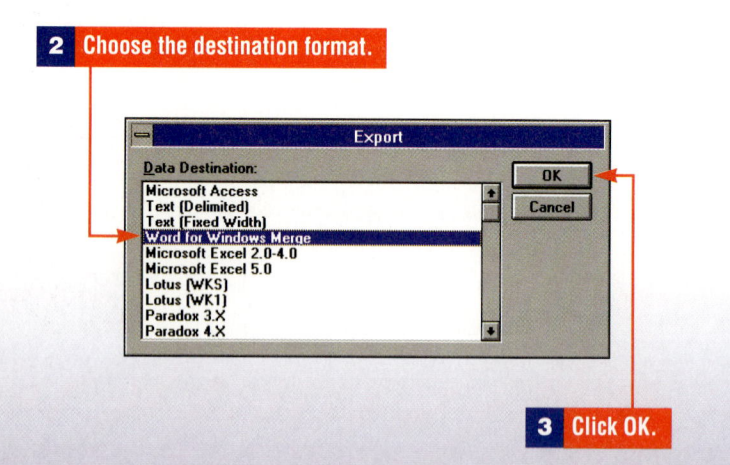

1 In the Database window, choose File, Export.

2 Choose the destination format.

3 Click OK.

Importing Data: Importing, Exporting, and Attaching

4 Select the table with the data to export.

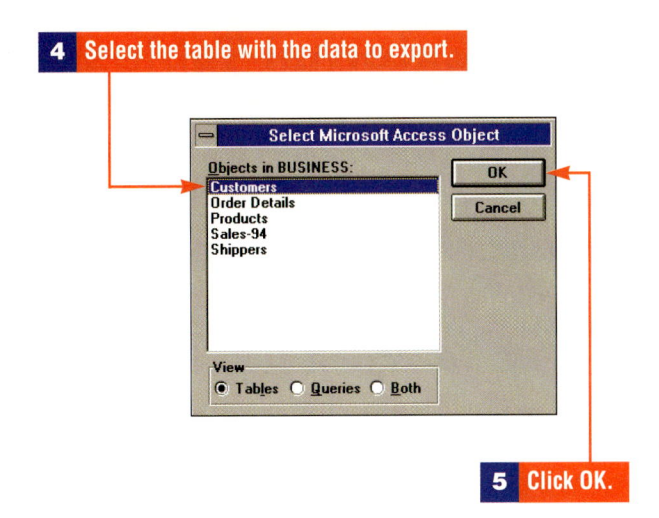

Select Microsoft Access Object

Objects in BUSINESS:
- Customers
- Order Details
- Products
- Sales-94
- Shippers

View: ● Tables ○ Queries ○ Both

5 Click OK.

---

6 Enter a file name for the new file.

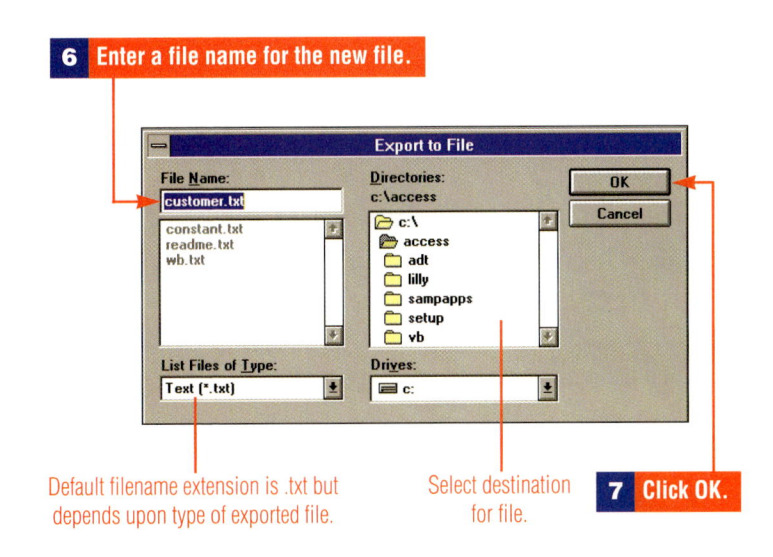

Export to File

File Name: customer.txt
- constant.txt
- readme.txt
- wb.txt

Directories: c:\access
- c:\
- access
- adt
- lilly
- sampapps
- setup
- vb

List Files of Type: Text (*.txt)

Drives: c:

Default filename extension is .txt but depends upon type of exported file.

Select destination for file.

7 Click OK.

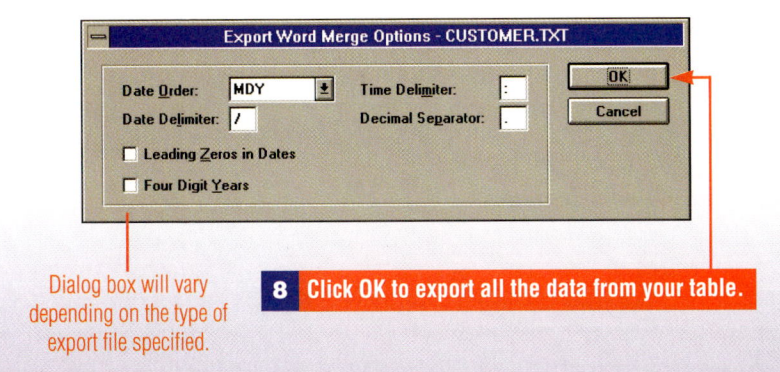

Export Word Merge Options - CUSTOMER.TXT

Date Order: MDY
Date Delimiter: /
Time Delimiter: :
Decimal Separator: .

☐ Leading Zeros in Dates
☐ Four Digit Years

Dialog box will vary depending on the type of export file specified.

8 Click OK to export all the data from your table.

Importing Data: Importing, Exporting, and Attaching

Attaching External Tables

Sometimes a database file is so big, or shared by so many people, that it isn't practical to copy the data using the Import command. In this case, the Attach command is useful. The data can reside in another storage area and still be analyzed in Access.

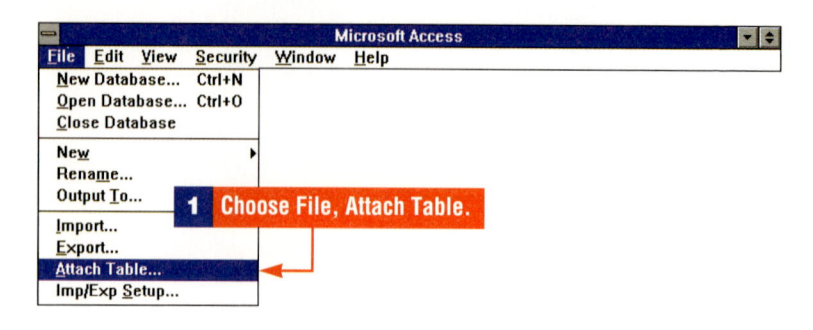

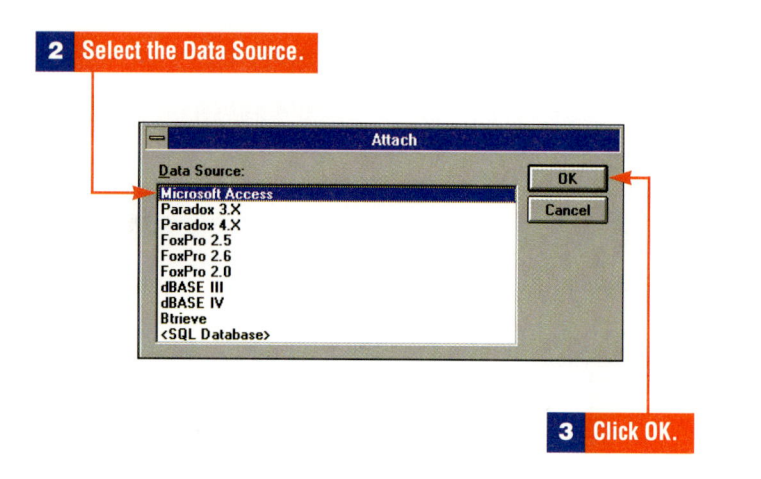

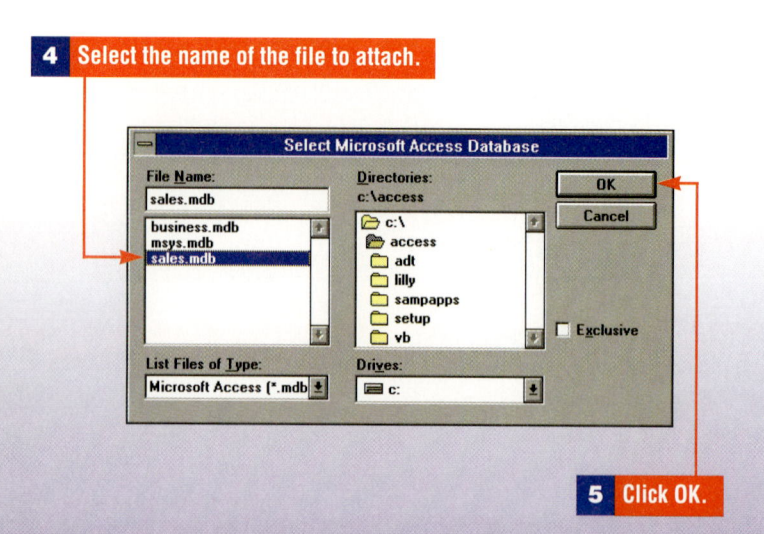

1 Choose File, Attach Table.

2 Select the Data Source.

3 Click OK.

4 Select the name of the file to attach.

5 Click OK.

Importing Data: Importing, Exporting, and Attaching

6 Select the name of the table you want to attach.

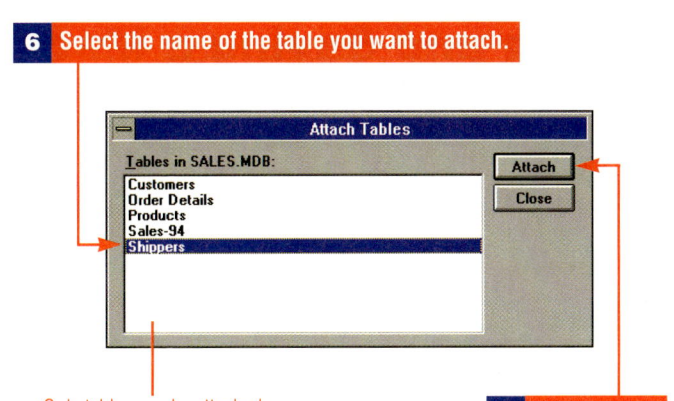

Attach Tables

Tables in SALES.MDB:
- Customers
- Order Details
- Products
- Sales-94
- **Shippers**

[Attach] [Close]

Only tables can be attached.

7 Click Attach.

8 Click OK to confirm attachment.

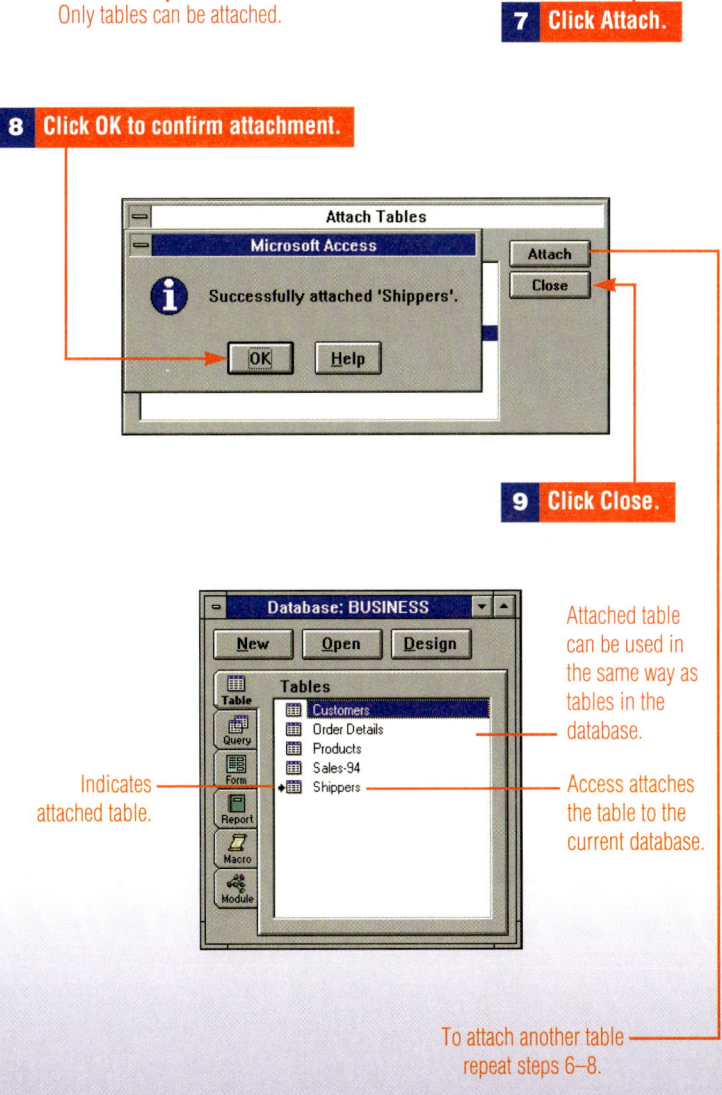

Attach Tables

Microsoft Access

Successfully attached 'Shippers'.

[OK] [Help]

[Attach] [Close]

9 Click Close.

Database: BUSINESS

[New] [Open] [Design]

Tables
- Customers
- Order Details
- Products
- Sales-94
- ◆ Shippers

Indicates attached table.

Attached table can be used in the same way as tables in the database.

Access attaches the table to the current database.

To attach another table repeat steps 6–8.

61

Macros: Creating, Running, and Attaching

Creating and Saving a Macro

Macros are simply names given to the instructions for a series of actions. For example, you might create a macro that sends a particular report to the printer while you are using a form. When you create a macro, you are asking Access to remember tasks in a specified order, so they can be repeated later.

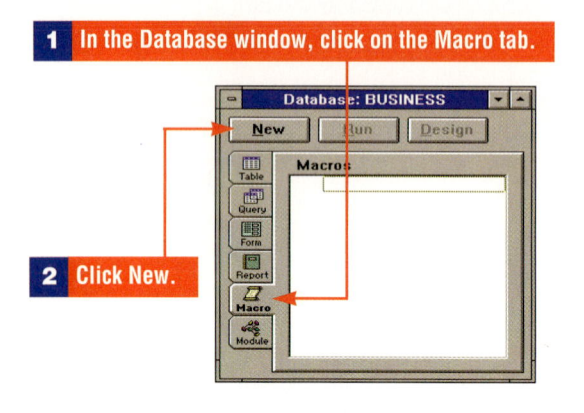

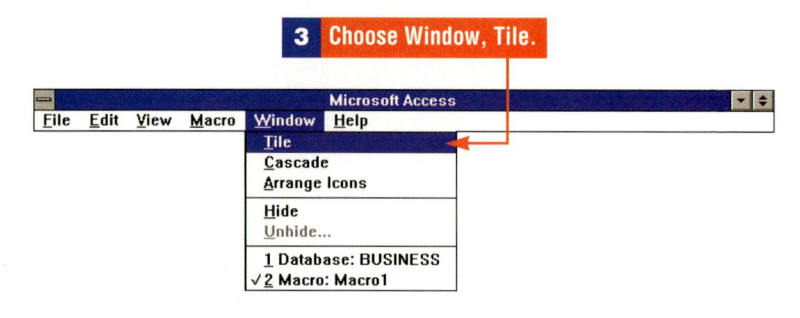

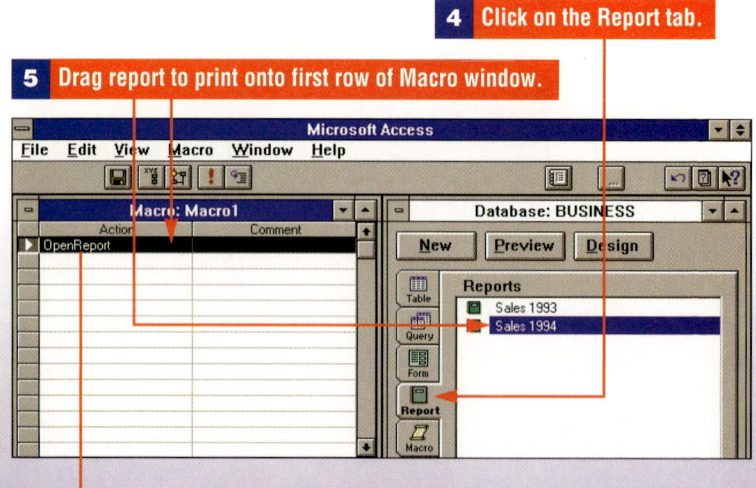

1 In the Database window, click on the Macro tab.

2 Click New.

3 Choose Window, Tile.

4 Click on the Report tab.

5 Drag report to print onto first row of Macro window.

This creates an OpenReport action for that report.

62

Macros: Creating, Running, and Attaching

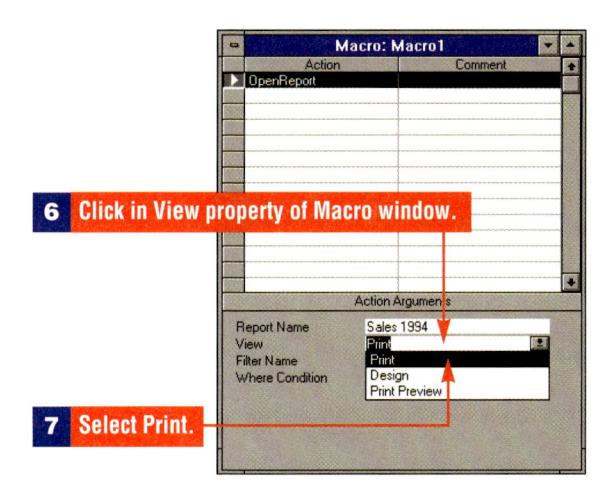

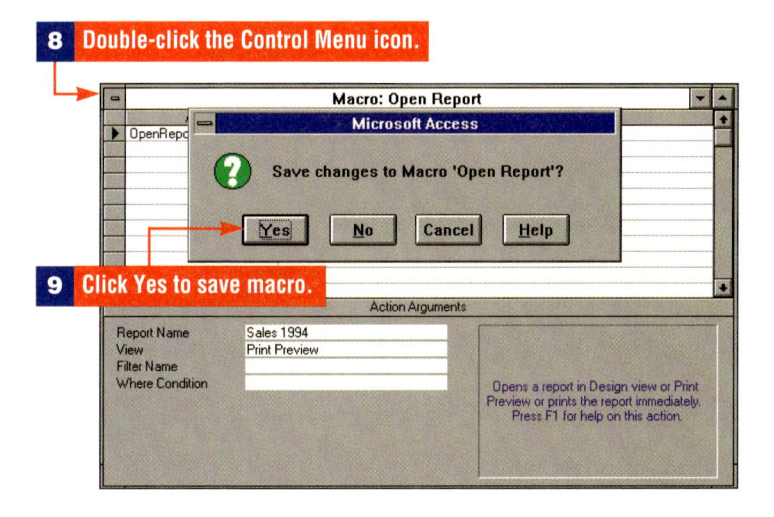

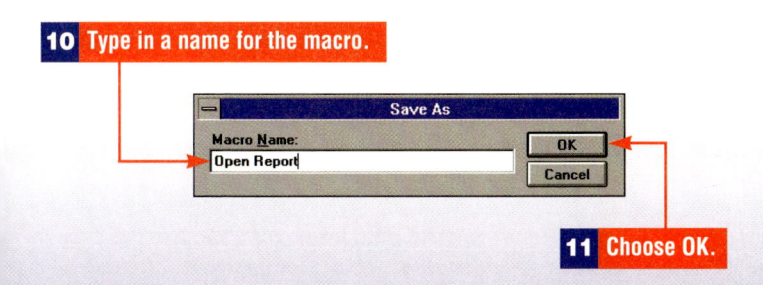

6 Click in View property of Macro window.

7 Select Print.

8 Double-click the Control Menu icon.

9 Click Yes to save macro.

10 Type in a name for the macro.

11 Choose OK.

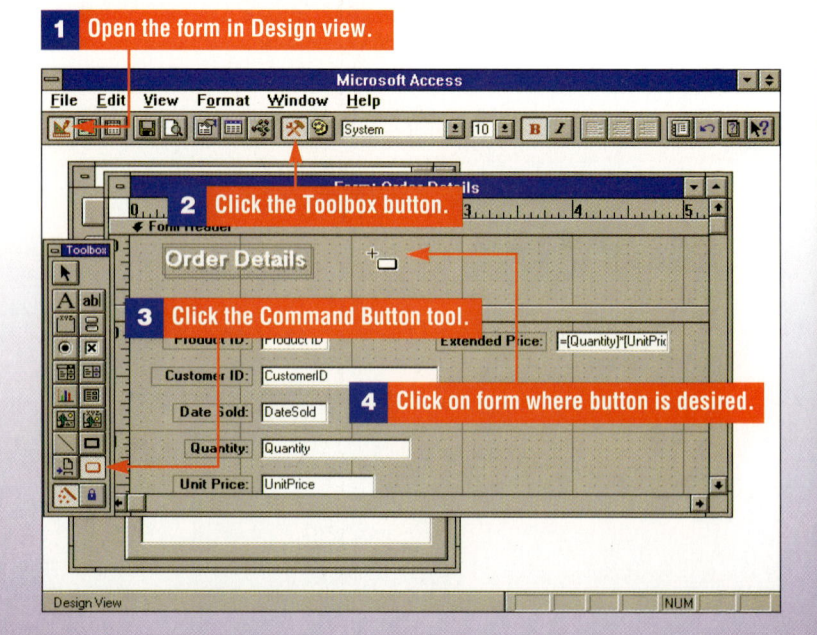

Macros: Creating, Running, and Attaching

Running a Macro

Once a macro has been saved and named, it is very simple to use the macro. Running a macro saves you the many steps it takes to accomplish a task.

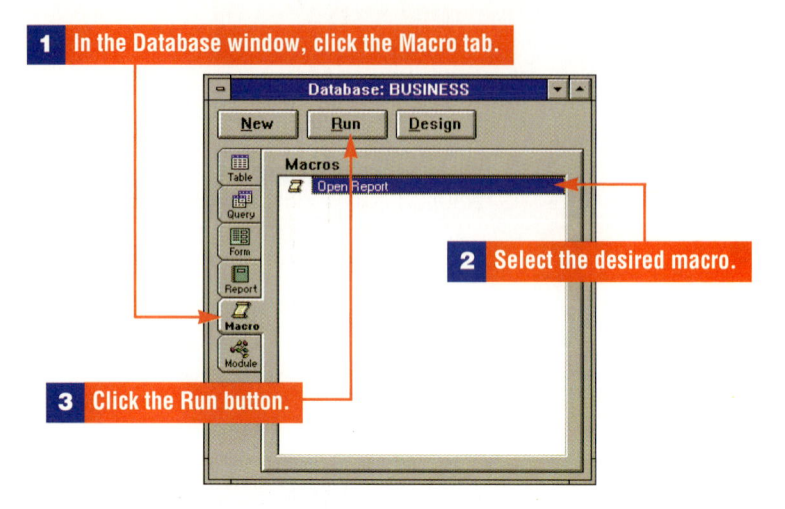

1 In the Database window, click the Macro tab.

2 Select the desired macro.

3 Click the Run button.

Attaching a Macro

Access allows you to attach a macro to a button so that you can run a macro from any location. Placing the button on a form then makes the macro available when you most need it. You could also attach the macro to a keyboard shortcut so that you could run the macro anytime.

To attach a macro to a button

1 Open the form in Design view.

2 Click the Toolbox button.

3 Click the Command Button tool.

4 Click on form where button is desired.

Macros: Creating, Running, and Attaching

5 In the Categories list, click Miscellaneous.

6 Under When button is pressed, click on Run Macro.

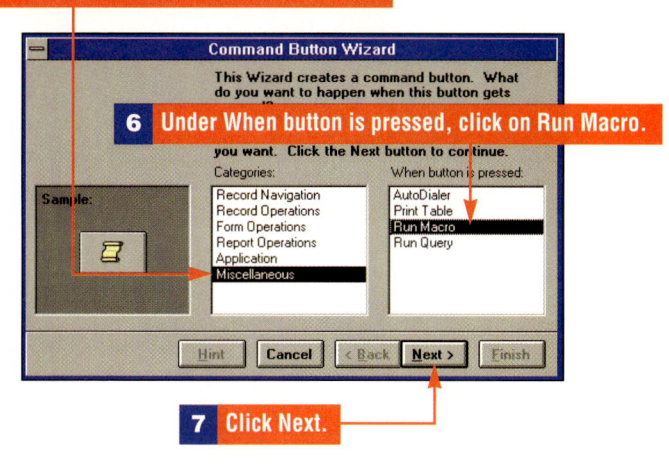

7 Click Next.

8 Click the macro you want this button to run.

9 Click Next.

10 Click Text.

11 Type in a label for the button.

Sample of text on a button.

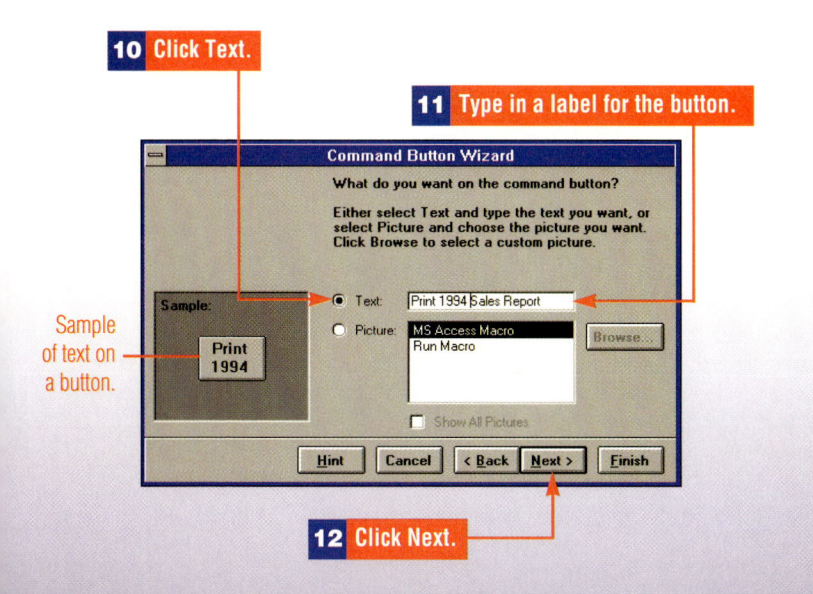

12 Click Next.

more ▶

65

Macros: Creating, Running, and Attaching

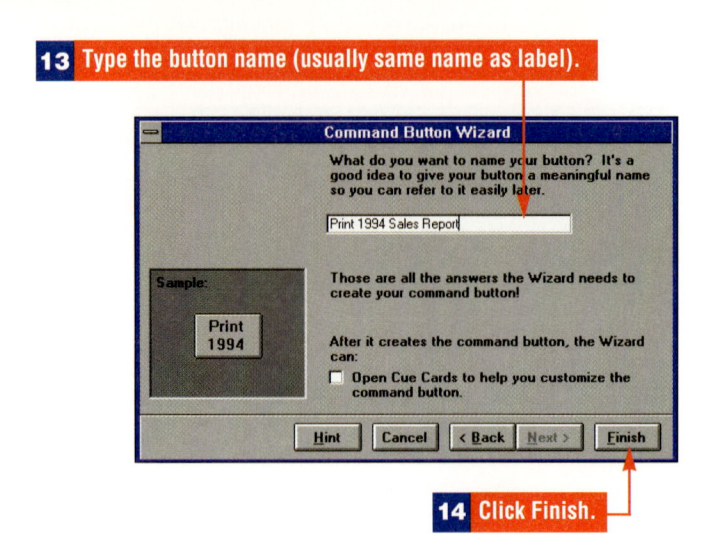

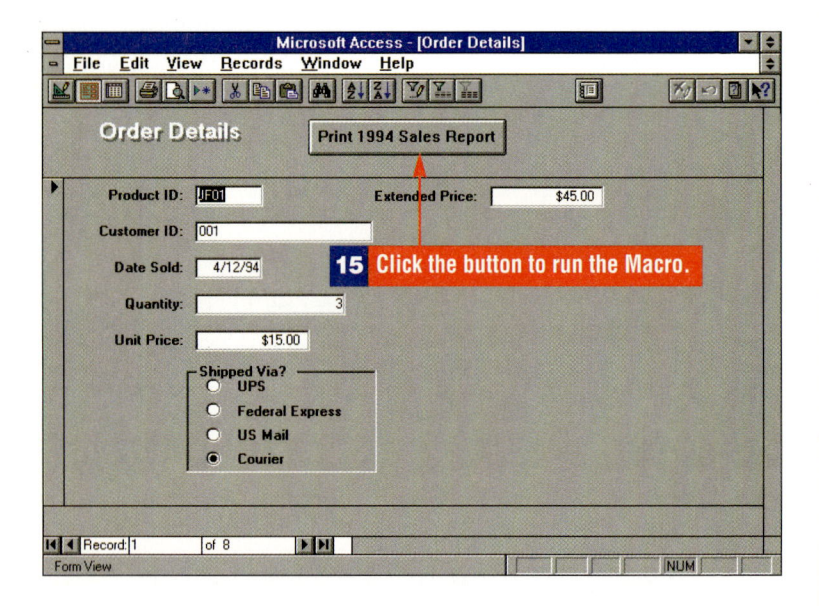

13 Type the button name (usually same name as label).

Command Button Wizard

What do you want to name your button? It's a good idea to give your button a meaningful name so you can refer to it easily later.

Print 1994 Sales Report

Sample:
Print 1994

Those are all the answers the Wizard needs to create your command button!

After it creates the command button, the Wizard can:
☐ Open Cue Cards to help you customize the command button.

[Hint] [Cancel] [< Back] [Next >] [Finish]

14 Click Finish.

Microsoft Access - [Order Details]

File Edit View Records Window Help

Order Details   [Print 1994 Sales Report]

Product ID: JF01   Extended Price: $45.00
Customer ID: 001
Date Sold: 4/12/94   **15** Click the button to run the Macro.
Quantity: 3
Unit Price: $15.00

Shipped Via?
○ UPS
○ Federal Express
○ US Mail
● Courier

Record: 1 of 8

Form View   NUM

Macros: Creating, Running, and Attaching

To attach a macro to a shortcut key

1 In the Database window, click the Macro tab.

2 Click the Macro you want to use.

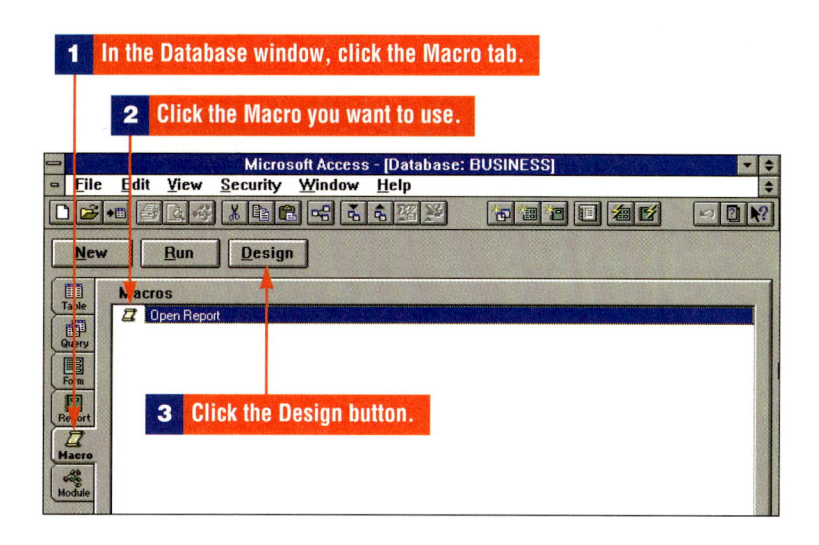

3 Click the Design button.

4 Click the Macro names button.

Use the caret ^ symbol to represent the Ctrl key.

Use the plus + sign to represent the Shift key.

Surround names of keys other than letters and numbers with braces { }.

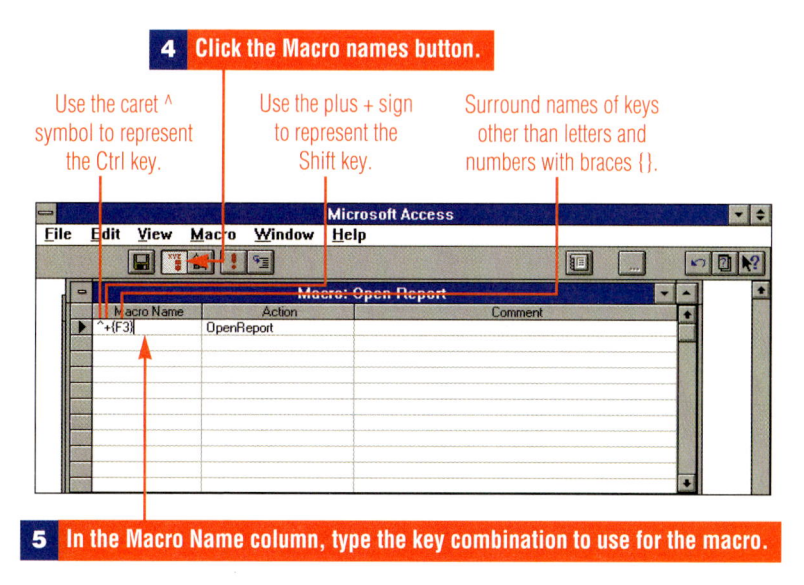

5 In the Macro Name column, type the key combination to use for the macro.

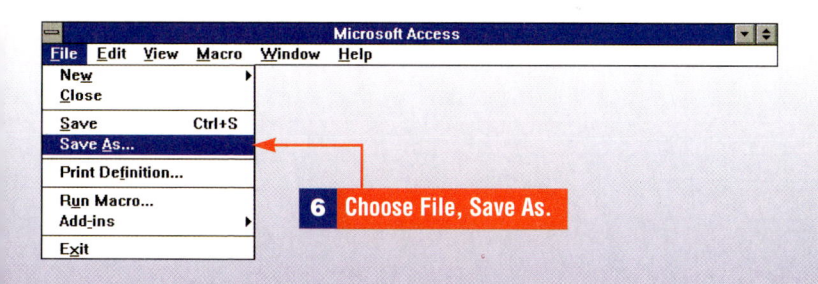

6 Choose File, Save As.

more ▶

Macros: Creating, Running, and Attaching

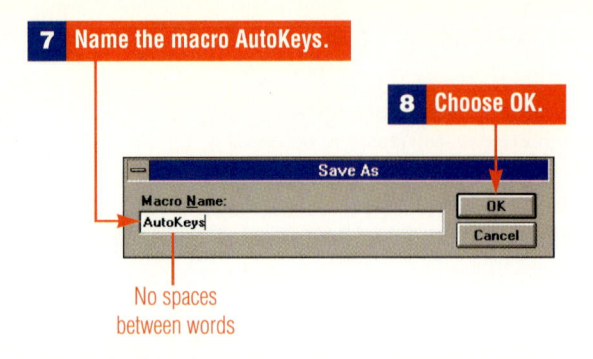

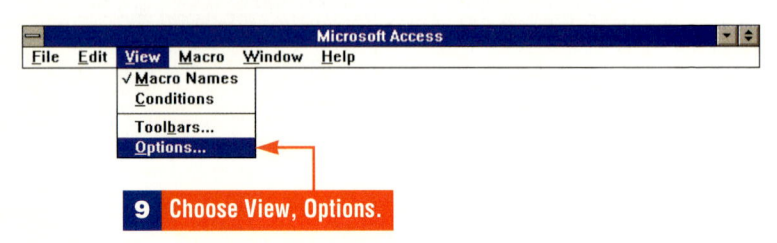

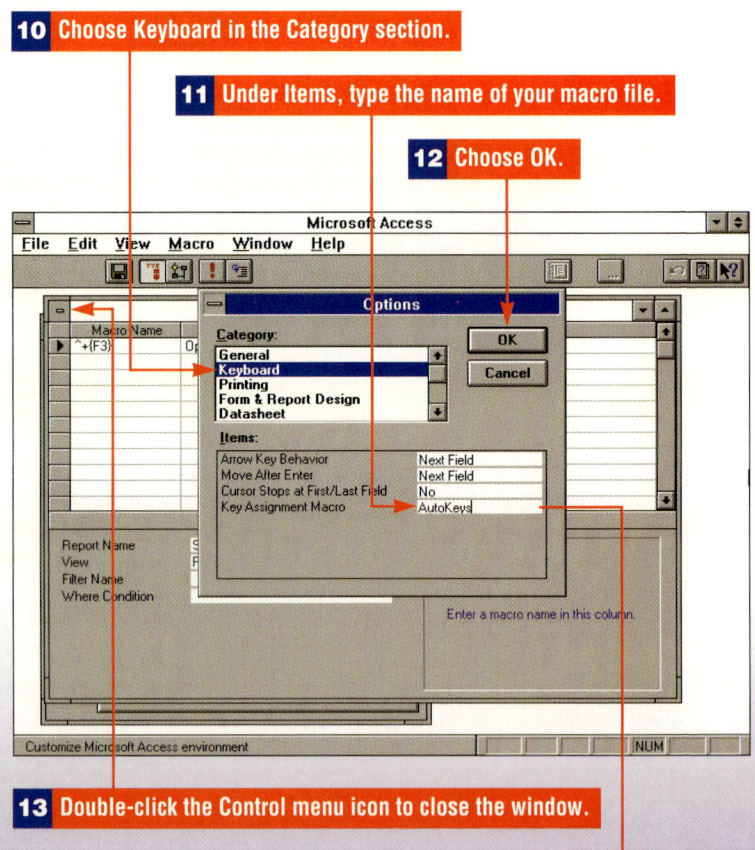

7 Name the macro AutoKeys.

8 Choose OK.

Save As
Macro Name: AutoKeys

No spaces between words

9 Choose View, Options.

10 Choose Keyboard in the Category section.

11 Under Items, type the name of your macro file.

12 Choose OK.

13 Double-click the Control menu icon to close the window.

AutoKeys is the default. This will tell Access 2.0 where you are saving your keyboard shortcuts.

68

Queries—Action Queries: Update, Make Table, Delete

Creating an Update Query

Change is inevitable in the business world. Suppose your freight costs increase considerably, and you need to raise your prices. An Update query will look for the affected database records and change the data in the table. When using any of the Action queries in Access, it is a good idea to first back up your data.

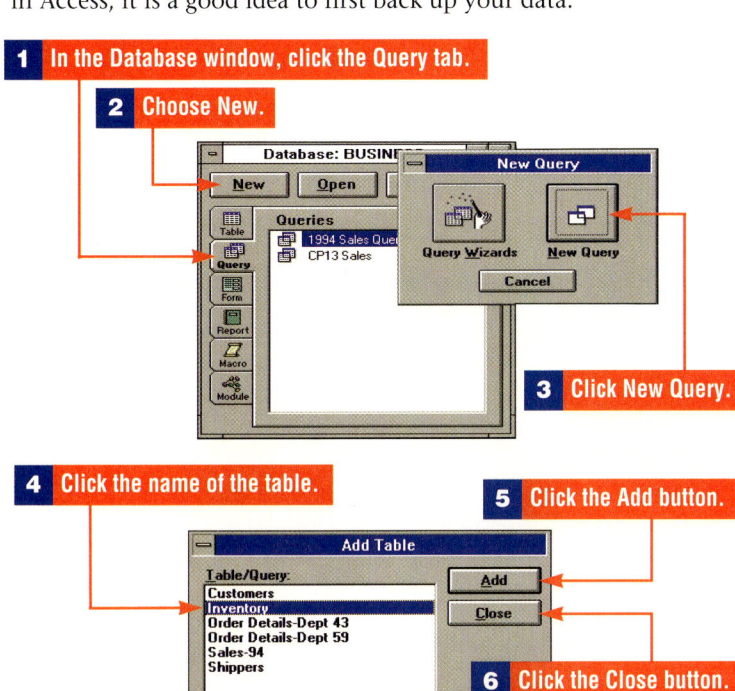

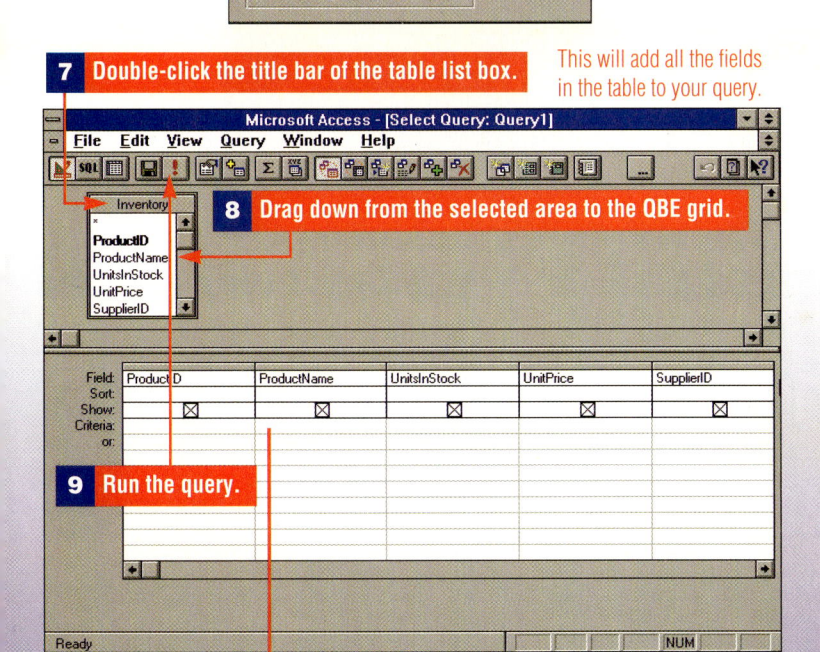

1 In the Database window, click the Query tab.

2 Choose New.

3 Click New Query.

4 Click the name of the table.

5 Click the Add button.

6 Click the Close button.

7 Double-click the title bar of the table list box.

This will add all the fields in the table to your query.

8 Drag down from the selected area to the QBE grid.

9 Run the query.

Enter a criteria in the criteria row if you want to select certain records.

more ▶

69

Queries—Action Queries: Update, Make Table, Delete

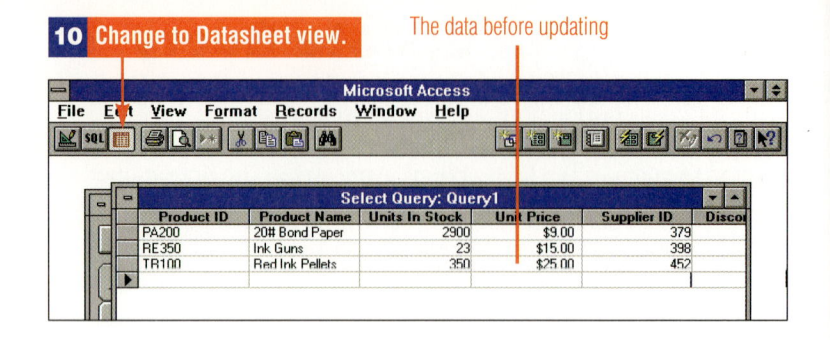

10 Change to Datasheet view.

The data before updating

Product ID	Product Name	Units In Stock	Unit Price	Supplier ID
PA200	20# Bond Paper	2900	$9.00	379
RE350	Ink Guns	23	$15.00	398
TR100	Red Ink Pellets	350	$25.00	452

11 Click the Update Query button.

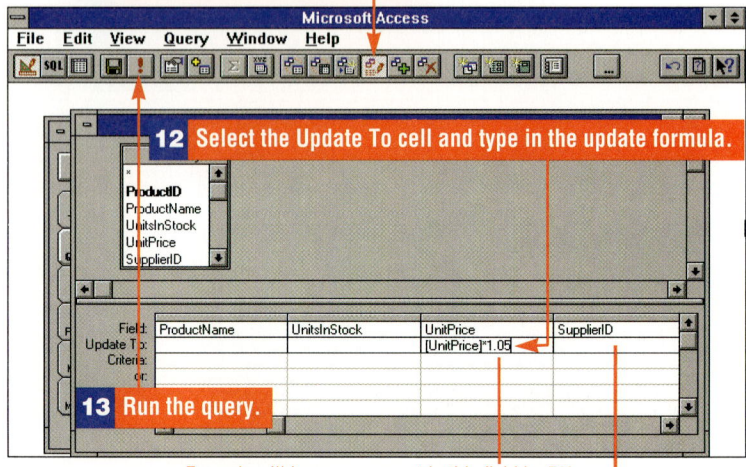

12 Select the Update To cell and type in the update formula.

Field:	ProductName	UnitsInStock	UnitPrice	SupplierID
Update To:			[UnitPrice]*1.05	
Criteria:				

13 Run the query.

Formula will increase amount in this field by 5%.
A new row is added to the QBE grid.

14 Click OK when Access tells you that the table will be updated.

You will not see the dynaset when you run this.

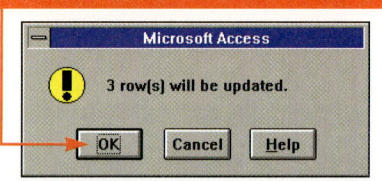

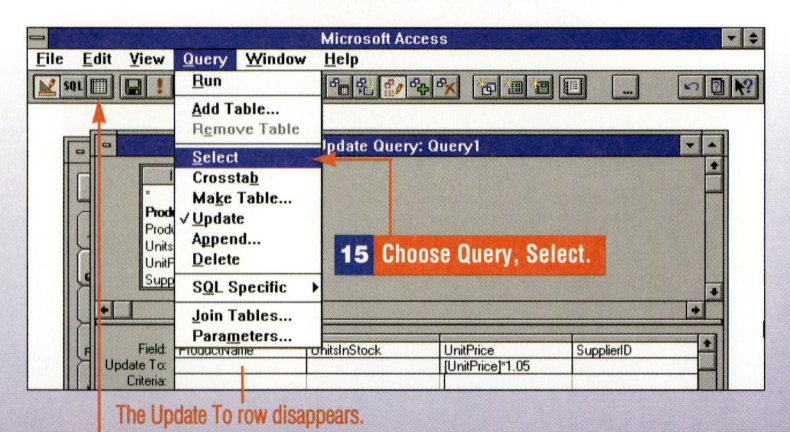

Microsoft Access: 3 row(s) will be updated. — OK, Cancel, Help

15 Choose Query, Select.

The Update To row disappears.

16 Switch to Datasheet view.

70

Queries—Action Queries: Update, Make Table, Delete

17 Double-click the Control Menu icon to close the query.

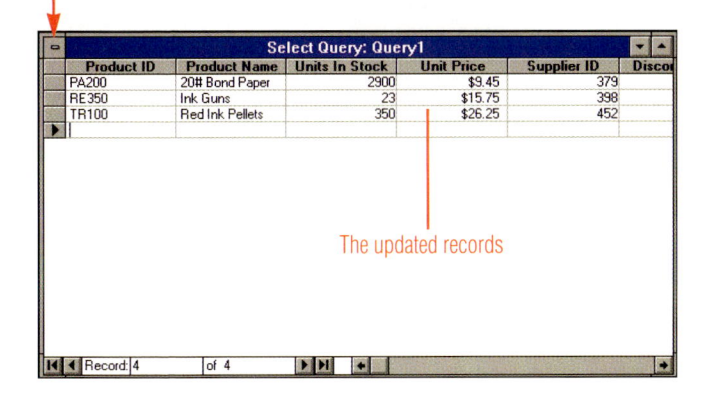

The updated records

18 Click No because query does not need to be saved.

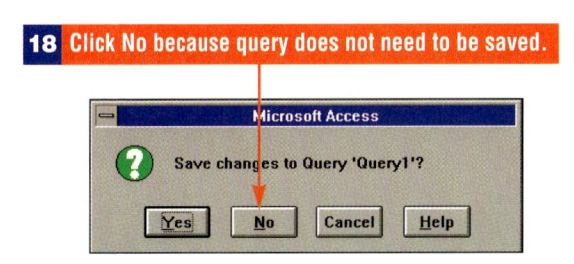

Creating a Make Table Query

Suppose that you need to make a table of the orders from a certain month. Or that you want to create a table with records from a certain department. To perform these operations, use a Make Table query. This type of query creates a new table and copies information from an existing table according to the specified criteria.

1 In the Database window, click the Query tab.

2 Choose New.

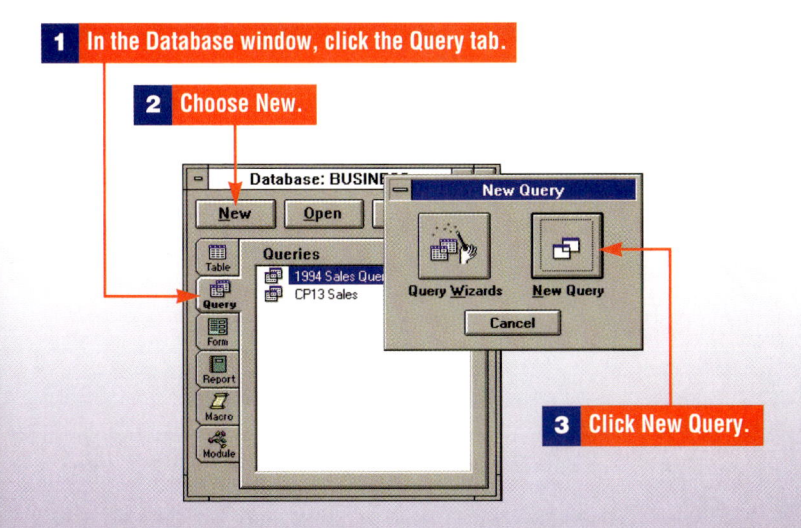

3 Click New Query.

more ▶

Queries—Action Queries: Update, Make Table, Delete

4 Click the name of the table.

5 Click the Add button.

Add Table

Table/Query:
- Customers
- Inventory
- **Order Details**
- Shippers

View: ● Tables ○ Queries ○ Both

6 Click the Close button.

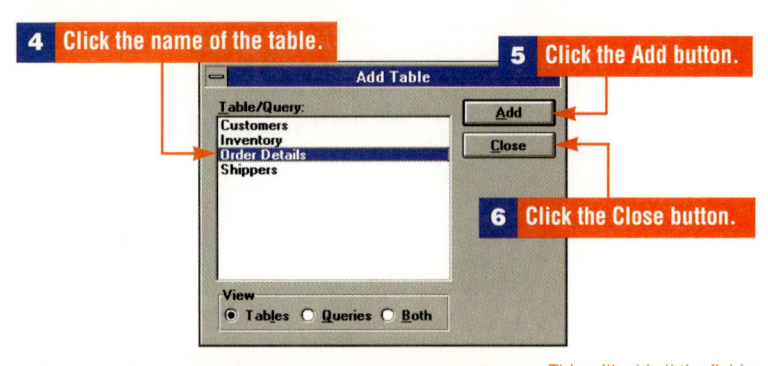

7 Double-click the title bar of the table list box.

This will add all the fields in the table to your query.

8 Drag down from the selected area to the QBE grid.

9 Run the query.

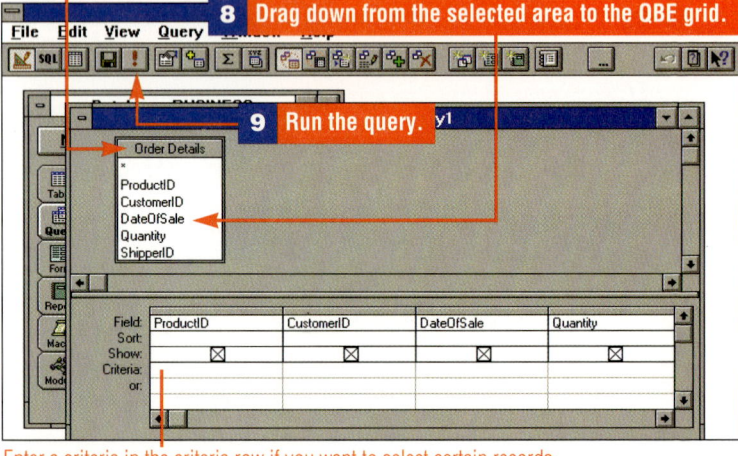

Order Details:
- ProductID
- CustomerID
- DateOfSale
- Quantity
- ShipperID

Field:	ProductID	CustomerID	DateOfSale	Quantity
Sort:				
Show:	☒	☒	☒	☒
Criteria:				
or:				

Enter a criteria in the criteria row if you want to select certain records.

10 Change to Datasheet view.

The data before updating

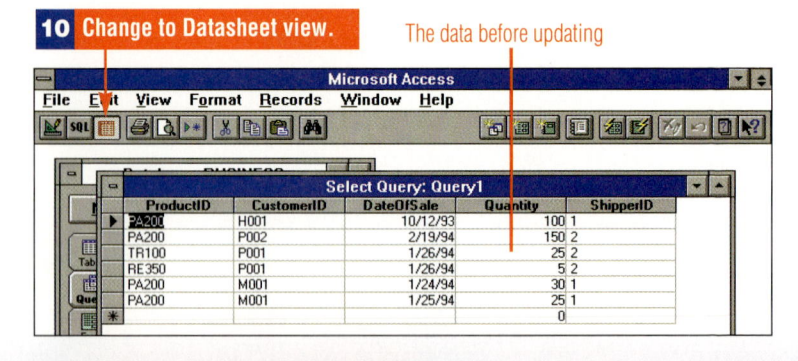

Select Query: Query1

ProductID	CustomerID	DateOfSale	Quantity	ShipperID
PA200	H001	10/12/93	100	1
PA200	P002	2/19/94	150	2
TR100	P001	1/26/94	25	2
RE350	P001	1/26/94	5	2
PA200	M001	1/24/94	30	1
PA200	M001	1/25/94	25	1
*			0	

11 Click the Make Table Query button.

12 Type a name for the new table.

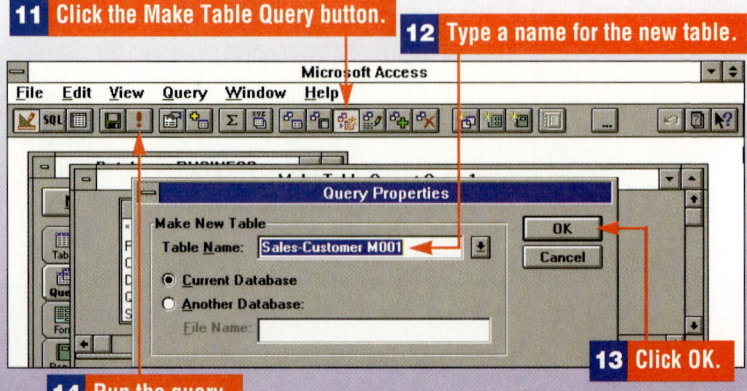

Query Properties

Make New Table
Table Name: Sales-Customer M001

● Current Database
○ Another Database:
File Name:

13 Click OK.

14 Run the query.

72

Queries—Action Queries: Update, Make Table, Delete

15 Click OK when Access tells you how many records will be copied.

16 Click the Database window button.

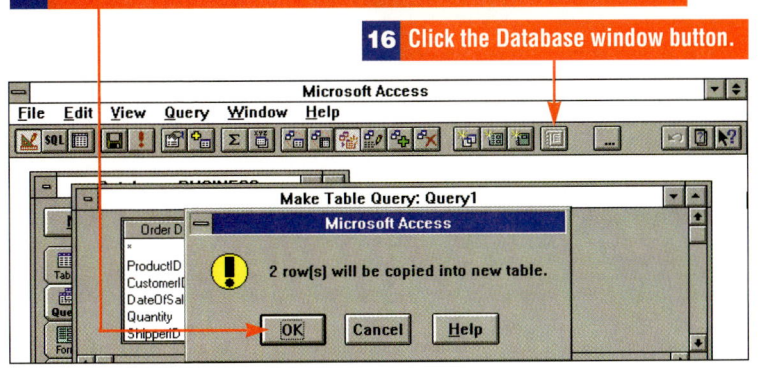

Make Table Query: Query1 — Microsoft Access: "2 row(s) will be copied into new table." [OK] [Cancel] [Help]

17 Click the Table tab.

18 Click the name of the new table.

19 Click Open.

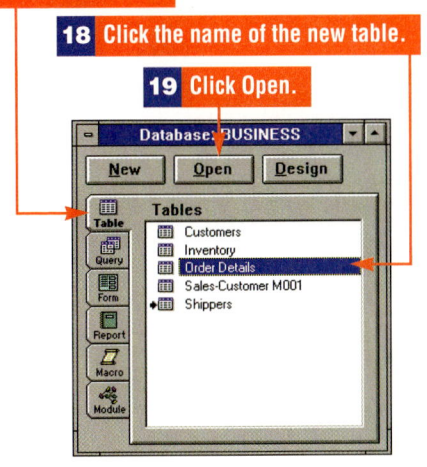

Database: BUSINESS — Tables: Customers, Inventory, Order Details, Sales-Customer M001, Shippers

20 Double-click the Control Menu icon to close the window.

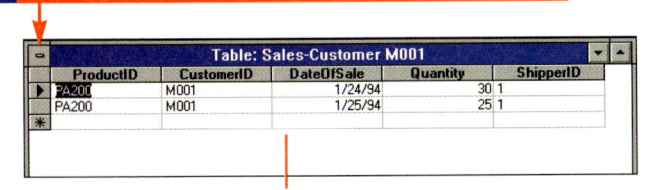

Table: Sales-Customer M001

ProductID	CustomerID	DateOfSale	Quantity	ShipperID
PA200	M001	1/24/94	30	1
PA200	M001	1/25/94	25	1

New table shows only data which matches the criteria.

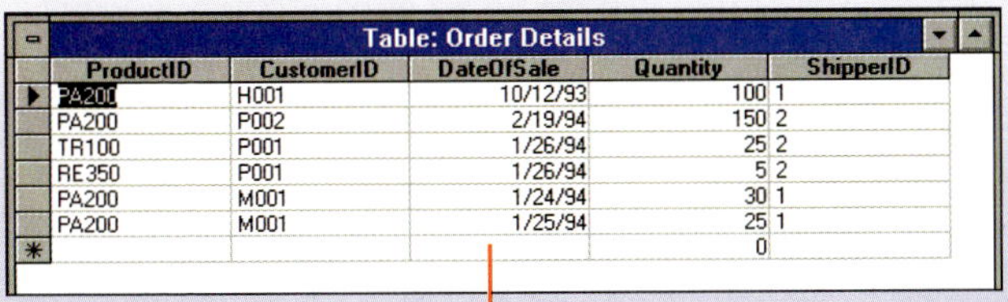

Table: Order Details

ProductID	CustomerID	DateOfSale	Quantity	ShipperID
PA200	H001	10/12/93	100	1
PA200	P002	2/19/94	150	2
TR100	P001	1/26/94	25	2
RE350	P001	1/26/94	5	2
PA200	M001	1/24/94	30	1
PA200	M001	1/25/94	25	1
			0	

Old table still has records which were copied to new table.

more ▶

Queries—Action Queries: Update, Make Table, Delete

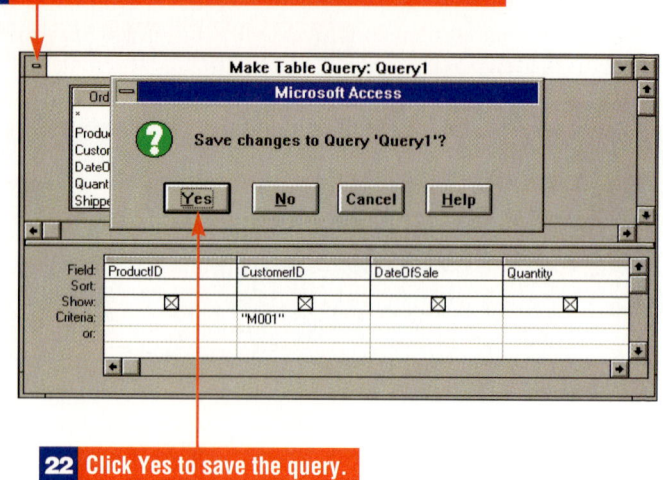

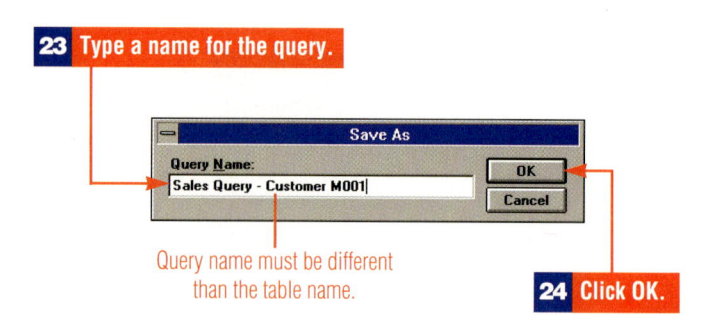

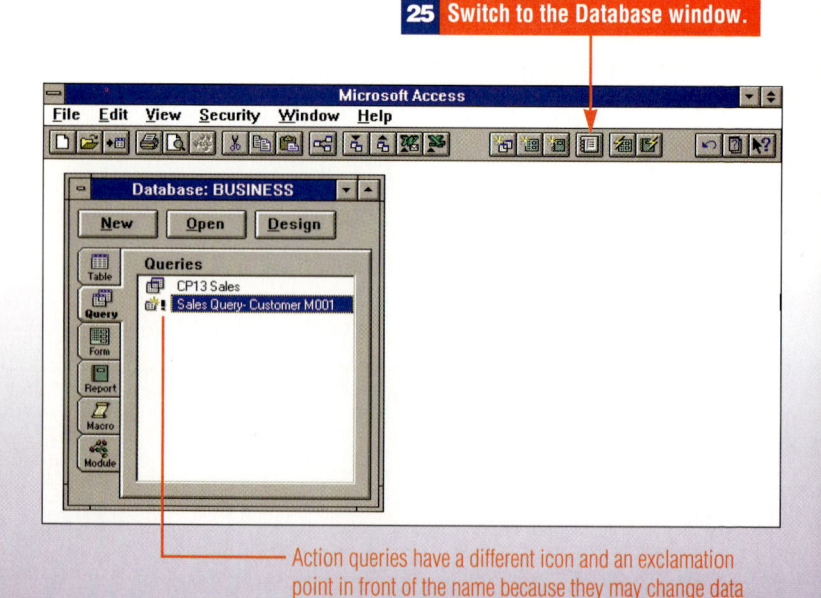

21 Double-click Control Menu icon to close the query.

[Dialog: Make Table Query: Query1 — Microsoft Access: "Save changes to Query 'Query1'?" with Yes, No, Cancel, Help buttons]

22 Click Yes to save the query.

23 Type a name for the query.

[Save As dialog — Query Name: Sales Query - Customer M001]

Query name must be different than the table name.

24 Click OK.

25 Switch to the Database window.

[Database: BUSINESS window showing Queries: CP13 Sales, Sales Query- Customer M001]

Action queries have a different icon and an exclamation point in front of the name because they may change data when opened.

Queries—Action Queries: Update, Make Table, Delete

Creating a Delete Query

A Delete query removes records from a table that match the same criteria. This is used, for example, if you would like to get rid of all of the product records of one supplier from your inventory table. Deleted records cannot be retrieved, so make a backup copy of your table before running a delete query.

1 In the Database window, click the Query tab.

2 Choose New.

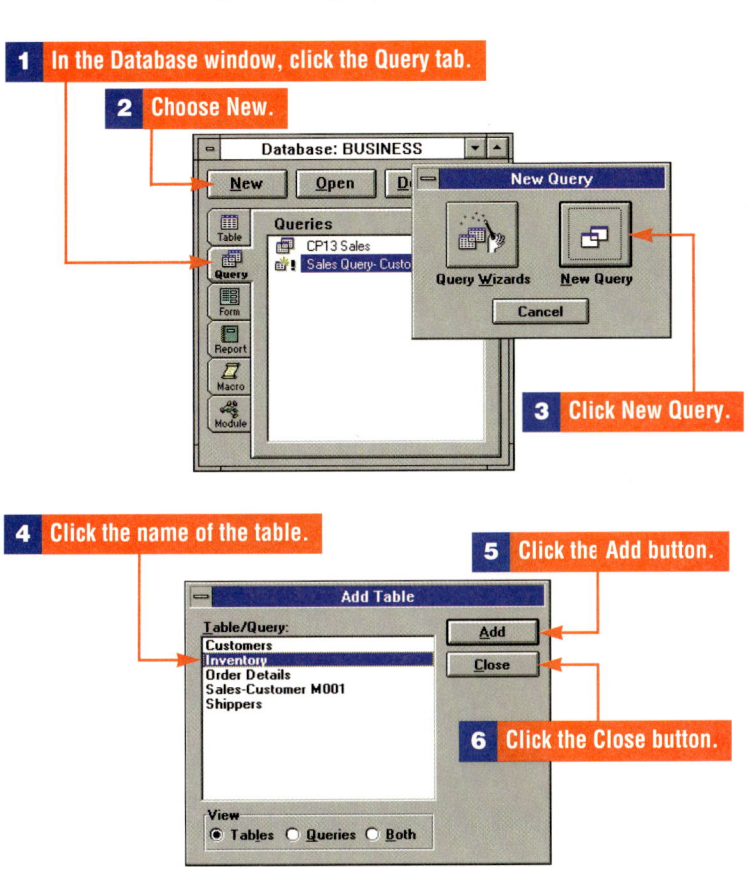

3 Click New Query.

4 Click the name of the table.

5 Click the Add button.

6 Click the Close button.

7 Double-click the title bar of the table list box.

This will add all the fields in the table to your query.

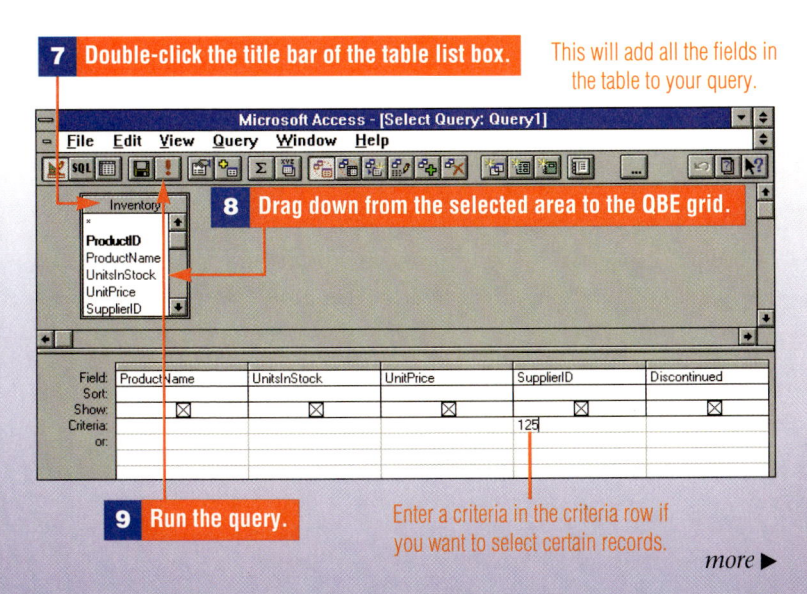

8 Drag down from the selected area to the QBE grid.

9 Run the query.

Enter a criteria in the criteria row if you want to select certain records.

more ▶

Queries—Action Queries: Update, Make Table, Delete

10 Change to Database view.

The data before records are deleted.

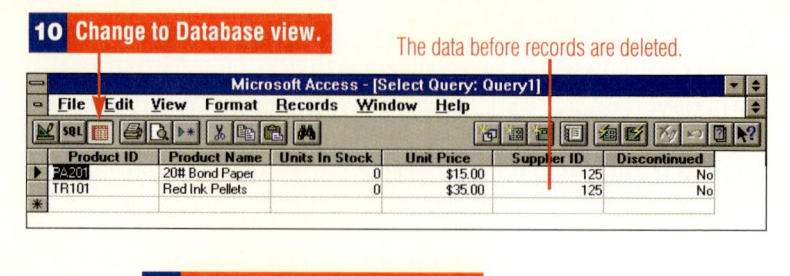

Product ID	Product Name	Units In Stock	Unit Price	Supplier ID	Discontinued
PA201	20# Bond Paper	0	$15.00	125	No
TR101	Red Ink Pellets	0	$35.00	125	No

11 Click the Delete Query button.

12 Run the query.

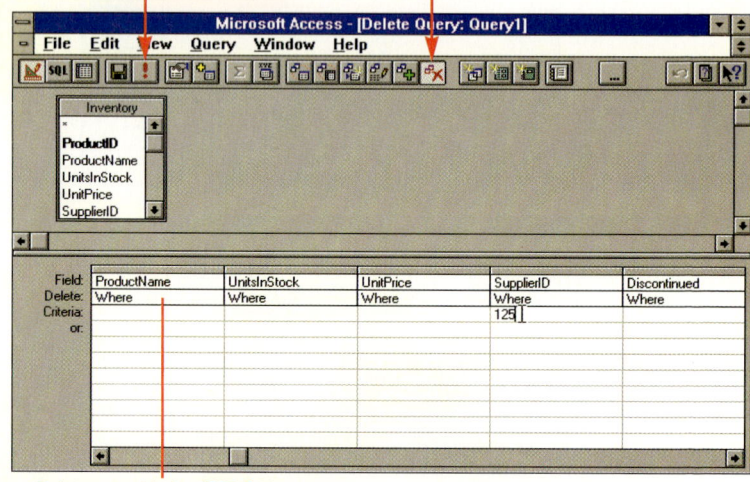

Microsoft Access - [Delete Query: Query1]

Inventory: ProductID, ProductName, UnitsInStock, UnitPrice, SupplierID

Field:	ProductName	UnitsInStock	UnitPrice	SupplierID	Discontinued
Delete:	Where	Where	Where	Where	Where
Criteria:				125	
or:					

Delete row added to QBE Grid.

13 Click OK when Access tells you how many records will be deleted.

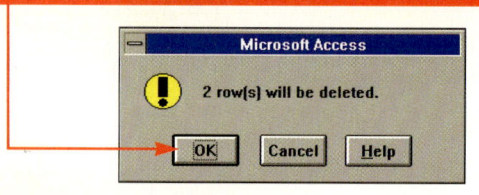

Microsoft Access: 2 row(s) will be deleted. [OK] [Cancel] [Help]

14 Click the Select button.

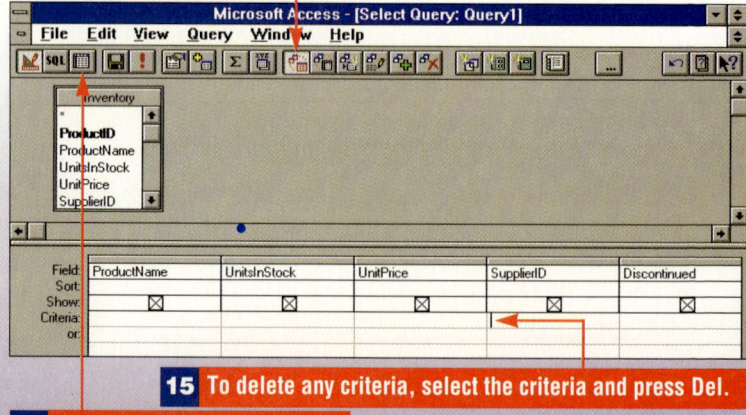

Microsoft Access - [Select Query: Query1]

Inventory: ProductID, ProductName, UnitsInStock, UnitPrice, SupplierID

Field:	ProductName	UnitsInStock	UnitPrice	SupplierID	Discontinued
Sort:					
Show:	☒	☒	☒	☒	☒
Criteria:					
or:					

15 To delete any criteria, select the criteria and press Del.

16 Click on the Datasheet button.

76

Queries—Action Queries: Update, Make Table, Delete

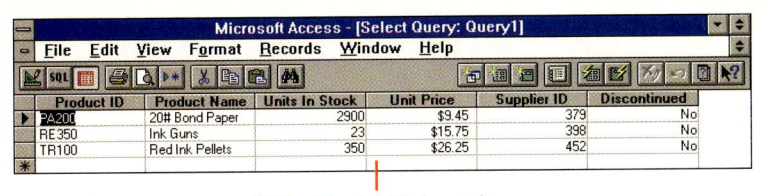

Table without deleted records

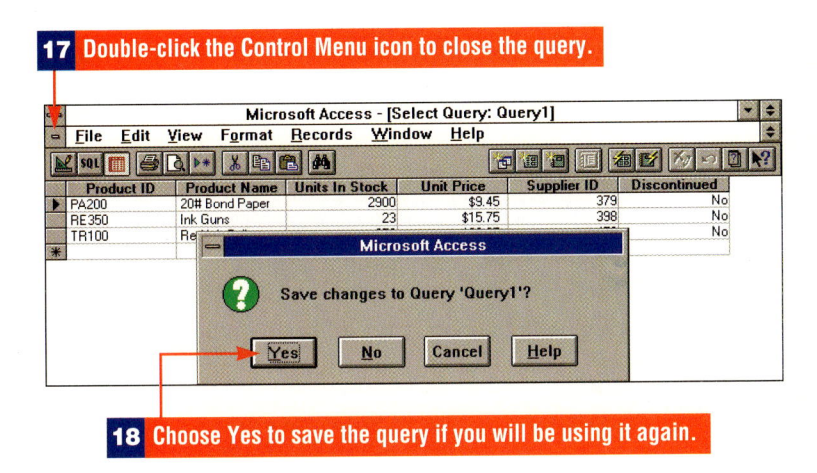

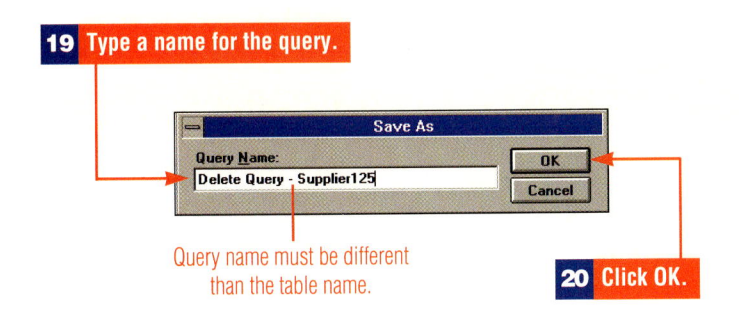

17 Double-click the Control Menu icon to close the query.

18 Choose Yes to save the query if you will be using it again.

19 Type a name for the query.

Query name must be different than the table name.

20 Click OK.

Queries—Action Queries: Update, Make Table, Delete

Creating an Archive Query Using the Query Wizard

An Archive query is a combination of a Make Table query and a Delete query. This type of query is very useful if you want to remove some records from a table but not from the database, such as last year's sales from the Sales table. You can copy records into a new table and then delete the records from the first table.

1 In the Database window, click the Query tab.

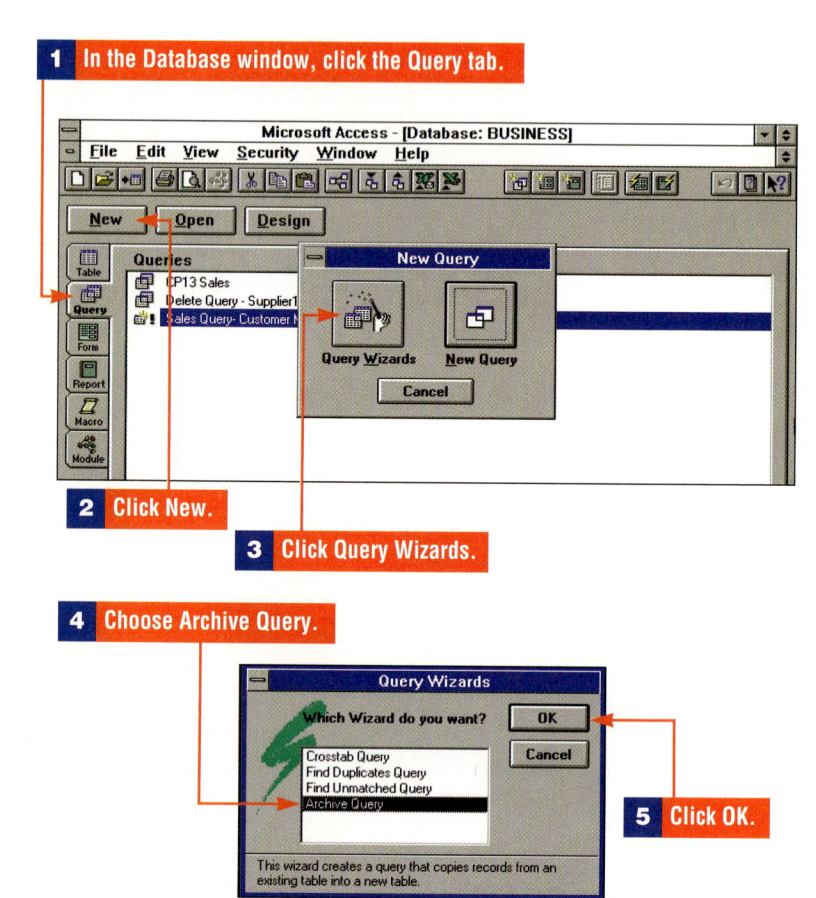

2 Click New.

3 Click Query Wizards.

4 Choose Archive Query.

5 Click OK.

6 Select the table to use.

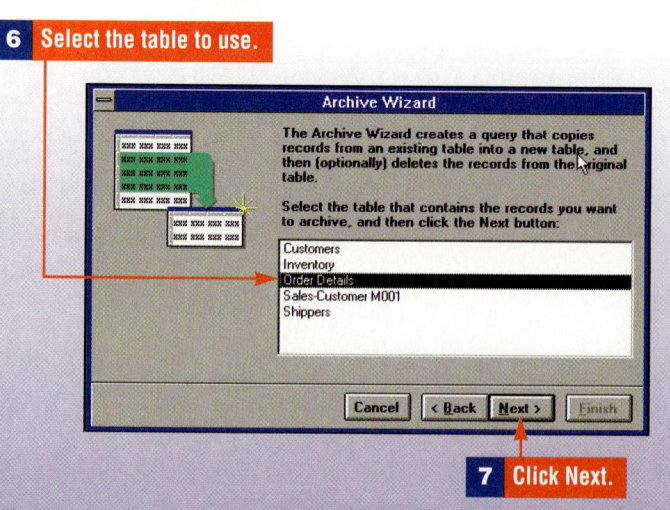

7 Click Next.

78

Queries—Action Queries: Update, Make Table, Delete

Click here to archive all records.

Click here for a list of operators.

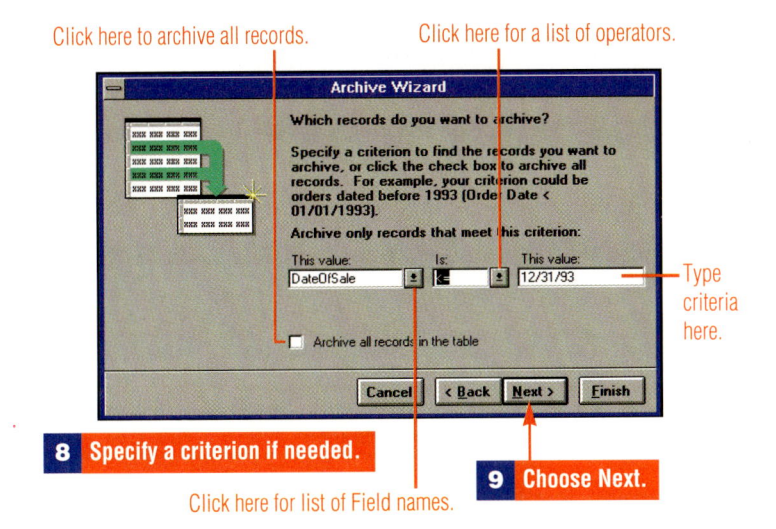

Archive Wizard

Which records do you want to archive?

Specify a criterion to find the records you want to archive, or click the check box to archive all records. For example, your criterion could be orders dated before 1993 (Order Date < 01/01/1993).

Archive only records that meet this criterion:

This value: DateOfSale
Is: <=
This value: 12/31/93 — Type criteria here.

☐ Archive all records in the table

8 Specify a criterion if needed.

Click here for list of Field names.

9 Choose Next.

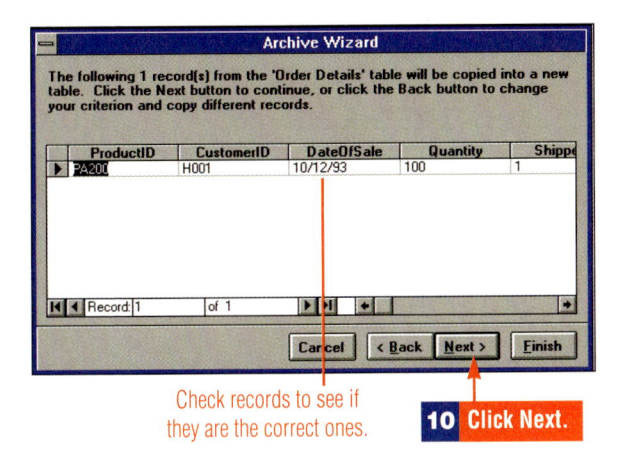

Archive Wizard

The following 1 record(s) from the 'Order Details' table will be copied into a new table. Click the Next button to continue, or click the Back button to change your criterion and copy different records.

ProductID	CustomerID	DateOfSale	Quantity	Shippe
PA200	H001	10/12/93	100	1

Record: 1 of 1

Check records to see if they are the correct ones.

10 Click Next.

---

11 Choose Yes to delete records from the original table.

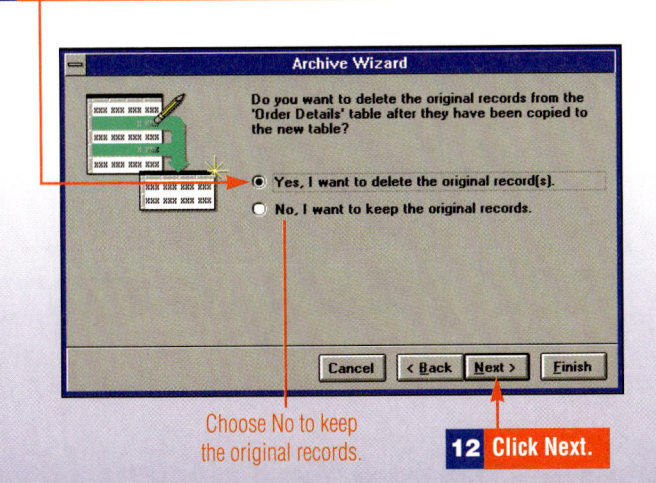

Archive Wizard

Do you want to delete the original records from the 'Order Details' table after they have been copied to the new table?

⦿ Yes, I want to delete the original record(s).
◯ No, I want to keep the original records.

Choose No to keep the original records.

12 Click Next.

more ▶

79

Queries—Action Queries: Update, Make Table, Delete

13 Give the archived table a name.

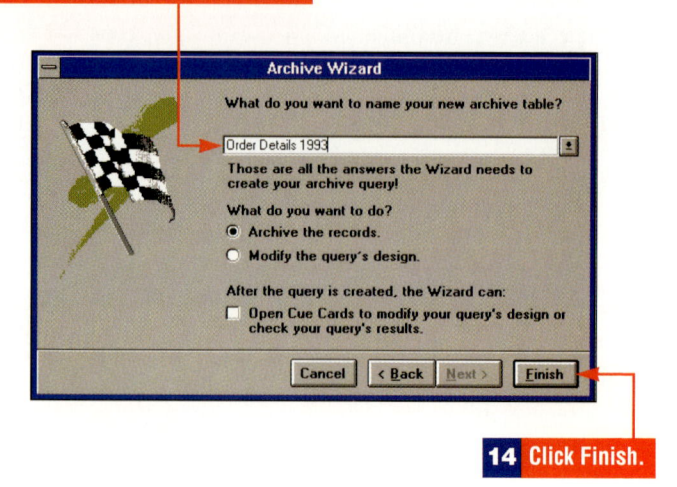

Archive Wizard

What do you want to name your new archive table?

`Order Details 1993`

Those are all the answers the Wizard needs to create your archive query!

What do you want to do?
- ◉ Archive the records.
- ○ Modify the query's design.

After the query is created, the Wizard can:
- ☐ Open Cue Cards to modify your query's design or check your query's results.

[Cancel] [< Back] [Next >] [Finish]

14 Click Finish.

15 Choose Yes to continue operation.

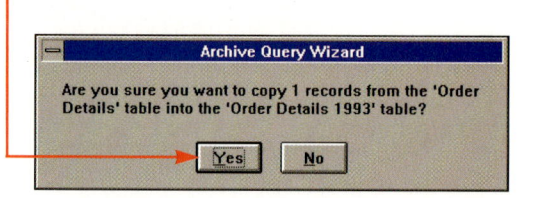

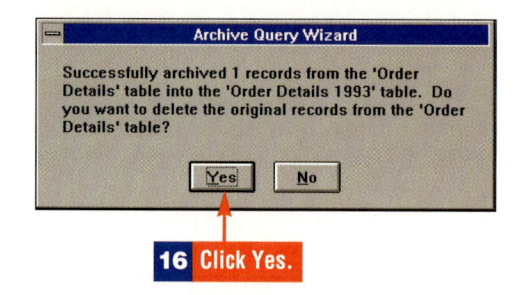

Archive Query Wizard

Are you sure you want to copy 1 records from the 'Order Details' table into the 'Order Details 1993' table?

[Yes] [No]

Archive Query Wizard

Successfully archived 1 records from the 'Order Details' table into the 'Order Details 1993' table. Do you want to delete the original records from the 'Order Details' table?

[Yes] [No]

16 Click Yes.

Queries—Action Queries: Update, Make Table, Delete

Creating an Append Query

An Append query is an Action query used to add records from one table to another. Suppose you have the sales records for two departments in two separate tables and these two departments merge. You will probably want to add the records of one department to the other so that all the records are together.

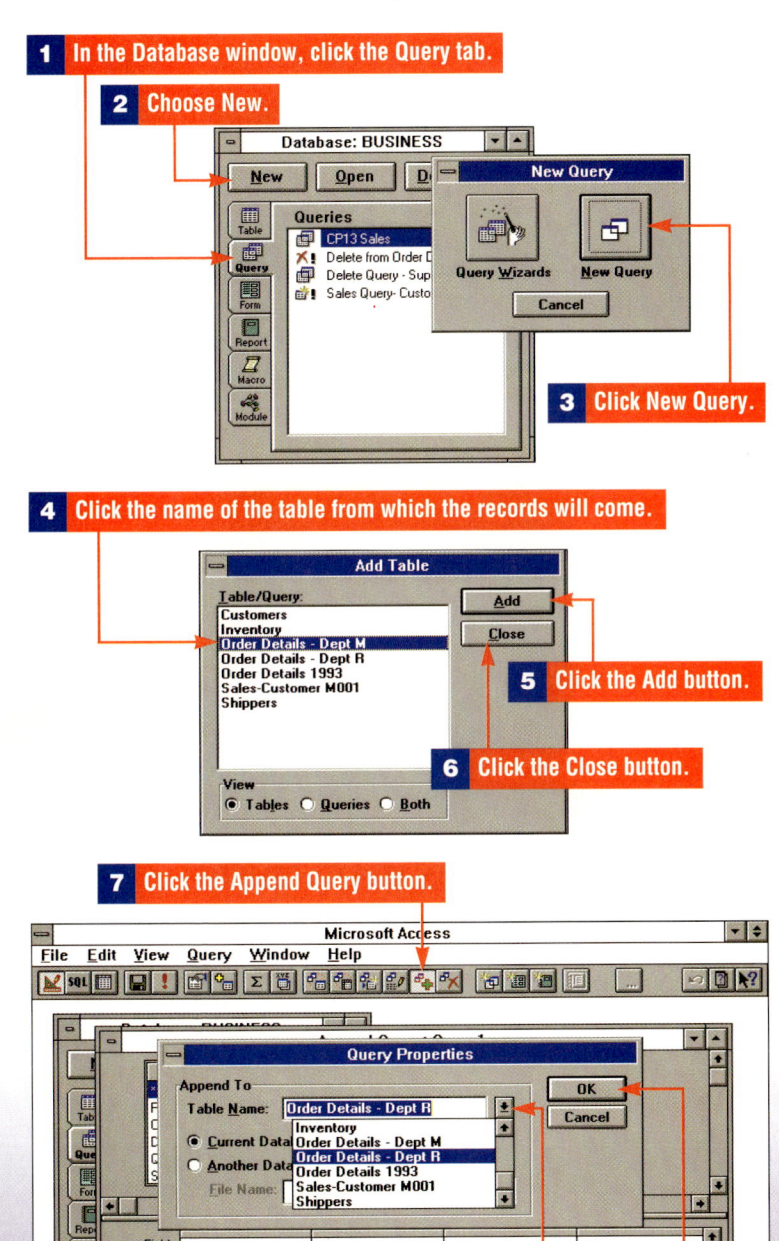

1 In the Database window, click the Query tab.

2 Choose New.

3 Click New Query.

4 Click the name of the table from which the records will come.

5 Click the Add button.

6 Click the Close button.

7 Click the Append Query button.

8 Select the name of the table to append the records to.

9 Click OK.

more ▶

81

Queries—Action Queries: Update, Make Table, Delete

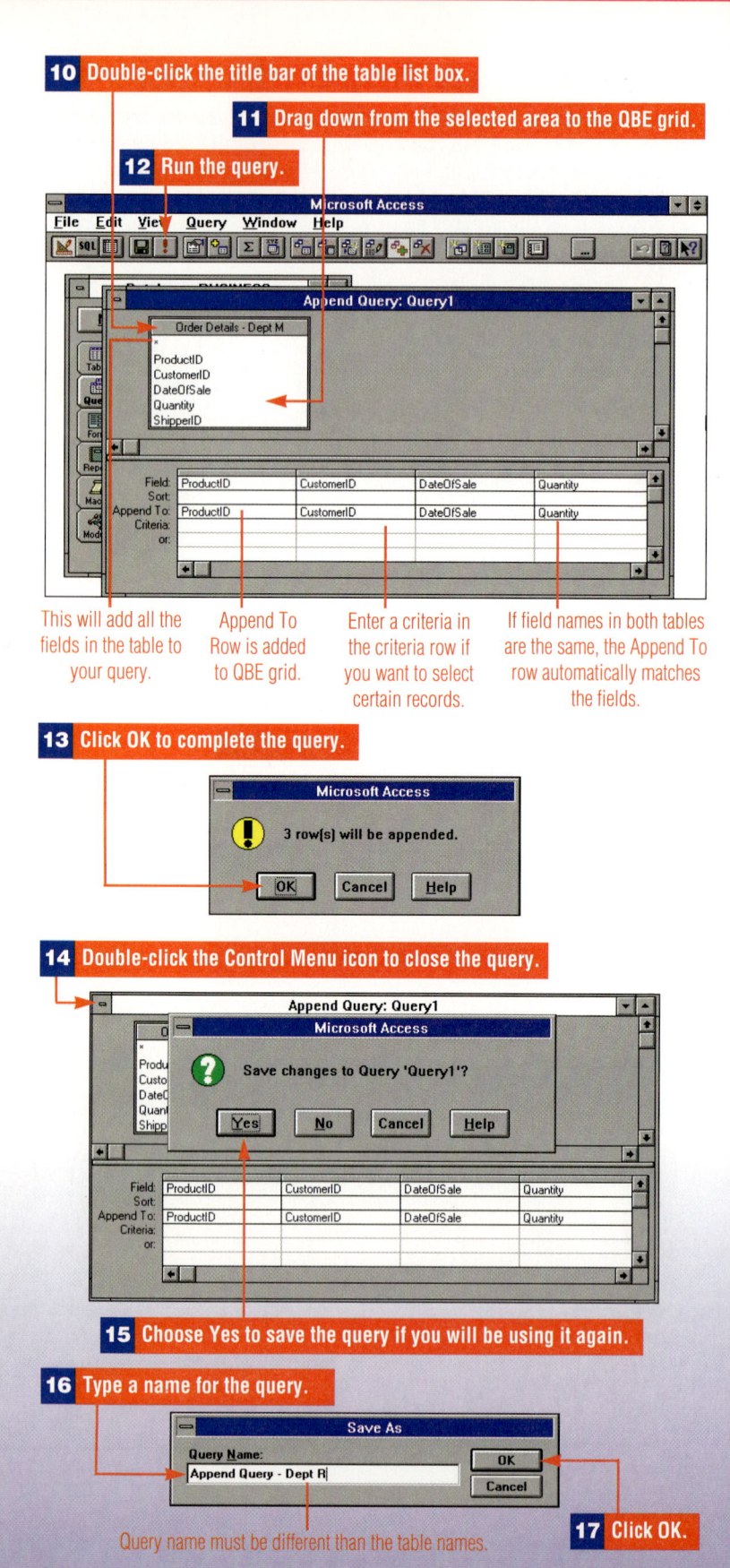

10 Double-click the title bar of the table list box.

11 Drag down from the selected area to the QBE grid.

12 Run the query.

This will add all the fields in the table to your query.

Append To Row is added to QBE grid.

Enter a criteria in the criteria row if you want to select certain records.

If field names in both tables are the same, the Append To row automatically matches the fields.

13 Click OK to complete the query.

14 Double-click the Control Menu icon to close the query.

15 Choose Yes to save the query if you will be using it again.

16 Type a name for the query.

Query name must be different than the table names.

17 Click OK.

82

Queries—Advanced Design: Empty Fields and Calculations

Searching for an Empty Field

Occasionally, when you enter data in a database, the information for a field is not available or the field is accidentally skipped, leaving a blank field in the database. Access provides a simple way of checking to see if there are any empty fields in a database.

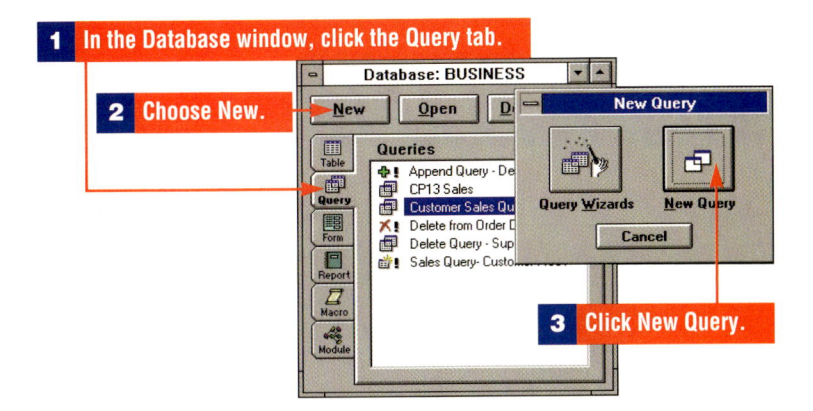

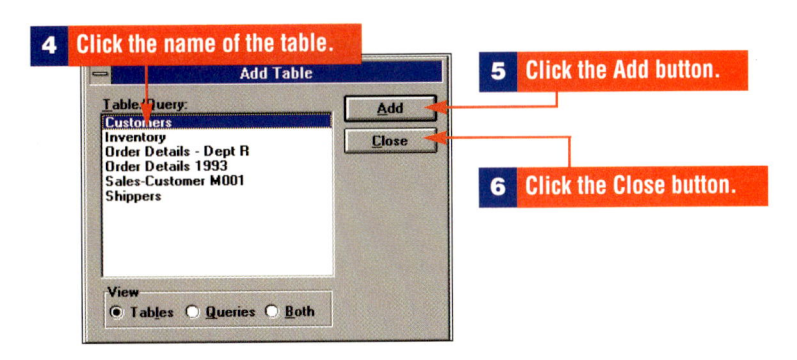

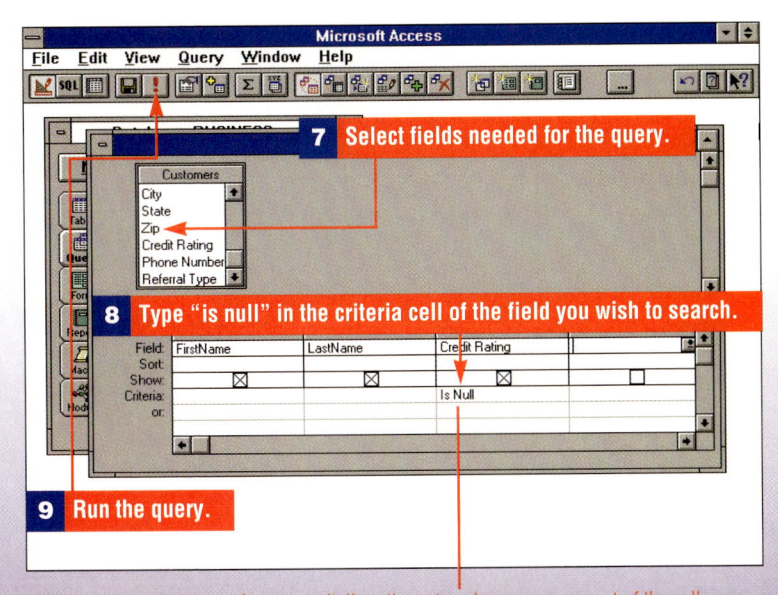

1 In the Database window, click the Query tab.

2 Choose New.

3 Click New Query.

4 Click the name of the table.

5 Click the Add button.

6 Click the Close button.

7 Select fields needed for the query.

8 Type "is null" in the criteria cell of the field you wish to search.

9 Run the query.

Type in lowercase letters. Access capitalizes the entry when you move out of the cell.

more ▶

83

Queries—Advanced Design: Empty Fields and Calculations

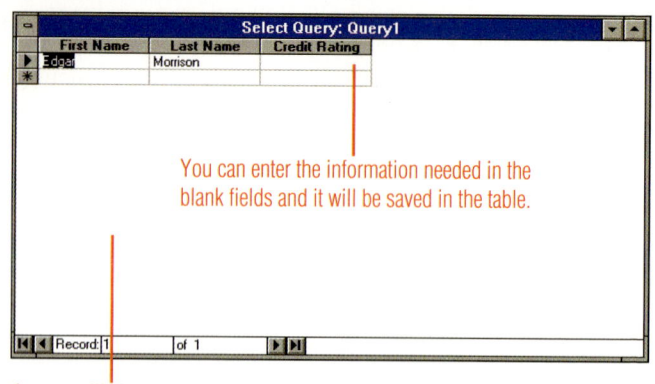

You can enter the information needed in the blank fields and it will be saved in the table.

The dynaset will show you all the records which are blank in that field.

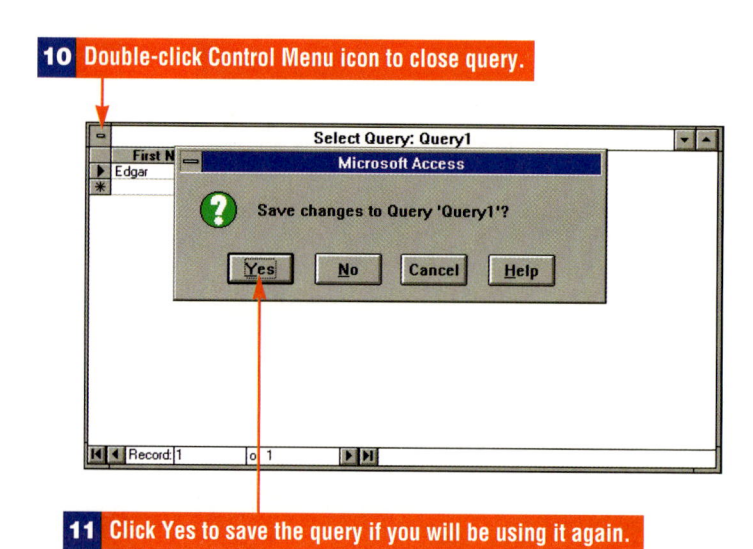

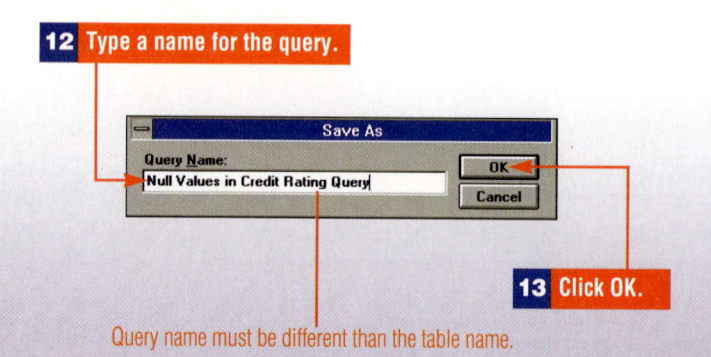

10 Double-click Control Menu icon to close query.

11 Click Yes to save the query if you will be using it again.

12 Type a name for the query.

Query name must be different than the table name.

13 Click OK.

84

Queries—Advanced Design: Empty Fields and Calculations

Searching Using Wildcards

In some queries, you may want to search for data based on a certain pattern of characters. For instance, you may want to search for all customers whose ZIP code starts with "66."/ To search for a pattern in the database field, use the asterisk "*" to stand for any number of characters, or the question mark "?" to stand for one character.

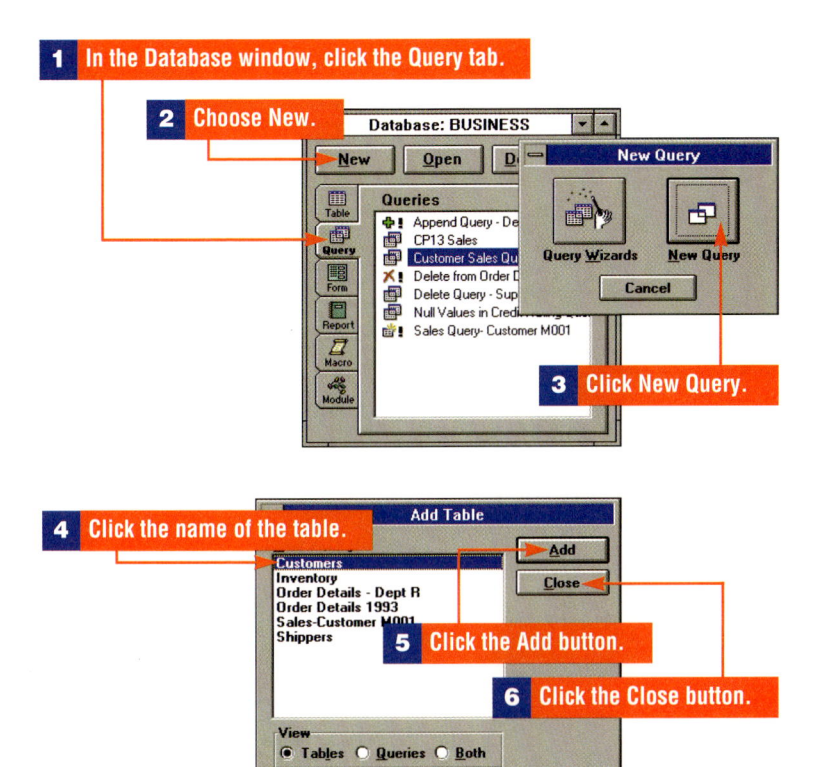

1 In the Database window, click the Query tab.

2 Choose New.

3 Click New Query.

4 Click the name of the table.

5 Click the Add button.

6 Click the Close button.

7 Double click the title bar of the table list box.

8 Drag down from the selected area to the QBE grid.

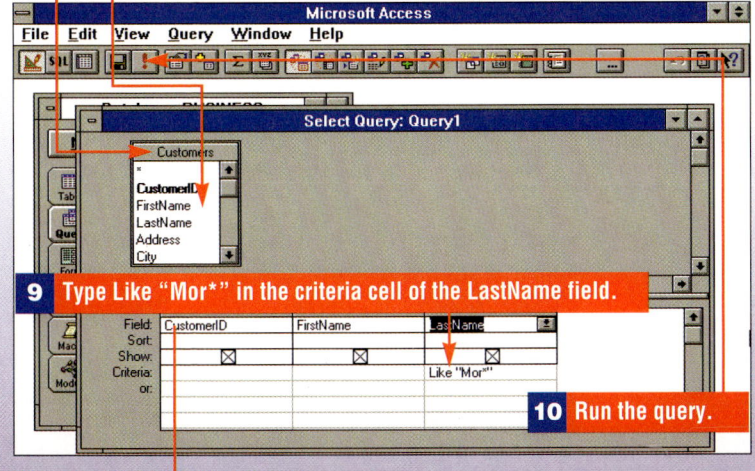

9 Type Like "Mor*" in the criteria cell of the LastName field.

10 Run the query.

This will add all the fields in the table to your query.

more ▶

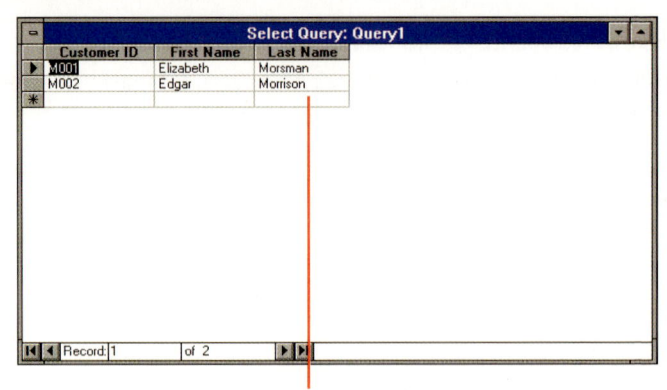

Queries—Advanced Design: Empty Fields and Calculations

The dynaset shows you all the records where the first three characters in the LastName field begins with "Mor."

11 Double-click the Control Menu icon to close.

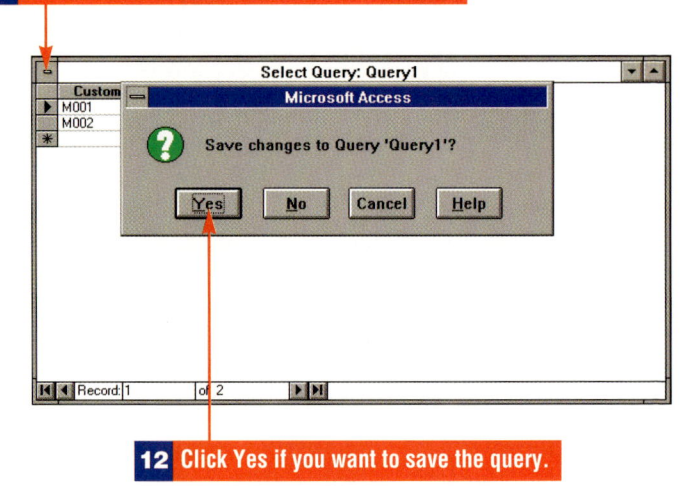

12 Click Yes if you want to save the query.

Wildcard Examples

If you enter "b?d", you will find bed, bad, bid.

If you enter "*in*", you will find winning, losing, or finds.

If you enter "01/*/94", you will find all the records in January 1994.

If you enter "not C*", you will find only records that do not begin with C.

Queries—Advanced Design: Empty Fields and Calculations

Finding Duplicate Records

You can use a Query Wizard to find records in your table that have the same information.

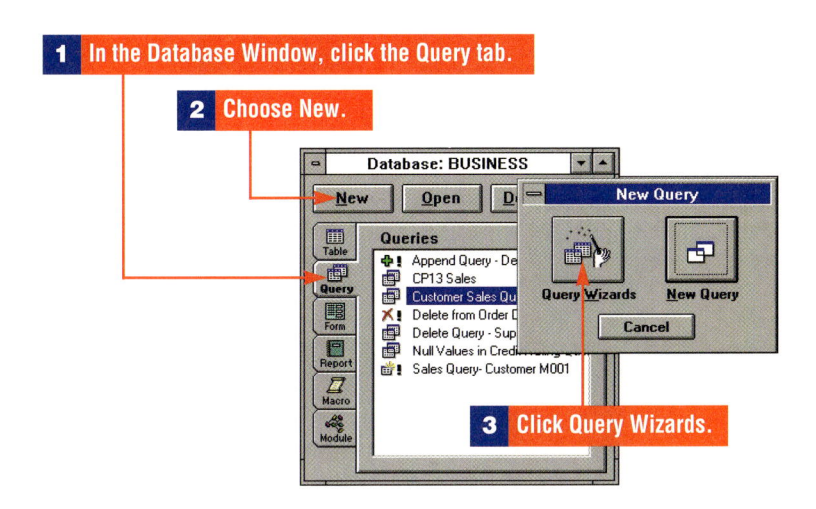

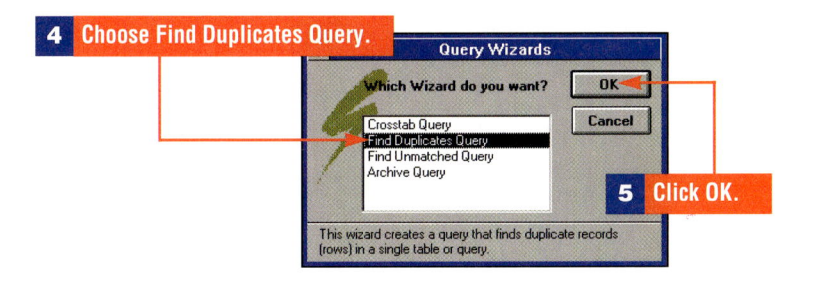

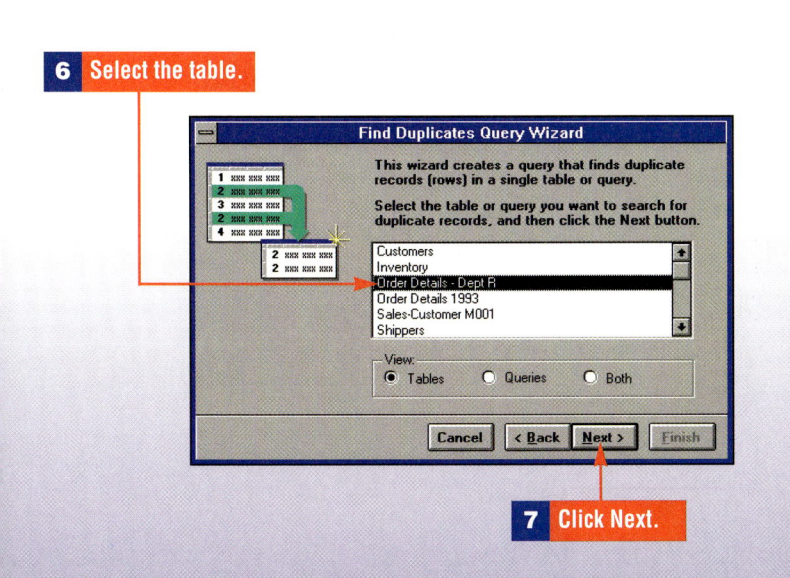

1 In the Database Window, click the Query tab.

2 Choose New.

3 Click Query Wizards.

4 Choose Find Duplicates Query.

5 Click OK.

6 Select the table.

7 Click Next.

more ▶

87

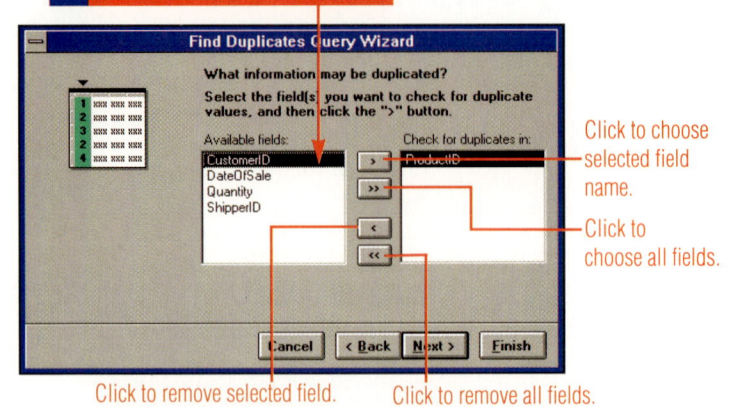

Queries—Advanced Design: Empty Fields and Calculations

8 Specify which field to search.

Find Duplicates Query Wizard

What information may be duplicated?

Select the field(s) you want to check for duplicate values, and then click the ">" button.

Available fields:
- CustomerID
- DateOfSale
- Quantity
- ShipperID

Check for duplicates in:
- ProductID

Click to choose selected field name.

Click to choose all fields.

Click to remove selected field. Click to remove all fields.

Find Duplicates Query Wizard

Do you want to see any additional information along with the duplicate values?

Select the additional field(s) you want to see in the query's results, and then click the ">" button. The wizard won't check these fields for duplicates.

Available fields:

Selected fields:
- CustomerID
- DateOfSale
- Quantity
- ShipperID

9 Click Next.

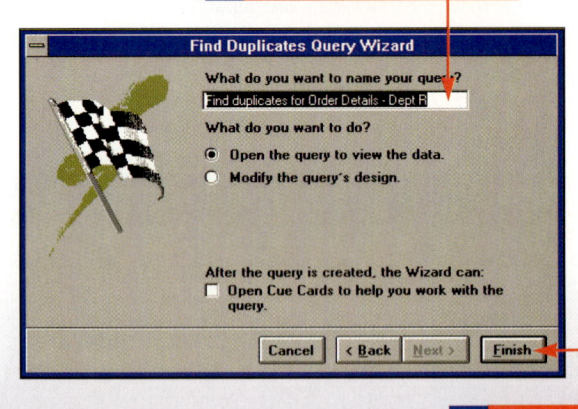

10 Type a name for the query.

Find Duplicates Query Wizard

What do you want to name your query?

Find duplicates for Order Details - Dept R

What do you want to do?
- ● Open the query to view the data.
- ○ Modify the query's design.

After the query is created, the Wizard can:
- ☐ Open Cue Cards to help you work with the query.

11 Click Finish.

12 Double-click Control Menu icon to close query.

Select Query: Find duplicates for Order Details - Dept R

ProductID	CustomerID	DateOfSale	Quantity	ShipperID
PA200	P002	2/19/94	500	3
PA200	H001	10/21/94	65	2
PA200	M002	2/25/94	70	2
PA200	M002	1/14/94	150	2
TR100	P001	1/26/94	45	2
TR100	M001	1/26/94	25	2
*			0	

List of records with the same Product ID

Queries—Advanced Design: Empty Fields and Calculations

Combining Information in a Field

When you have a customer's name in two or more separate fields, at times you may want to combine the information in these fields into one temporary field. Access calls this concatenating. You can accomplish this by using the ampersand "&" character with the field names.

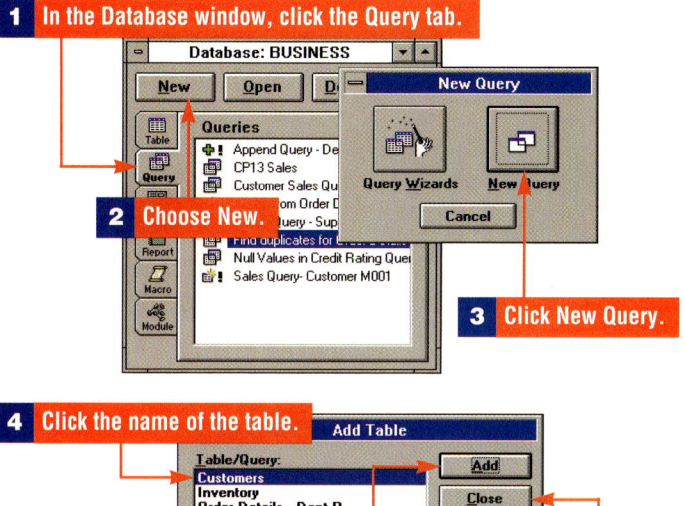

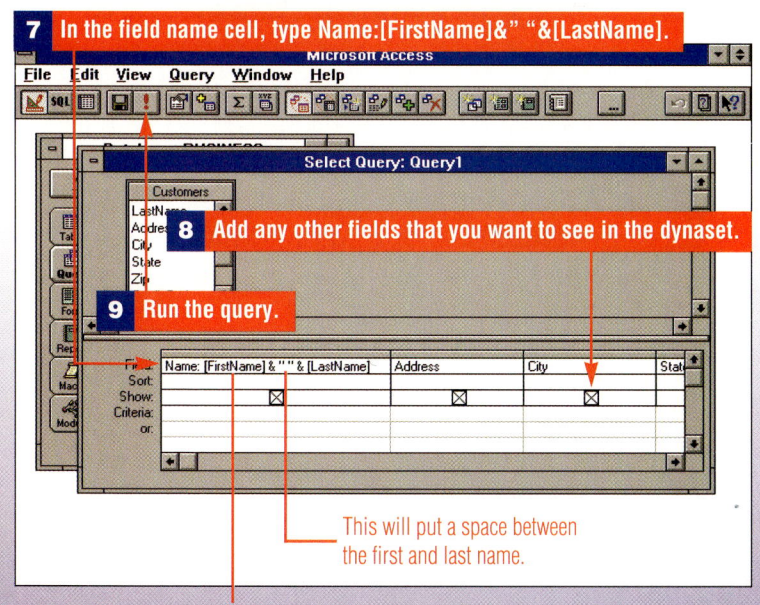

1 In the Database window, click the Query tab.

2 Choose New.

3 Click New Query.

4 Click the name of the table.

5 Click the Add button.

6 Click the Close button.

7 In the field name cell, type Name:[FirstName]&" "&[LastName].

8 Add any other fields that you want to see in the dynaset.

9 Run the query.

This will put a space between the first and last name.

Name: Creates a temporary label for the concatenated field.
All field names must be enclosed in square brackets.

more ▶

89

Queries—Advanced Design: Empty Fields and Calculations

The dynaset will give you a temporary field with the first and last names in the same field.

This field is not saved in the table. If you need to see the name data like this again, save the query and run it later.

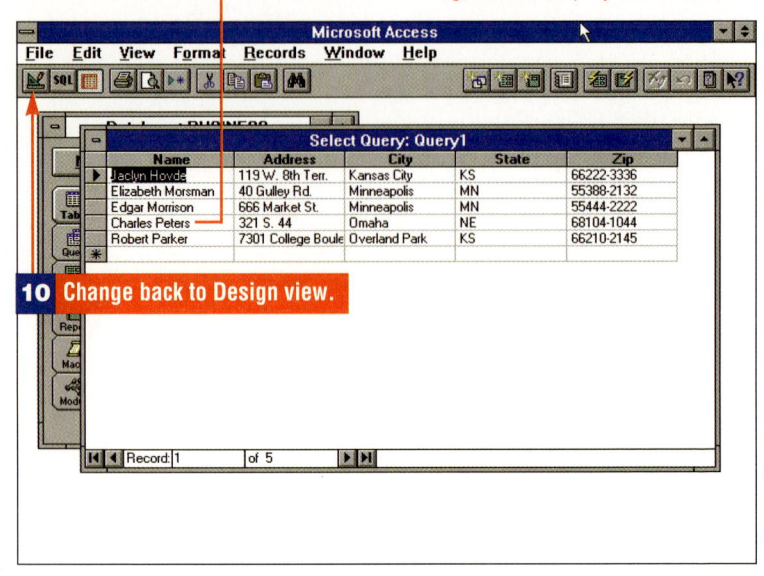

10 Change back to Design view.

To zoom the window, click in the cell to edit, and press Shift + F2.

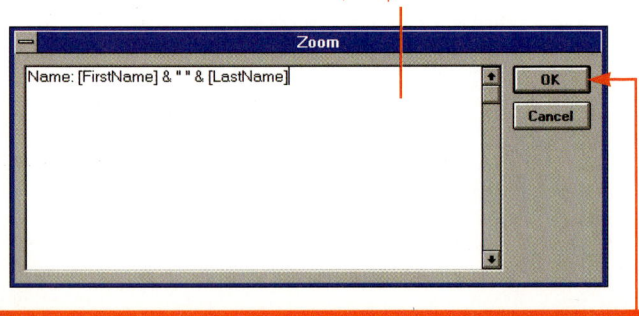

Zoom contents: `Name: [FirstName] & " " & [LastName]`

11 Click OK to close Zoom window and place edited information in the cell.

12 Double-click Control Menu icon to close the query.

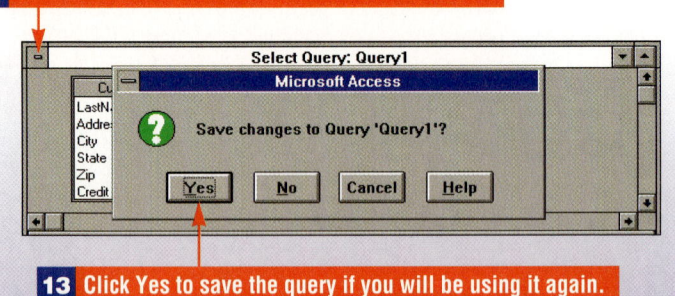

Save changes to Query 'Query1'?

13 Click Yes to save the query if you will be using it again.

Queries—Advanced Design: Empty Fields and Calculations

14 Type a name for the query.

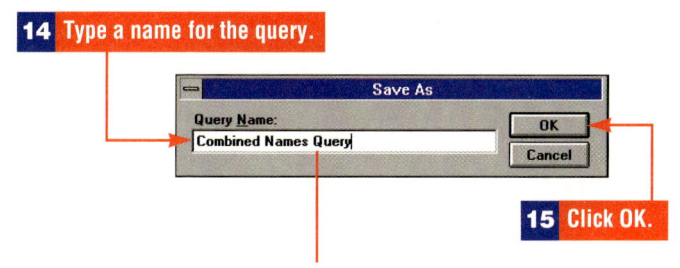

Save As
Query Name: Combined Names Query

15 Click OK.

Query name must be different than the table name.

Performing a Calculation in a Query Using Expressions

You cannot create a calculated field in a table. However, you can easily create a calculated field in a query. It will then be available later for a report or a form. For example, when you know the price and the quantity of an item, you can type an expression which calculates the extended price by multiplying price times quantity.

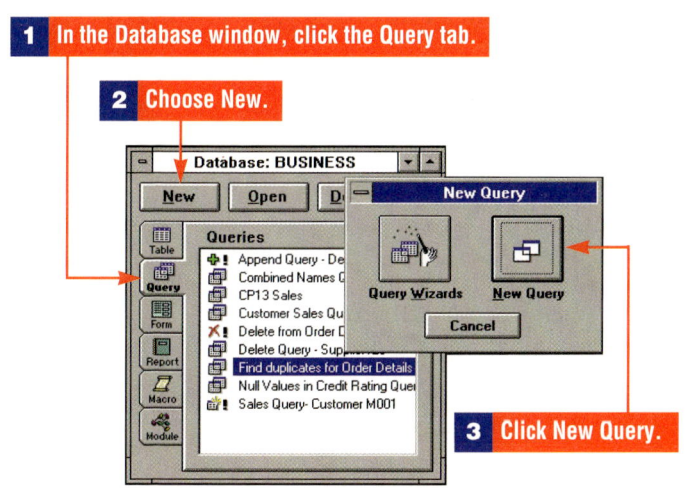

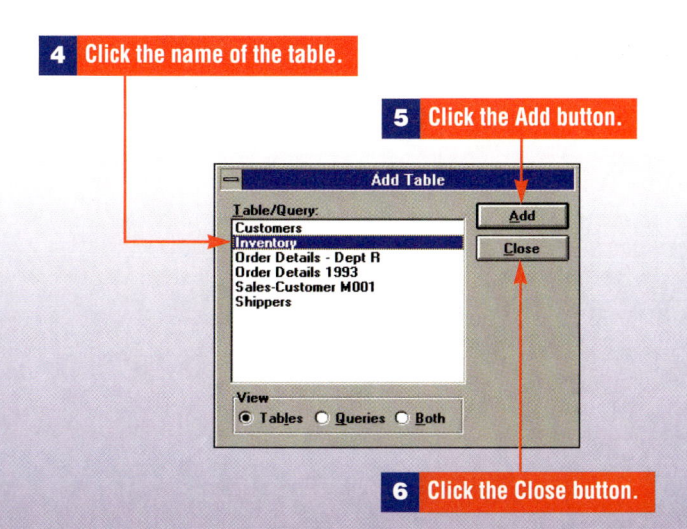

1 In the Database window, click the Query tab.

2 Choose New.

3 Click New Query.

4 Click the name of the table.

5 Click the Add button.

6 Click the Close button.

more ▶

91

Queries—Advanced Design: Empty Fields and Calculations

7 Add all the fields you want to show in this query.

8 In a field name cell, type Total Price:[UnitsInStock]*[UnitPrice].

9 Run the query.

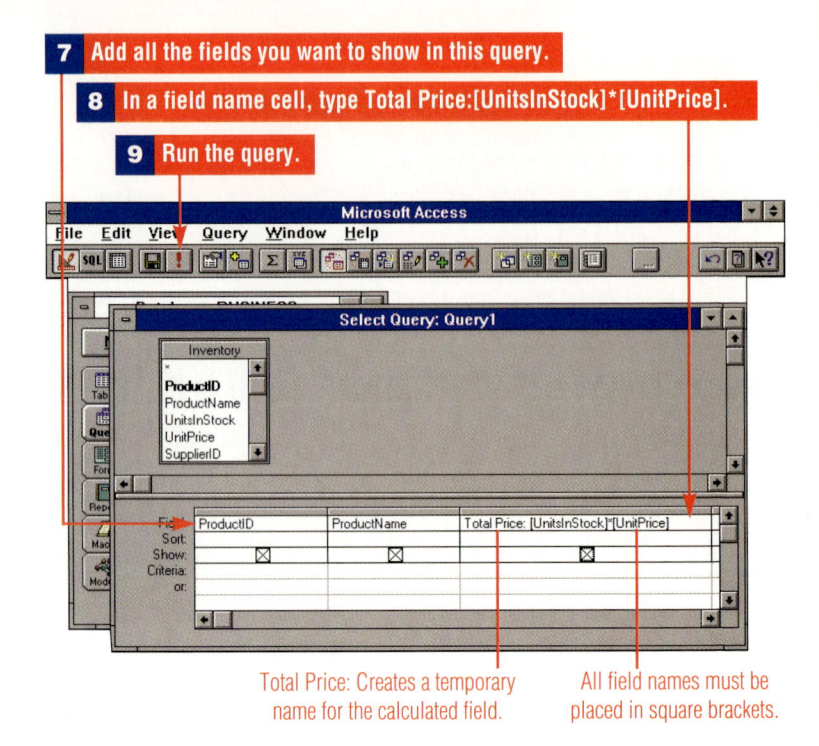

Total Price: Creates a temporary name for the calculated field.

All field names must be placed in square brackets.

If you change one of the fields on which the calculation is based, the calculation will be updated.

You cannot change the calculation in the datasheet view.

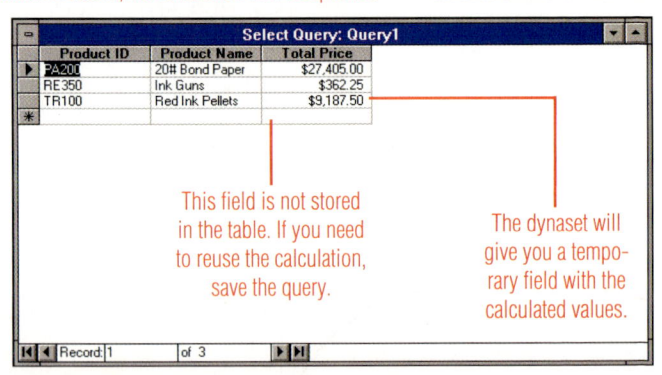

This field is not stored in the table. If you need to reuse the calculation, save the query.

The dynaset will give you a temporary field with the calculated values.

10 Double-click Control Menu icon to close the query.

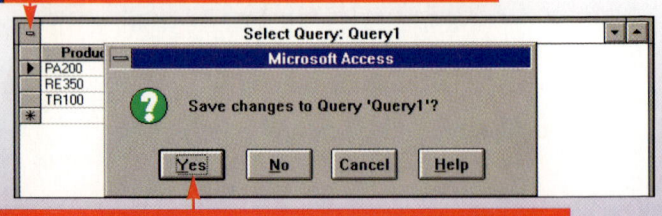

11 Choose Yes to save the query if you will be using it again.

12 Type a name for the query.

Query name must be different than the table name.

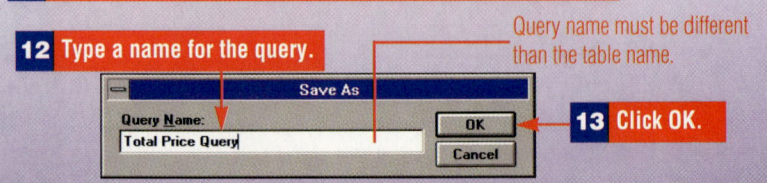

13 Click OK.

92

Queries—Advanced Design: Empty Fields and Calculations

Adding a Parameter to a Query

To use different criteria each time you run a query, you can set up a parameter. A parameter allows you to enter a different criteria every time you run a query. For example, you may want to look up all products by one supplier today, but use the same query to look up another supplier next time.

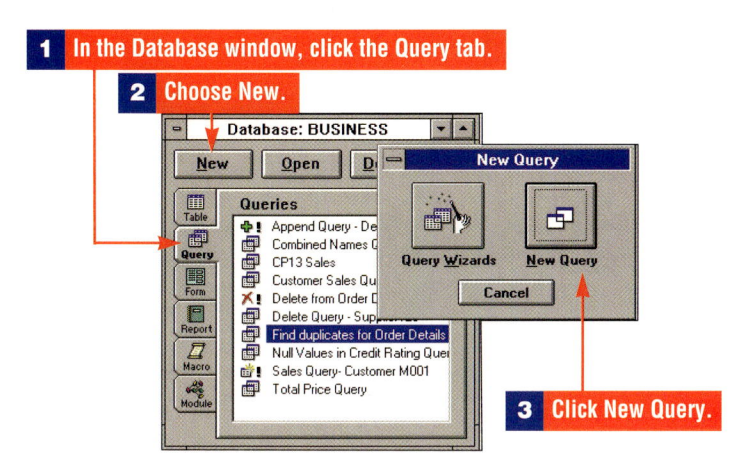

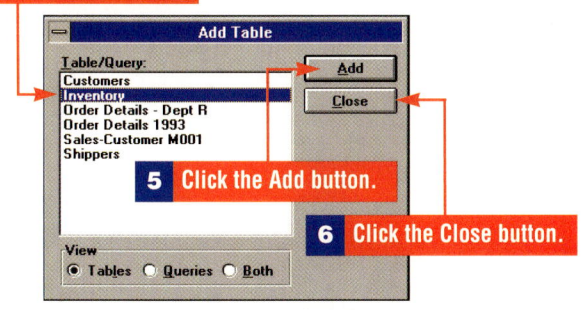

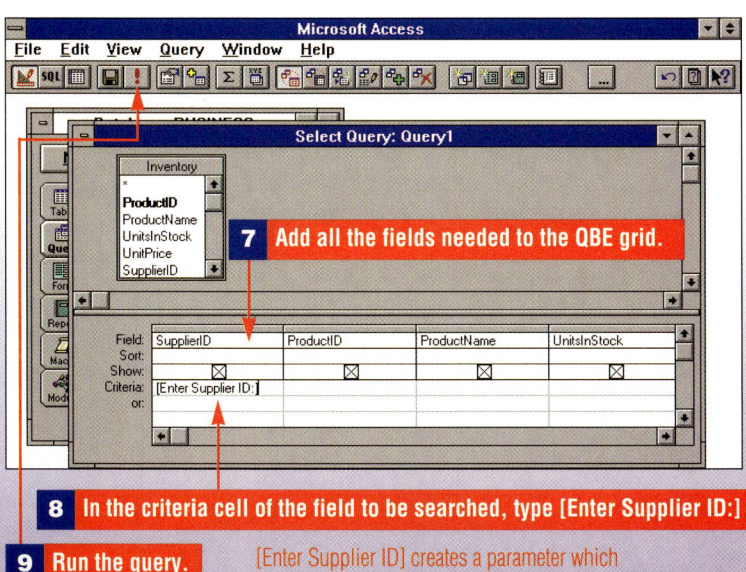

1 In the Database window, click the Query tab.

2 Choose New.

3 Click New Query.

4 Click the name of the table.

5 Click the Add button.

6 Click the Close button.

7 Add all the fields needed to the QBE grid.

8 In the criteria cell of the field to be searched, type [Enter Supplier ID:]

9 Run the query.

[Enter Supplier ID] creates a parameter which Access displays each time the query is run.

more ▶

93

Queries—Advanced Design: Empty Fields and Calculations

10 Type in the Supplier ID desired.

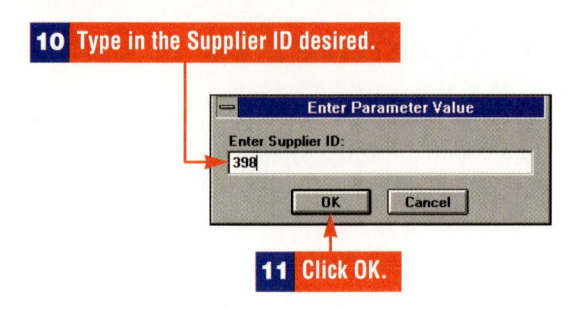

Enter Parameter Value

Enter Supplier ID:
398

OK   Cancel

11 Click OK.

Dynasheet of the desired data

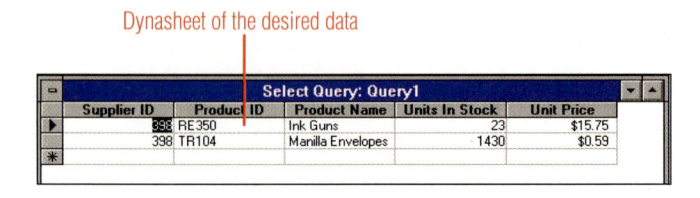

Supplier ID	Product ID	Product Name	Units In Stock	Unit Price
398	RE350	Ink Guns	23	$15.75
398	TR104	Manilla Envelopes	1430	$0.59

12 Double-click Control Menu icon to close the query.

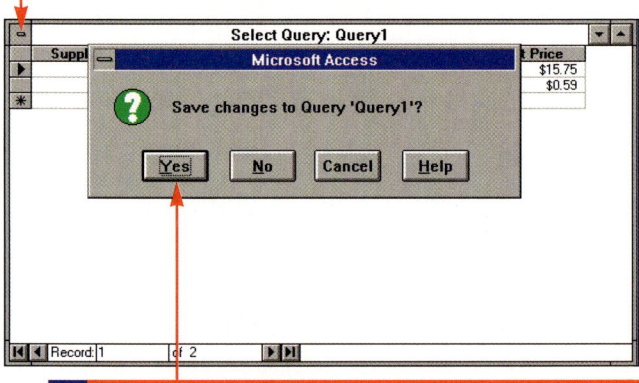

Microsoft Access

Save changes to Query 'Query1'?

Yes   No   Cancel   Help

13 Choose Yes to save the query if you will be using it again.

14 Type a name for the query.

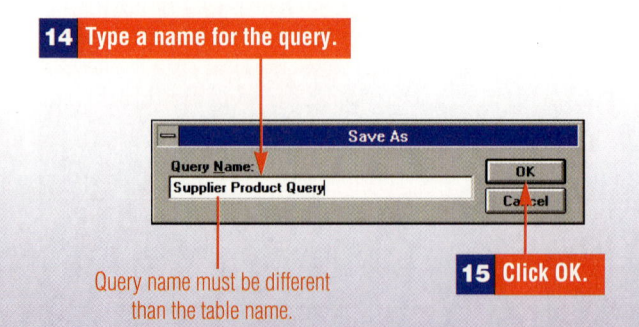

Save As

Query Name:
Supplier Product Query

OK   Cancel

Query name must be different than the table name.

15 Click OK.

Queries—Advanced Design: Empty Fields and Calculations

Summarizing Data

Frequently, you need to quickly calculate totals and averages or count the number of records which match a certain criteria. You can perform these calculations with a totals or aggregate query. When you run this type of query, you cannot update the dynaset.

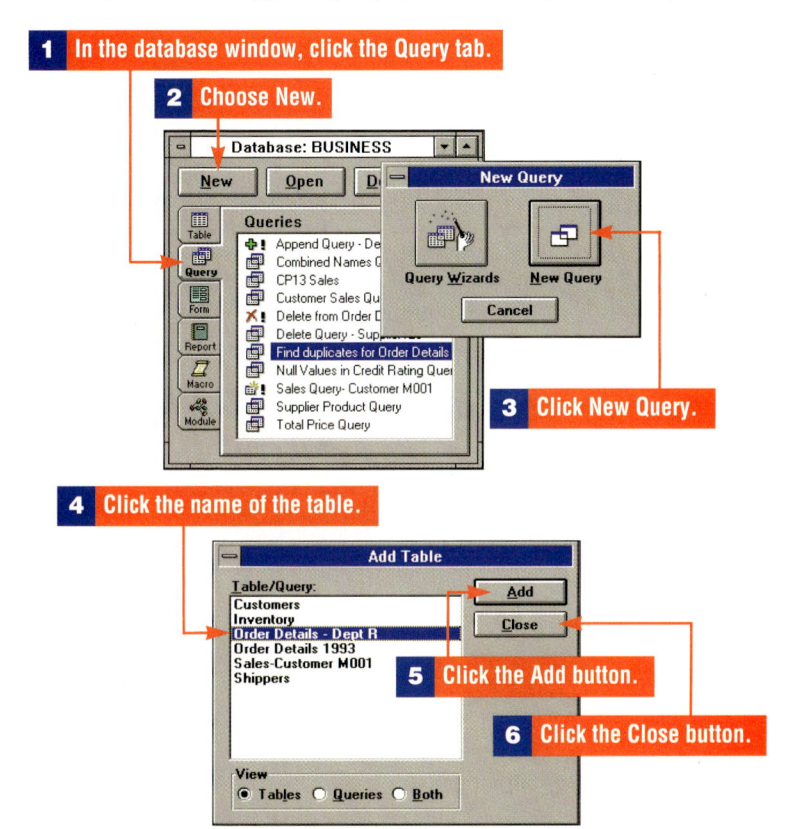

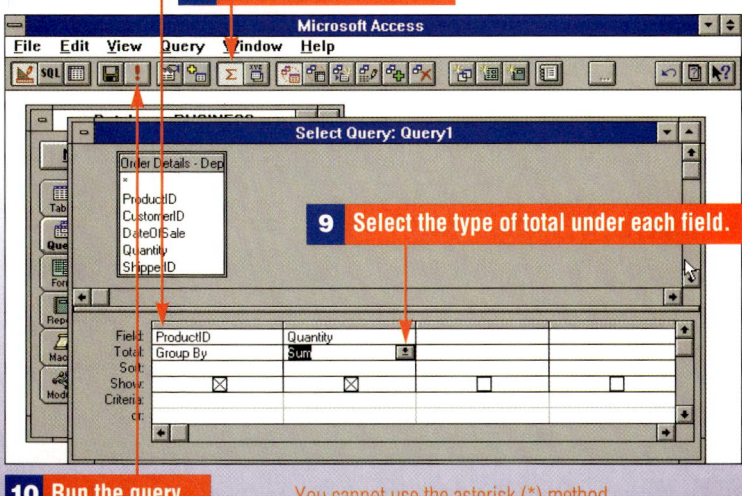

1 In the database window, click the Query tab.

2 Choose New.

3 Click New Query.

4 Click the name of the table.

5 Click the Add button.

6 Click the Close button.

7 Add the fields to the QBE grid.

8 Click the Totals button.

9 Select the type of total under each field.

10 Run the query.

You cannot use the asterisk (*) method of choosing fields for a totals query.

more ▶

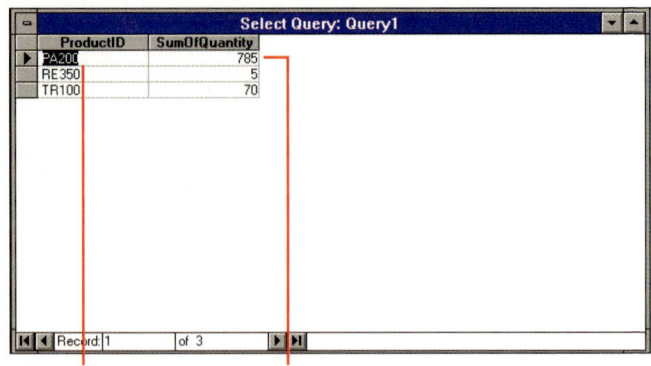

Queries—Advanced Design: Empty Fields and Calculations

Dynaset is now grouped by Product ID.

Access creates a new column heading for each calculation.

11 Double-click Control Menu icon to close the query.

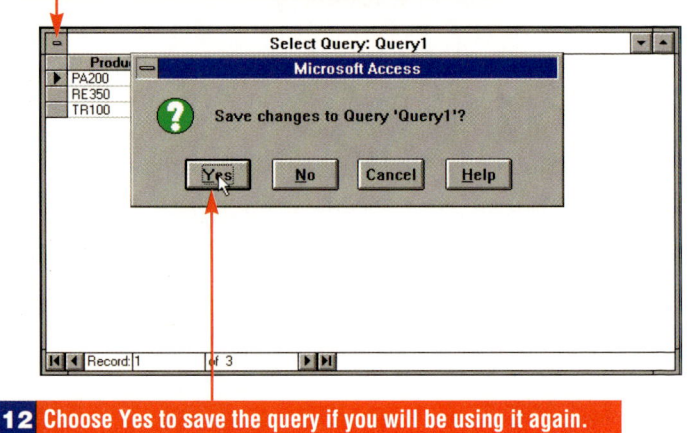

12 Choose Yes to save the query if you will be using it again.

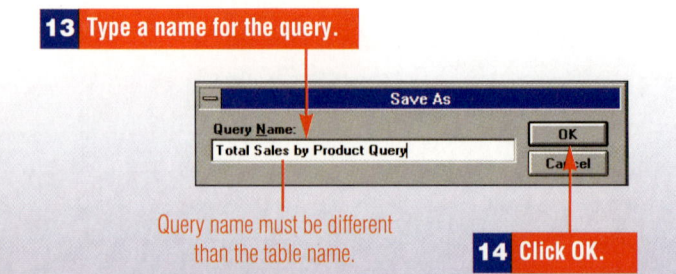

13 Type a name for the query.

Query name must be different than the table name.

14 Click OK.

96

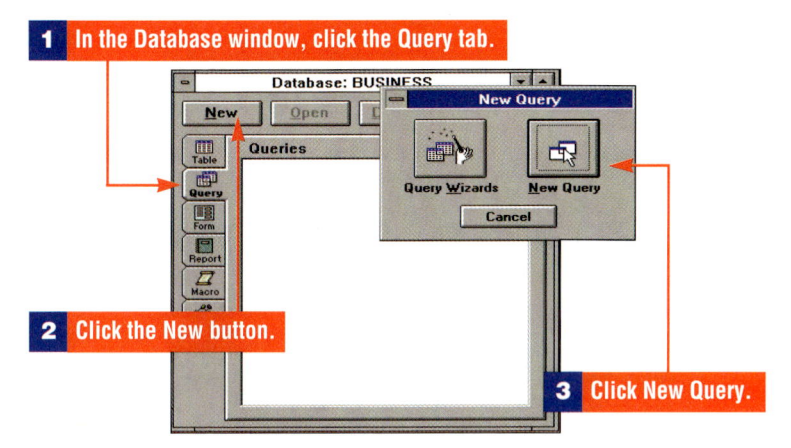

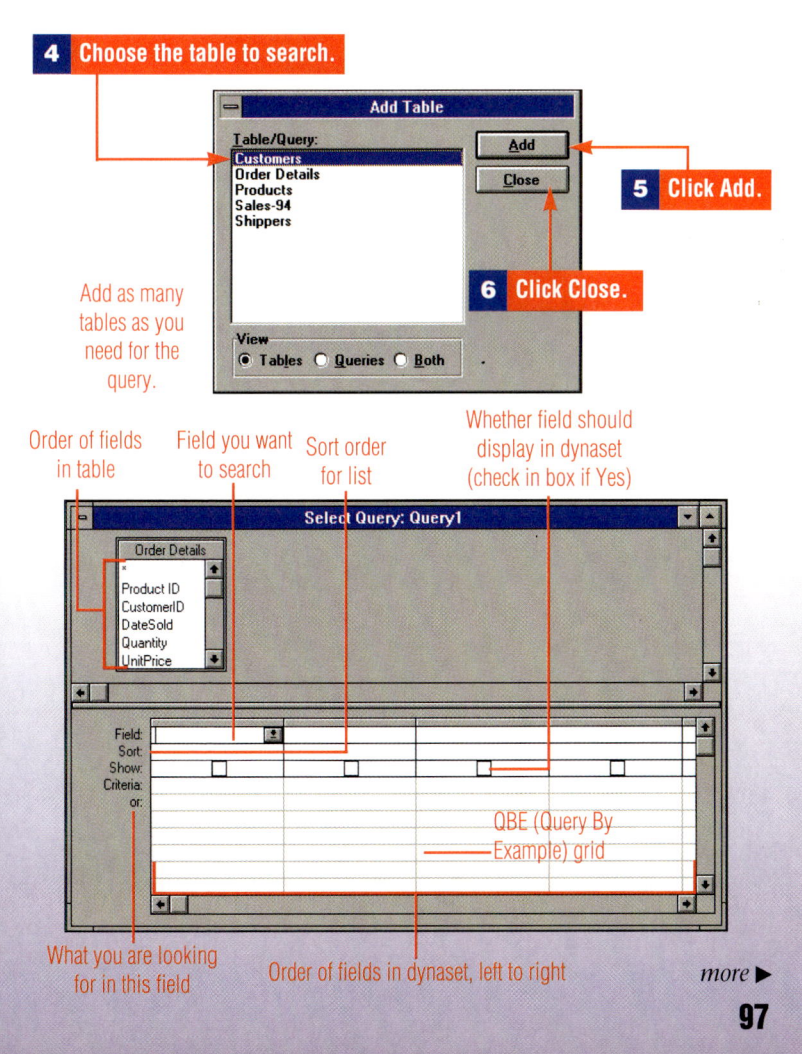

Queries—Select Query: Creating and Editing

Creating a Select Query

You create a select query to enable Access to ask questions about the information in your database. When you run a select query, Access displays a dynaset that contains the resulting records and fields.

To create a select query

1 In the Database window, click the Query tab.

2 Click the New button.

3 Click New Query.

4 Choose the table to search.

5 Click Add.

6 Click Close.

Add as many tables as you need for the query.

Order of fields in table

Field you want to search

Sort order for list

Whether field should display in dynaset (check in box if Yes)

QBE (Query By Example) grid

What you are looking for in this field

Order of fields in dynaset, left to right

more ▶

97

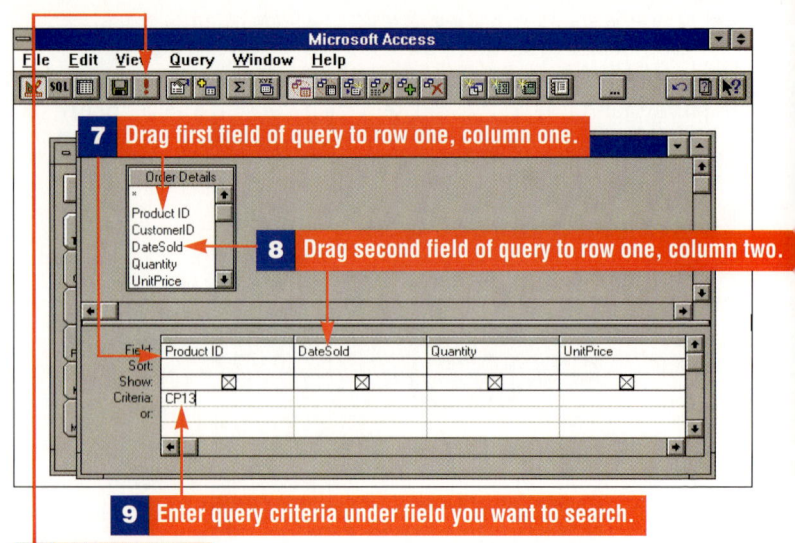

Queries—Select Query: Creating and Editing

7 Drag first field of query to row one, column one.

8 Drag second field of query to row one, column two.

9 Enter query criteria under field you want to search.

10 Run the query.

Scroll field list and add all the fields you want to include.

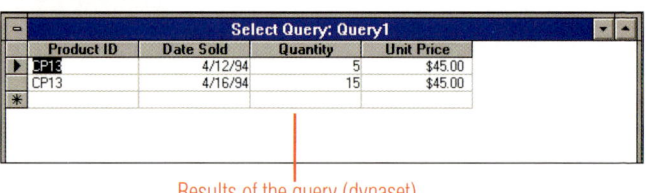

Results of the query (dynaset)

To sort records in a query

1 Switch to Design view.

2 In the Sort row, click the Sort cell below the field to sort.

3 Choose Ascending from the list.

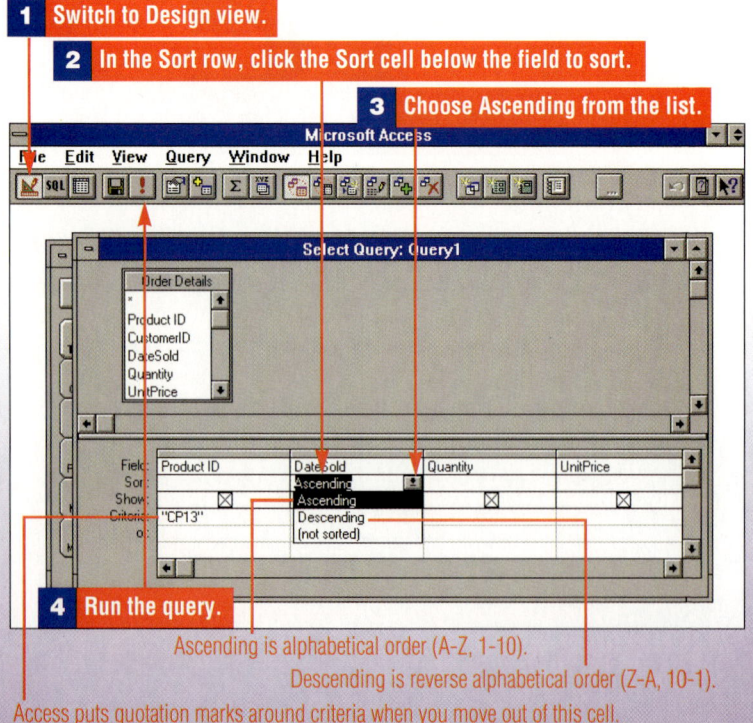

4 Run the query.

Ascending is alphabetical order (A-Z, 1-10).

Descending is reverse alphabetical order (Z-A, 10-1).

Access puts quotation marks around criteria when you move out of this cell.

98

Queries—Select Query: Creating and Editing

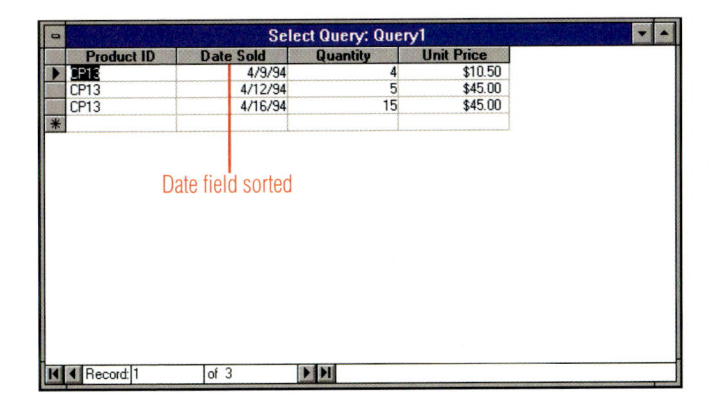

Date field sorted

To close and save a query

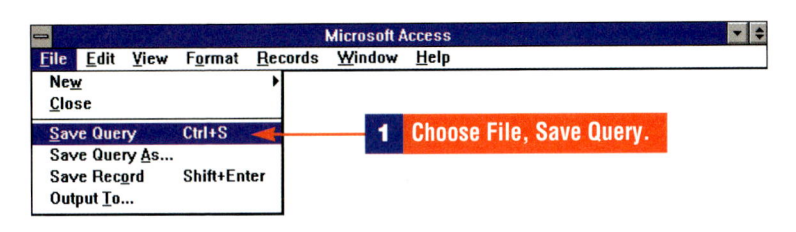

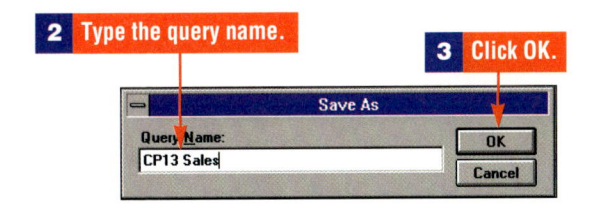

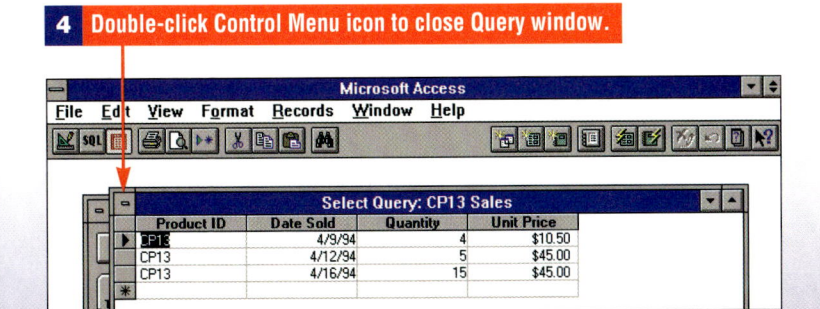

1 Choose File, Save Query.

2 Type the query name.

3 Click OK.

4 Double-click Control Menu icon to close Query window.

Queries—Select Query: Creating and Editing

To select multiple fields for the QBE grid

1 To select several fields, hold the Ctrl key while selecting the fields desired.

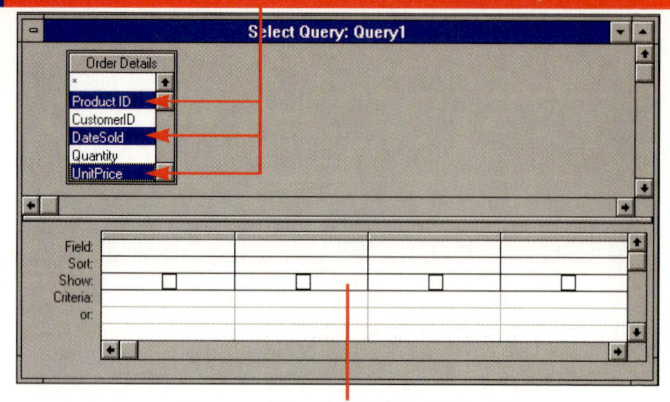

Drag any of the selected fields to the grid.

2 To select all table fields, drag the asterisk from the top of the field list.

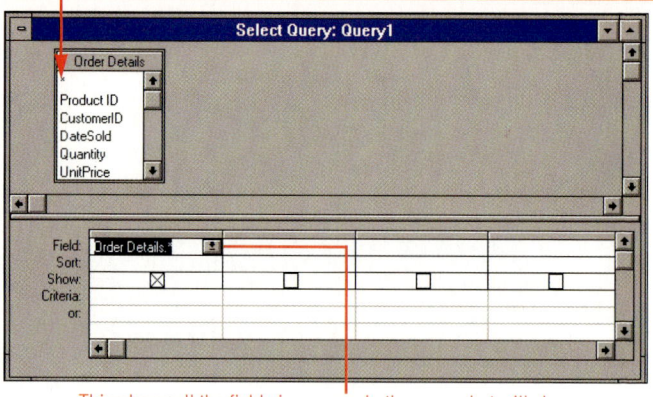

This places all the fields in a group in the query, but will show them all in the dynaset. Cannot sort or identify criteria.

To open and reuse a query

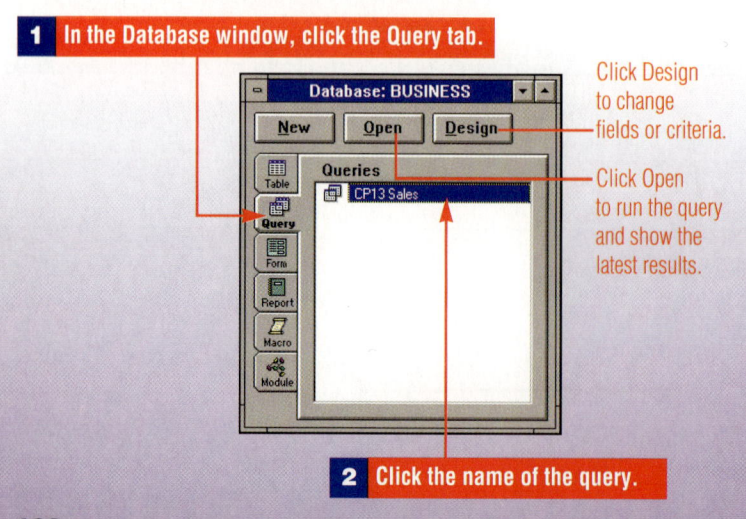

1 In the Database window, click the Query tab.

Click Design to change fields or criteria.

Click Open to run the query and show the latest results.

2 Click the name of the query.

Queries—Select Query: Creating and Editing

To print the results of a query

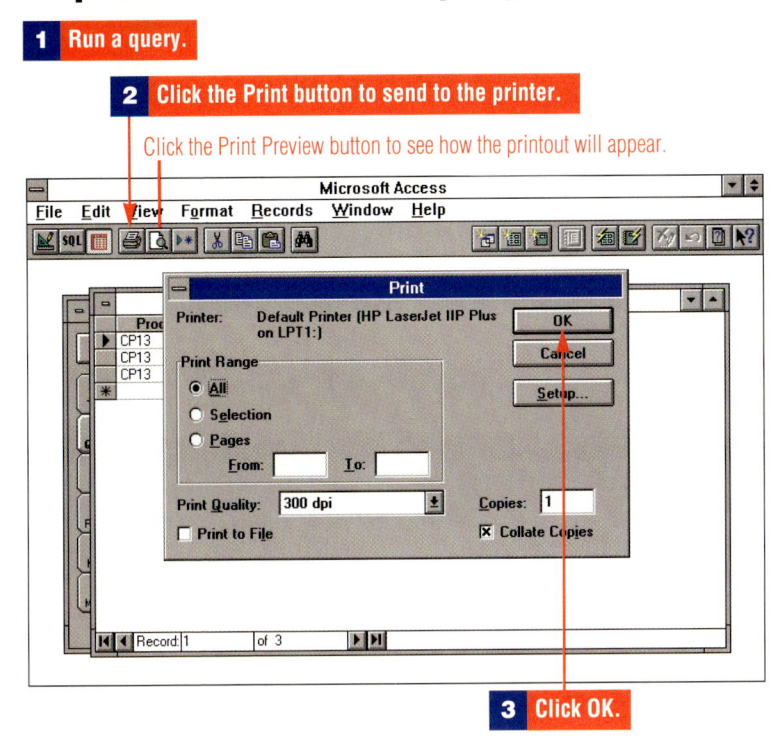

1 Run a query.

2 Click the Print button to send to the printer.

Click the Print Preview button to see how the printout will appear.

3 Click OK.

To print only certain records

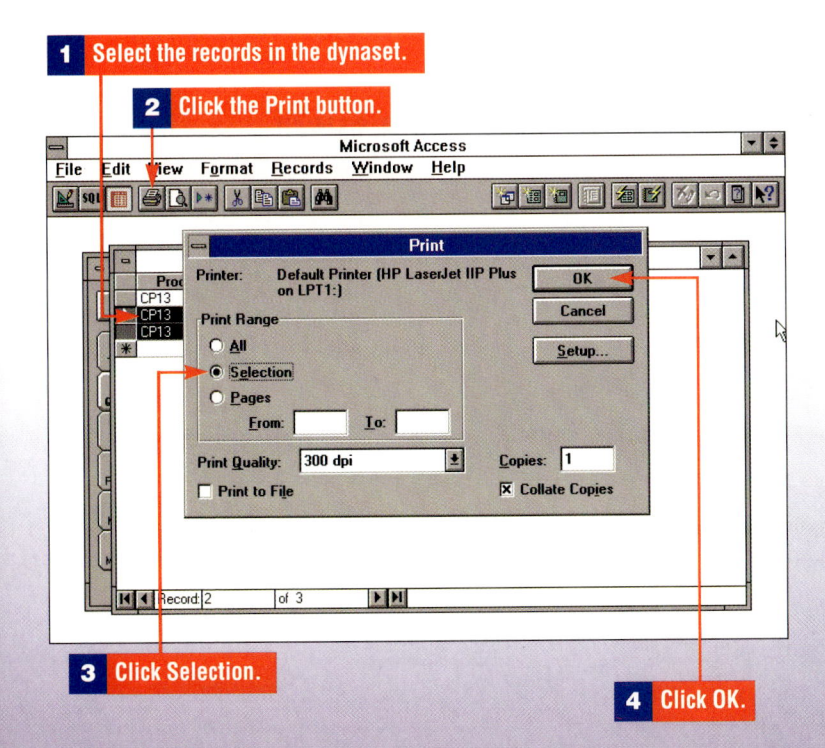

1 Select the records in the dynaset.

2 Click the Print button.

3 Click Selection.

4 Click OK.

101

Queries—Select Query: Creating and Editing

Editing the Query

After you have created and saved the query, you may need to modify it. By opening the query in Design view or clicking on the Design View button while viewing the dynaset, you will be able to make any necessary adjustments.

To insert a field in a query

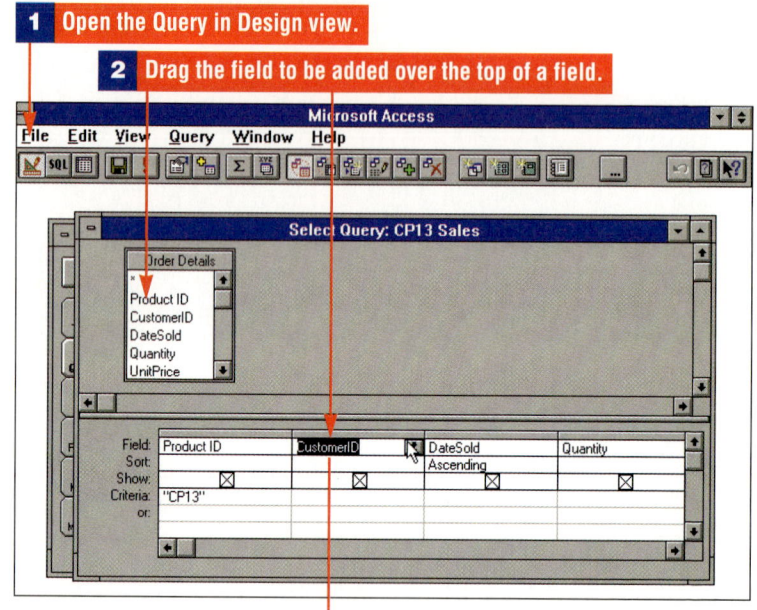

1 Open the Query in Design view.

2 Drag the field to be added over the top of a field.

The new field will make a new column and push the adjacent fields to the right.

To delete a field from a query

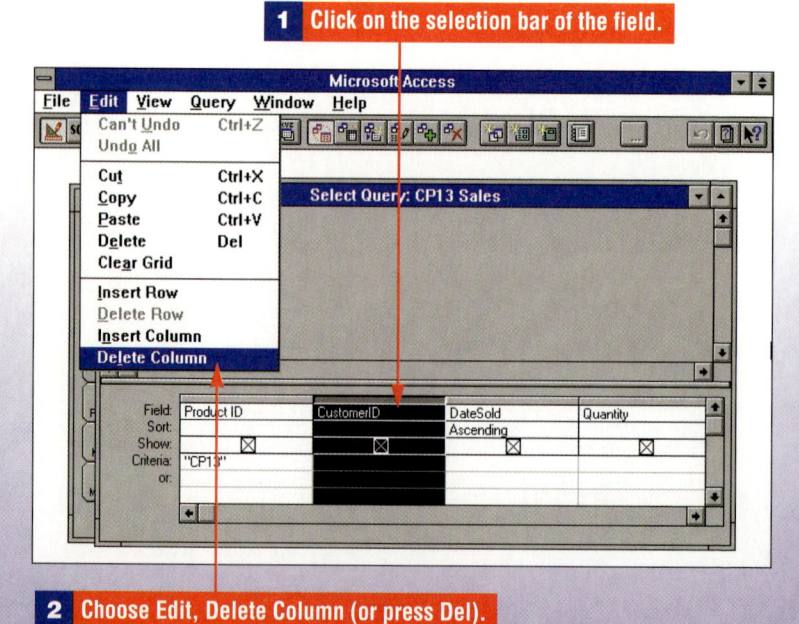

1 Click on the selection bar of the field.

2 Choose Edit, Delete Column (or press Del).

102

Queries—Select Query: Creating and Editing

To change a criteria

1 Drag over the criteria to change and retype.

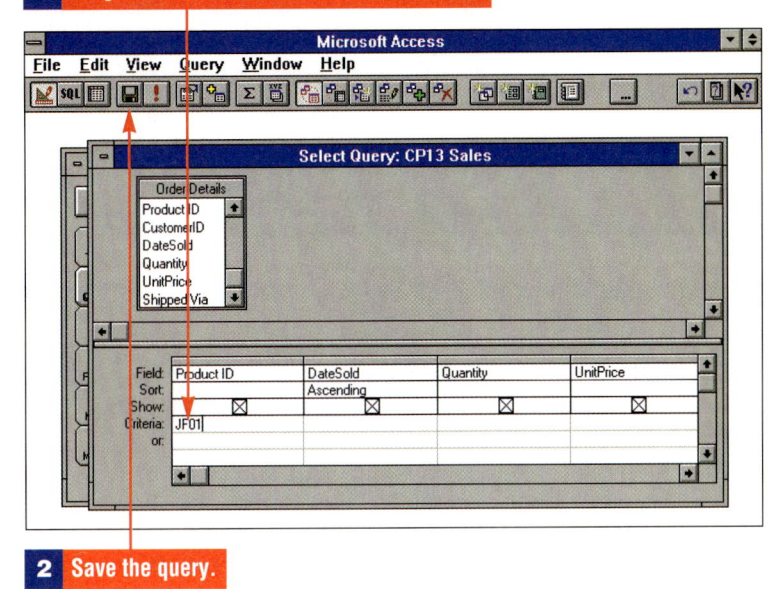

2 Save the query.

To move fields in a query

1 Click the selection bar of the field you want to move.

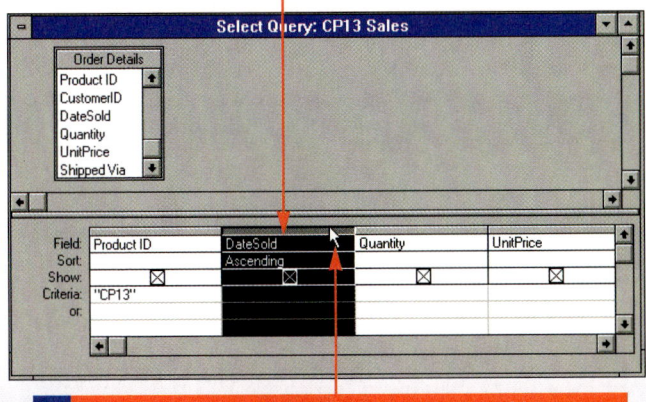

2 Move the mouse on top of the bar to show a white arrow.

more ▶

Queries—Select Query: Creating and Editing

3 Drag the arrow until the dark line is placed where field is to go.

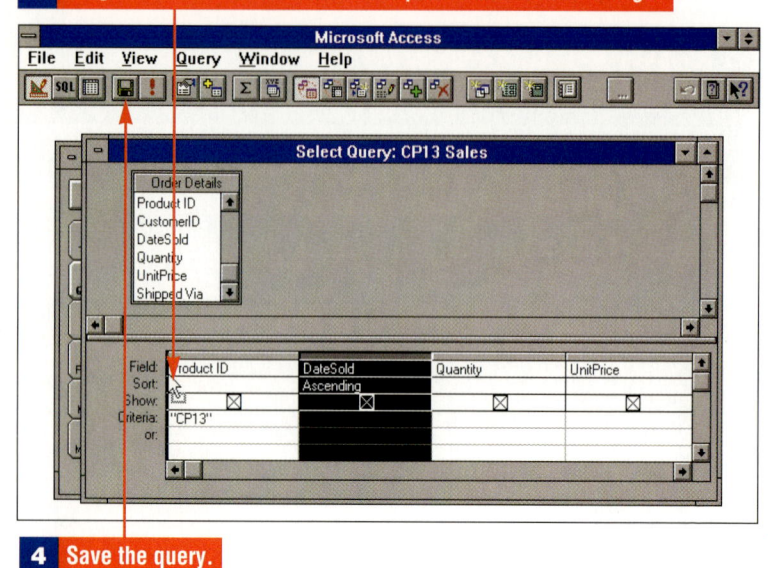

4 Save the query.

To update data using a select query dynaset

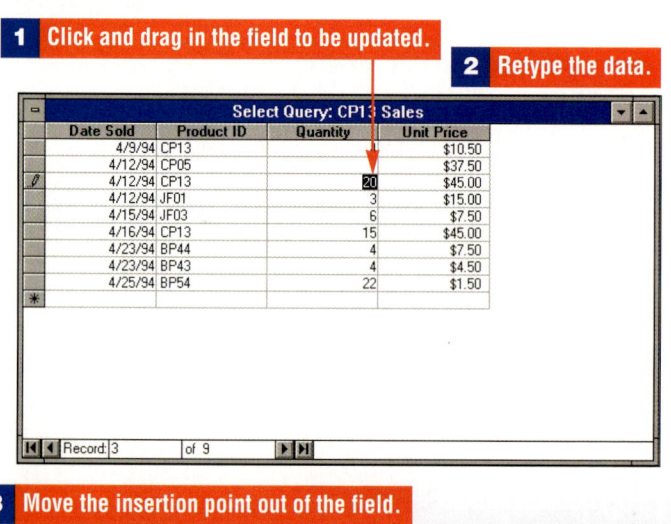

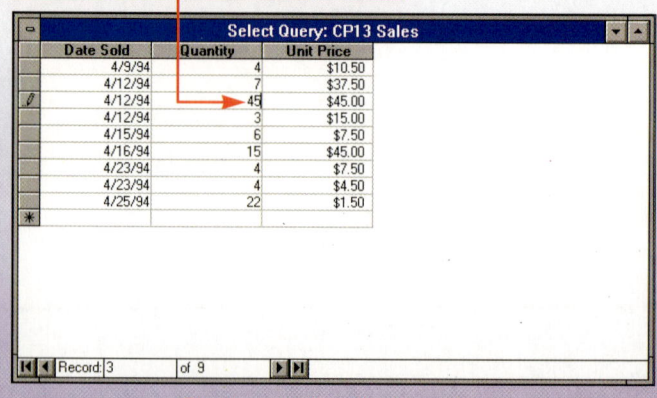

1 Click and drag in the field to be updated.

2 Retype the data.

3 Move the insertion point out of the field.

The changed information is saved.

104

Queries—Select Query: Creating and Editing

To add another table to the query

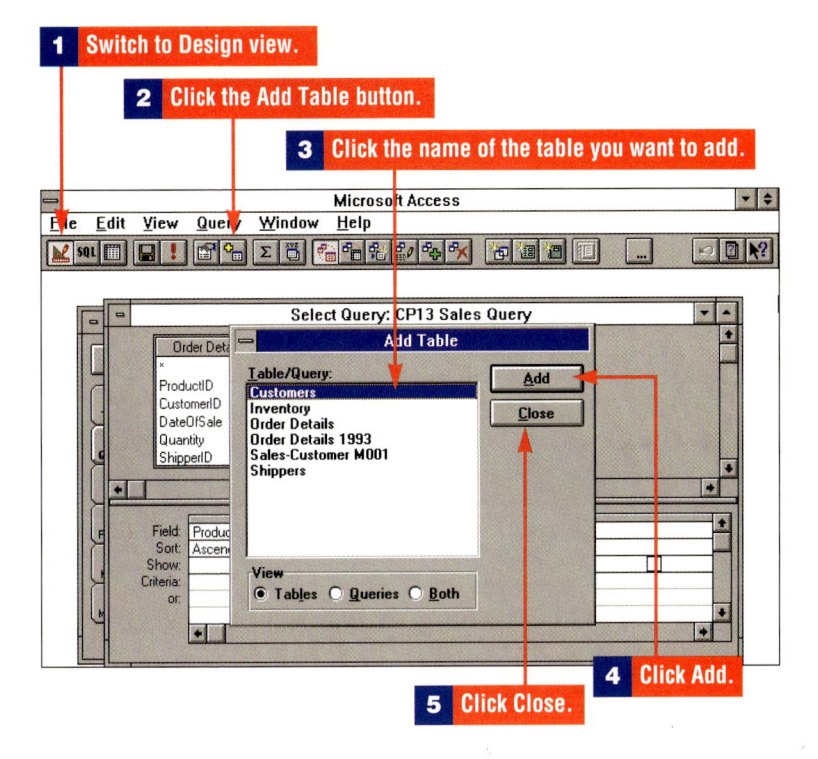

1 Switch to Design view.

2 Click the Add Table button.

3 Click the name of the table you want to add.

4 Click Add.

5 Click Close.

To delete a table from a query

1 Click on the table you want to delete.

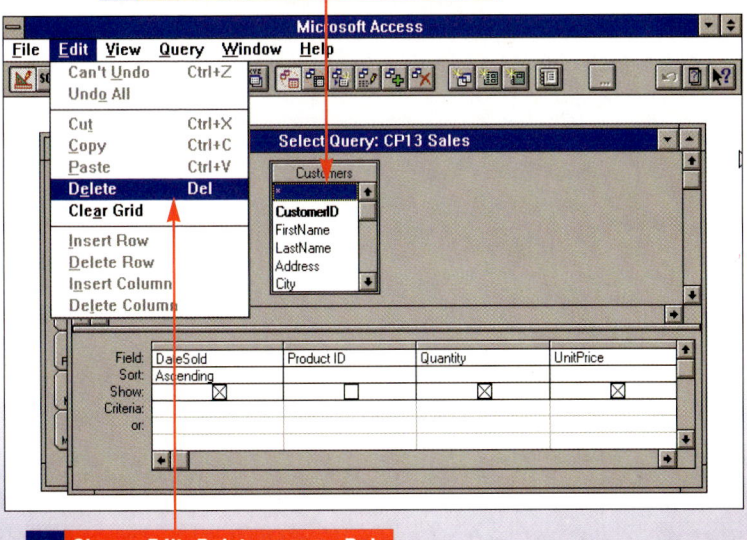

2 Choose Edit, Delete or press Del.

105

Queries—Select Query: Creating and Editing

To change a column width

1 Move mouse pointer to right border of the column.

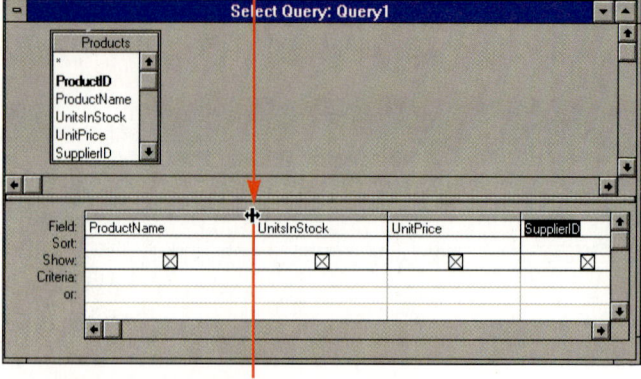

Mouse pointer will look like a two-way arrow.

2 Press left mouse button and drag line to desired width.

To give a field a customized name

1 Switch to Design view.

2 In Field cell, type new name followed by a colon in front of field name.

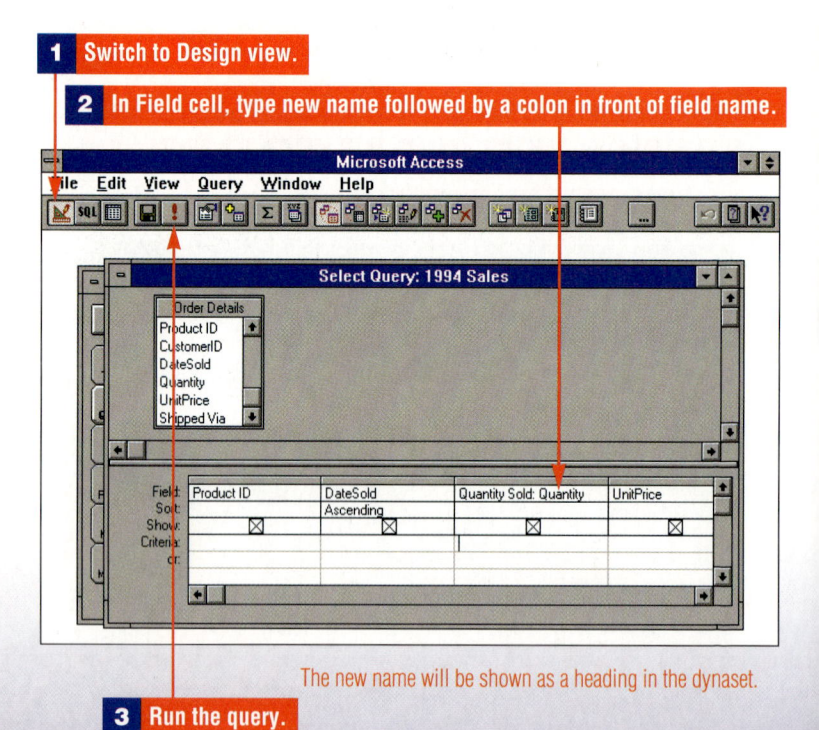

The new name will be shown as a heading in the dynaset.

3 Run the query.

106

Queries—Select Query: Creating and Editing

Hiding a Field

Hiding a field is useful if you want to quickly select every field, but don't need to show one of the fields; or if you select all the fields with the asterisk and want to enter criteria on a specific field.

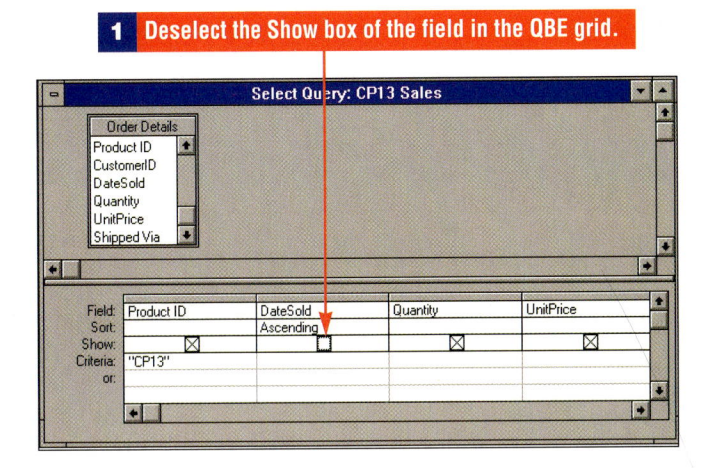

1 Deselect the Show box of the field in the QBE grid.

Defining Multiple Criteria

Access allows you to specify several criteria for one field. You might want to find all customers who live in Indiana *or* Ohio. You might also want to find all customers who live in Indiana *and* spent over $150.

To create an Or search for the same field

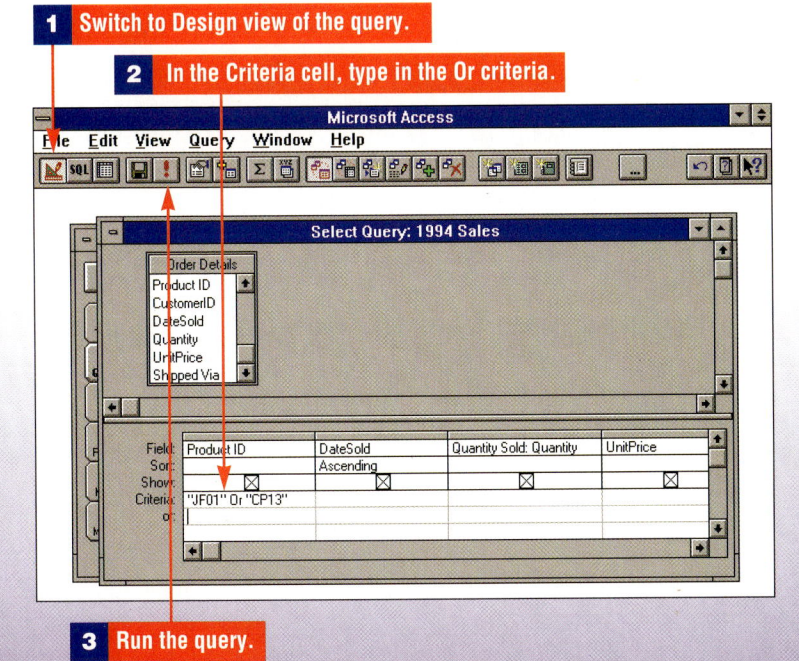

1 Switch to Design view of the query.

2 In the Criteria cell, type in the Or criteria.

3 Run the query.

If you do not type in the quotation marks and capitalize Or, Access will do it for you.

more ▶

107

Queries—Select Query: Creating and Editing

Results show records that match one criteria or the other.

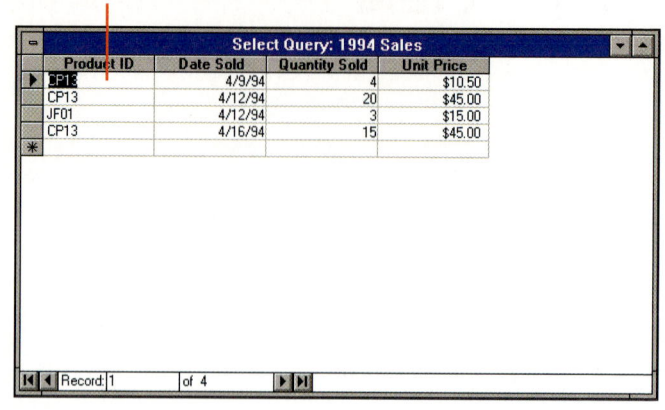

To use the Or search in different fields

1 Switch to Design view.

2 Type the criteria for one field in the Criteria cell.

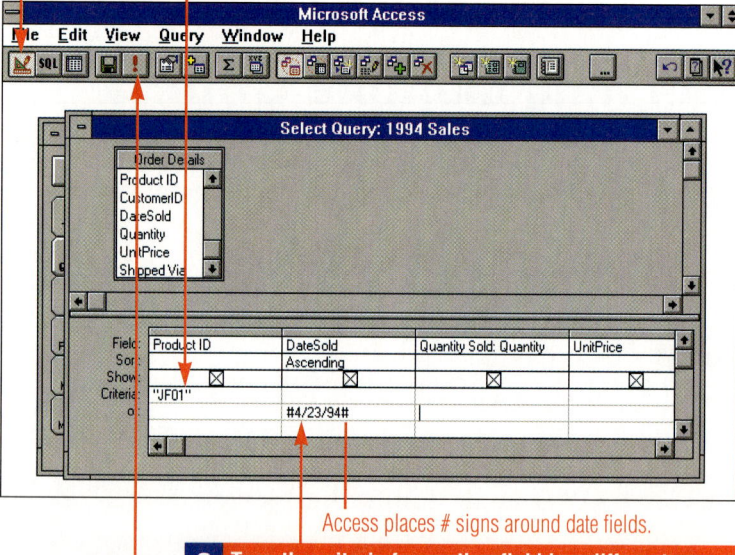

Access places # signs around date fields.

3 Type the criteria for another field in a different row.

4 Run the query.

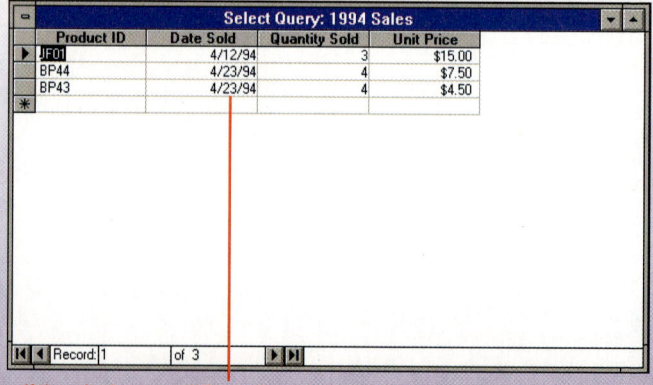

If the criteria are on different lines, Access will match one or the other.

Queries—Select Query: Creating and Editing

To use the And criteria for different fields

1 Switch to Design view.

2 Type the criteria for one field in the Criteria cell.

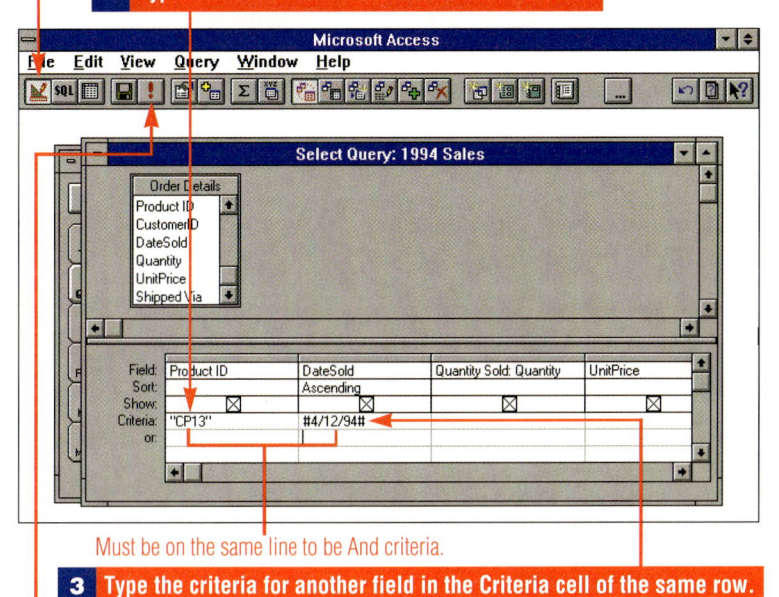

Must be on the same line to be And criteria.

3 Type the criteria for another field in the Criteria cell of the same row.

4 Run the query.

The results show only records that match both criteria.

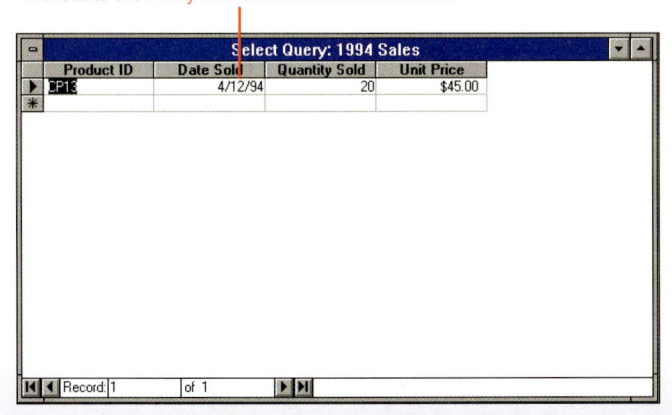

109

Relationships: Defining, Using in Queries and Subforms

Defining Relationships

The most common type of relationship set up between two tables is a one-to-many relationship. An example would be between a table which contains information about customers (customer number, name, address) and the Order Details table (customer number, order information). The customer table would be the One side of the relationship (known as the primary table) and the Order Details table would be on the Many side (known as a related table). One customer can have many sales, but one sale can have only one customer. Setting up relationships between tables saves storage space, time, and makes combining tables in forms, queries, and reports much easier. Related tables must have at least one common field.

To define a one-to-many relationship between two tables

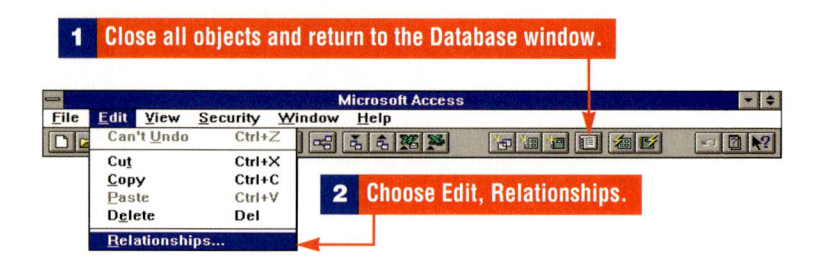

1 Close all objects and return to the Database window.

2 Choose Edit, Relationships.

If necessary, click the Add Table button to open the dialog box.

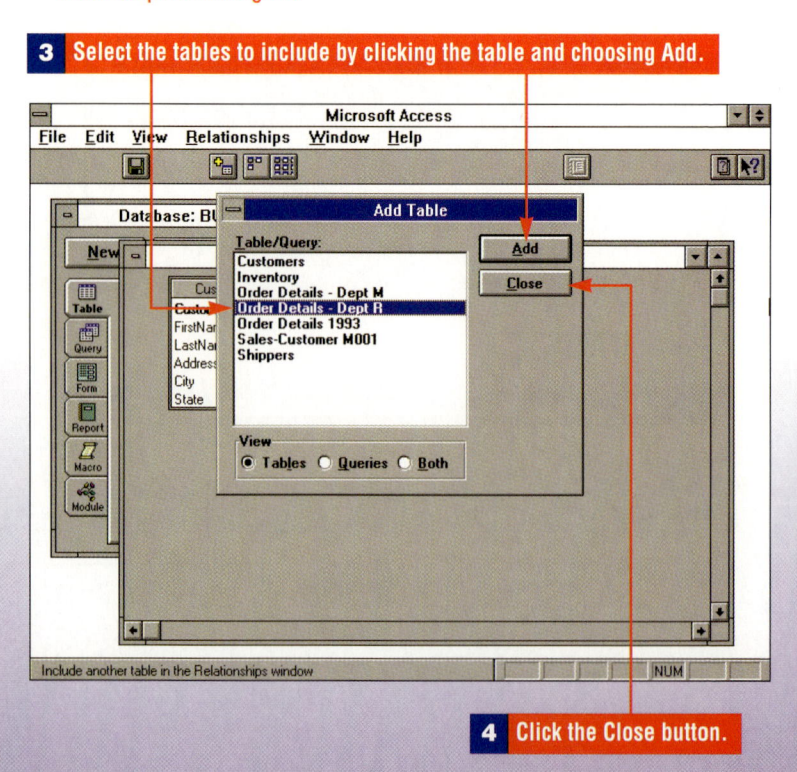

3 Select the tables to include by clicking the table and choosing Add.

4 Click the Close button.

Relationships: Defining, Using in Queries and Subforms

5 Drag from common field in primary table to same field in related table.

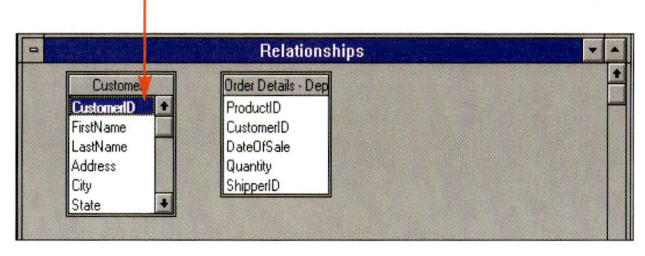

The Relationships window

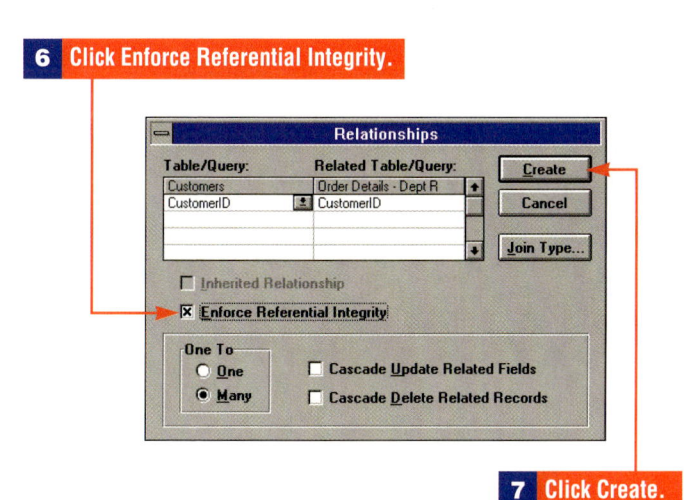

6 Click Enforce Referential Integrity.

7 Click Create.

8 Double-click the Control Menu icon to close the window.

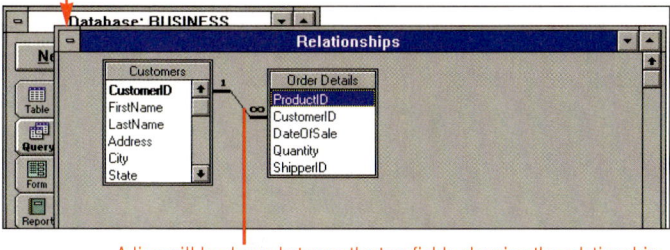

A line will be drawn between the two fields showing the relationship.

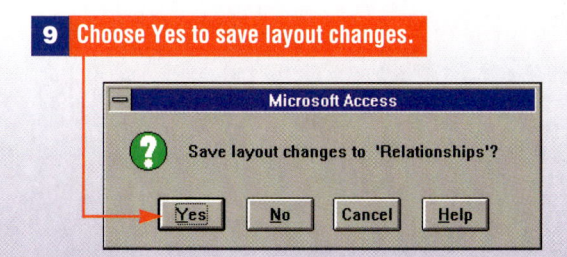

9 Choose Yes to save layout changes.

111

Relationships: Defining, Using in Queries and Subforms

To delete a relationship

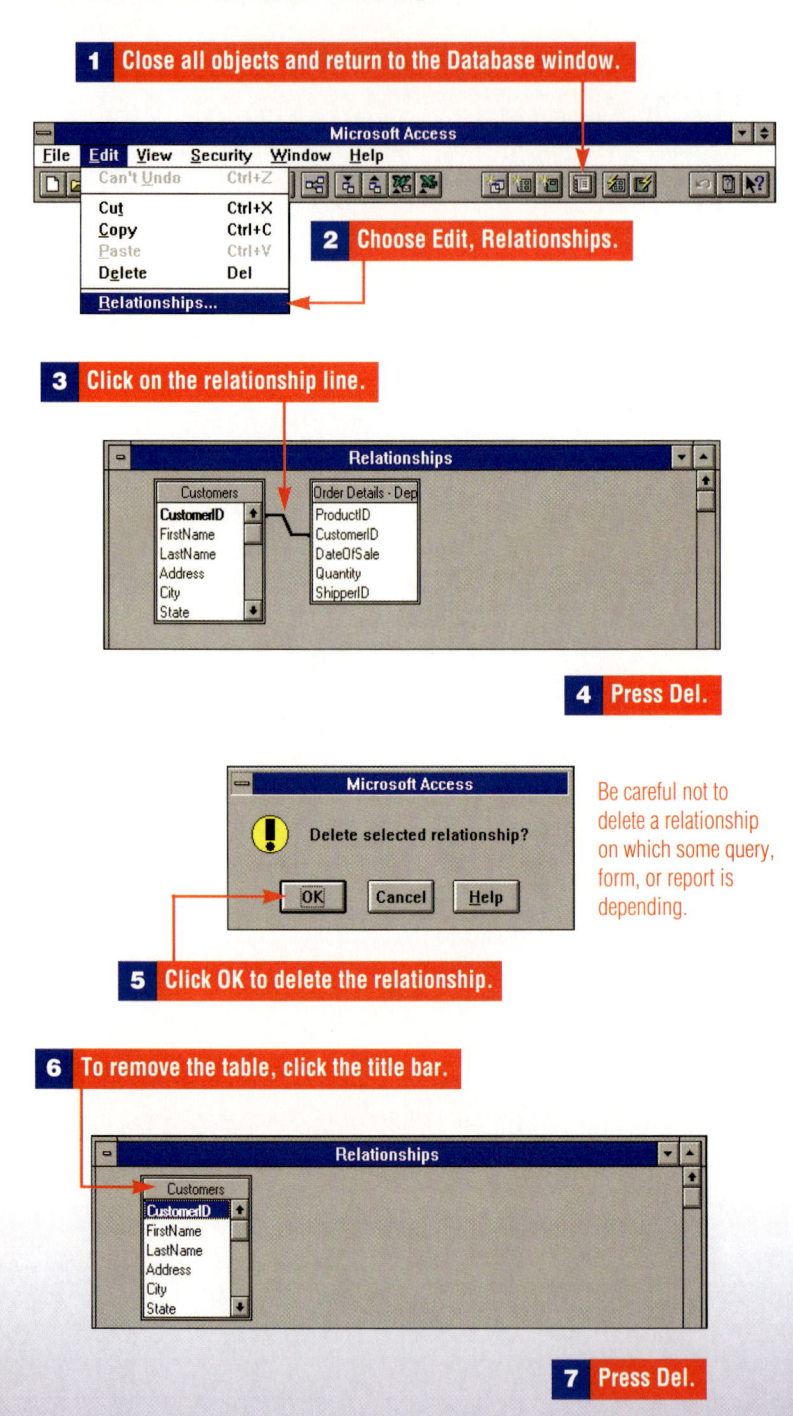

1 Close all objects and return to the Database window.

2 Choose Edit, Relationships.

3 Click on the relationship line.

4 Press Del.

5 Click OK to delete the relationship.

Be careful not to delete a relationship on which some query, form, or report is depending.

6 To remove the table, click the title bar.

7 Press Del.

112

Relationships: Defining, Using in Queries and Subforms

8 Double-click the Control Menu icon to close the window.

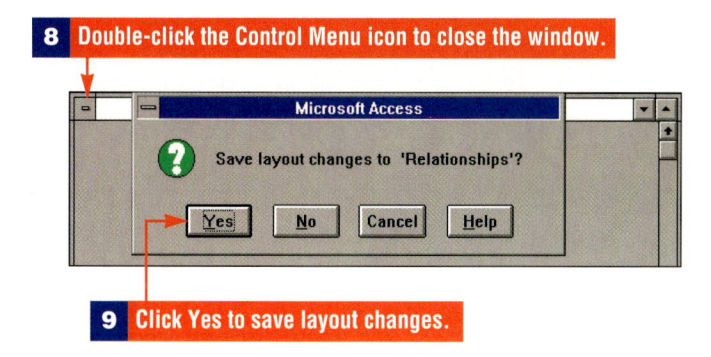

Microsoft Access dialog: Save layout changes to 'Relationships'? — Yes / No / Cancel / Help

9 Click Yes to save layout changes.

Using Multiple Tables in a Query

One of the most common uses of relationships is to create a multiple table query. Consider a query in which you see all the sales per customer, showing the customer name instead of just the Customer ID.

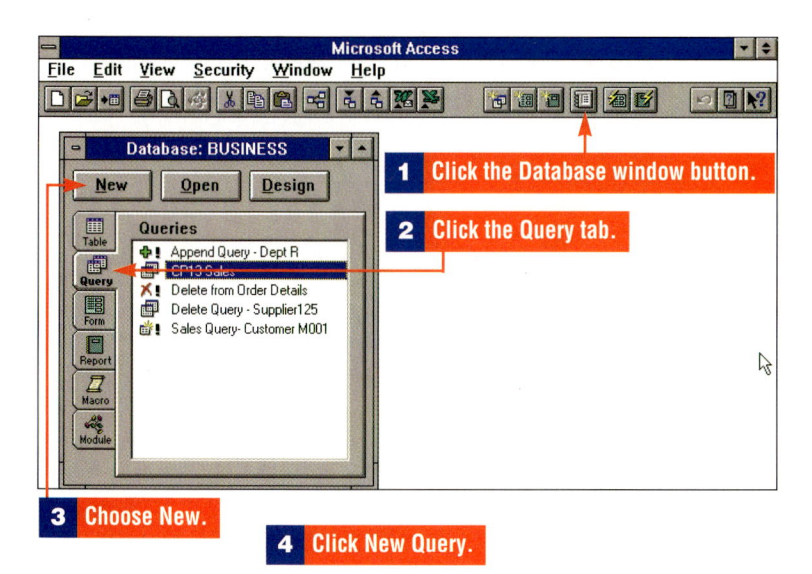

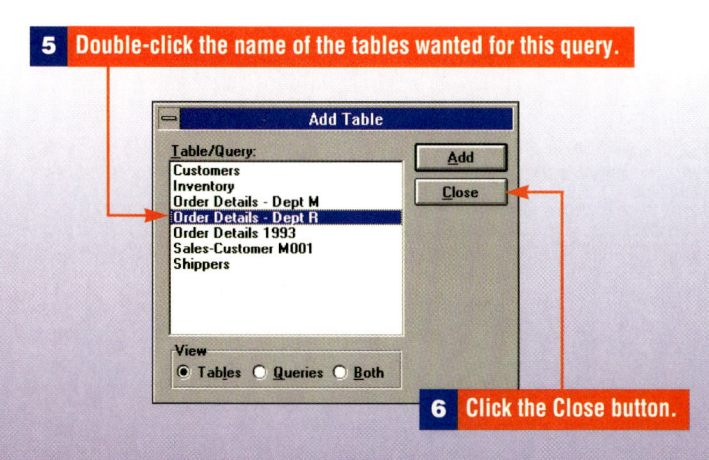

1 Click the Database window button.

2 Click the Query tab.

3 Choose New.

4 Click New Query.

5 Double-click the name of the tables wanted for this query.

6 Click the Close button.

more ▶

113

Relationships: Defining, Using in Queries and Subforms

7 Add fields desired from each table.

8 Click the Table Names button.

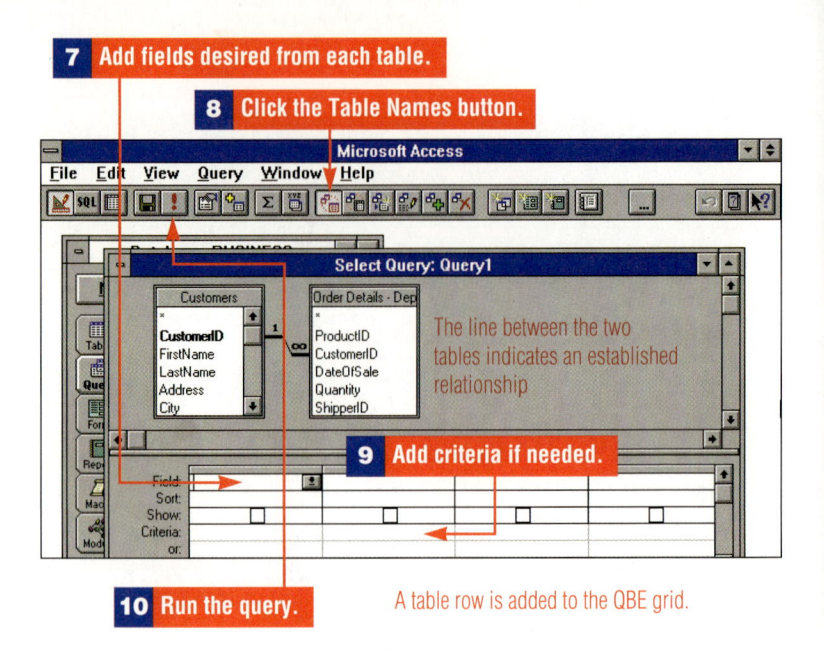

The line between the two tables indicates an established relationship

9 Add criteria if needed.

10 Run the query.

A table row is added to the QBE grid.

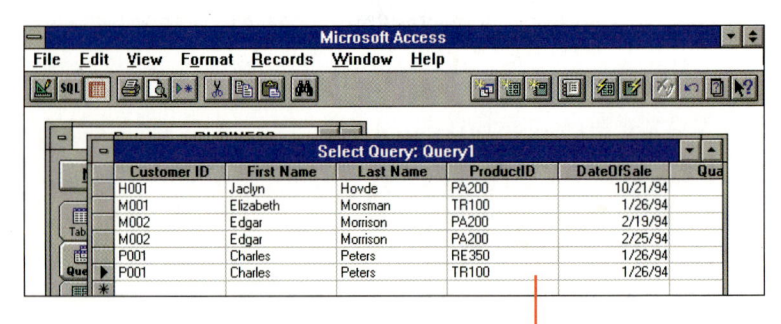

The dynaset showing fields from two tables

11 Double-click the Control Menu icon to close the query.

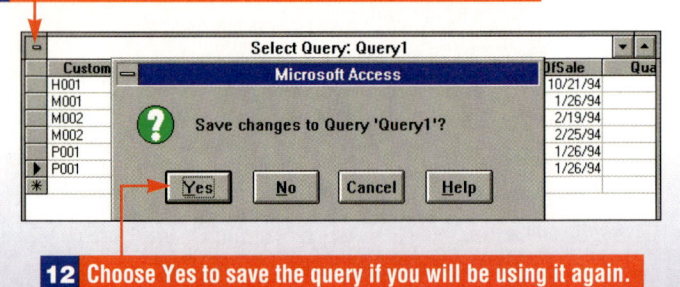

12 Choose Yes to save the query if you will be using it again.

13 Type a name for the query.

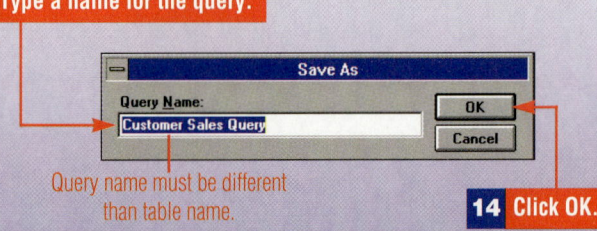

Query name must be different than table name.

14 Click OK.

Relationships: Defining, Using in Queries and Subforms

Creating a Subform in a Form

A subform is a form inside another form. In order for a subform to show the correct information on the main form, the two tables used must have a relationship. Creating a main form/subform is easily done using a Form Wizard.

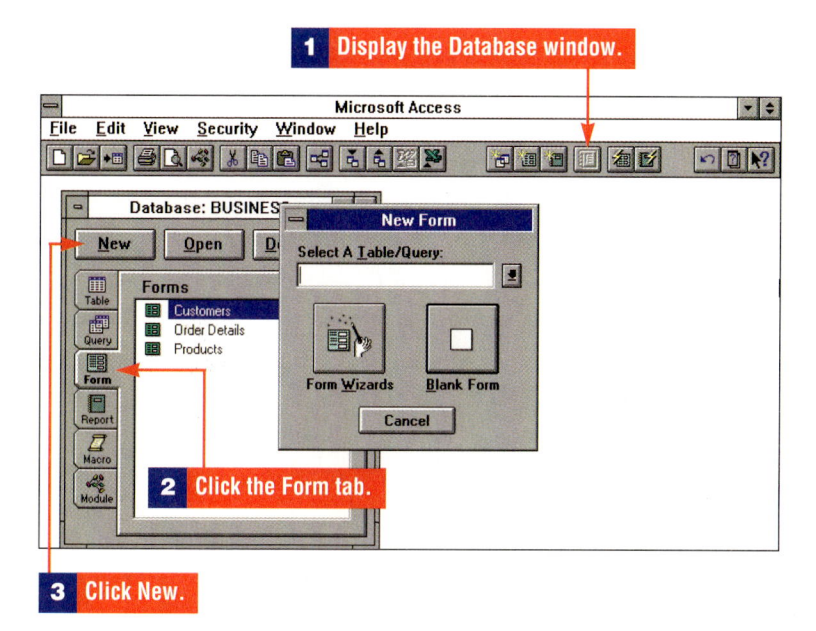

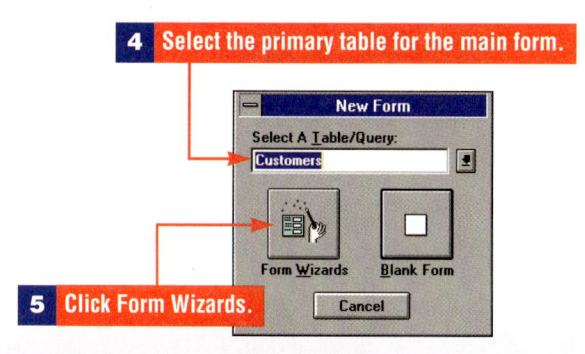

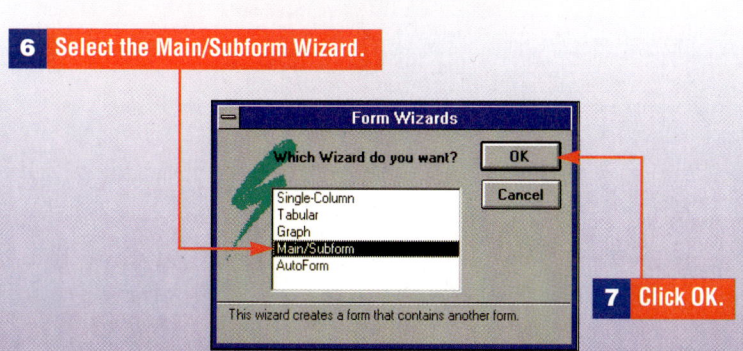

1 Display the Database window.

2 Click the Form tab.

3 Click New.

4 Select the primary table for the main form.

5 Click Form Wizards.

6 Select the Main/Subform Wizard.

7 Click OK.

more ▶

115

Relationships: Defining, Using in Queries and Subforms

Example of a subform in a form

8 Select the table for the subform.

Main/Subform Wizard

This Wizard creates a form that contains another form.
The data for your main form comes from: Customers

Which table or query contains the data for the subform?

- Customers
- Inventory
- **Order Details - Dept R**
- Order Details 1993

View:
◉ Tables   ○ Queries   ○ Both

[Hint] [Cancel] [< Back] [Next >] [Finish]

9 Click Next.

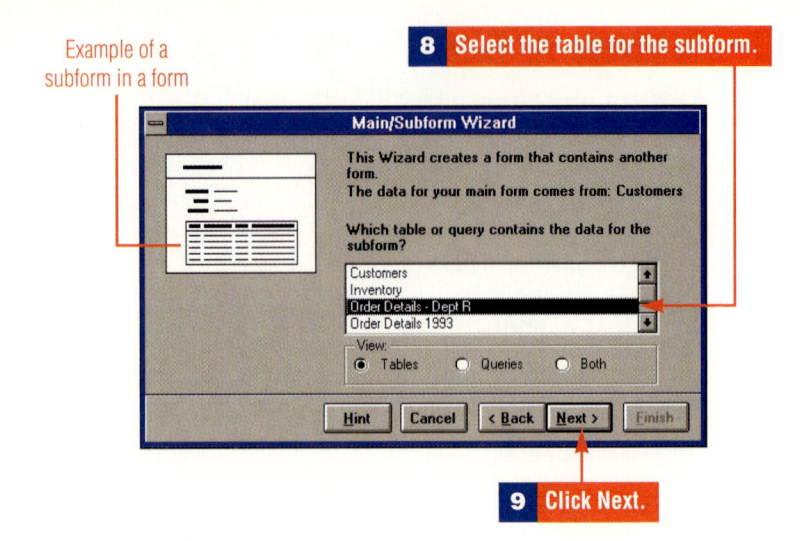

10 Select fields to be used in the main form.

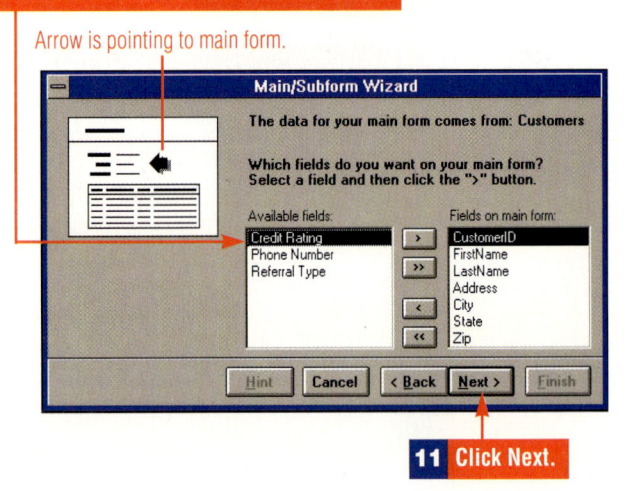

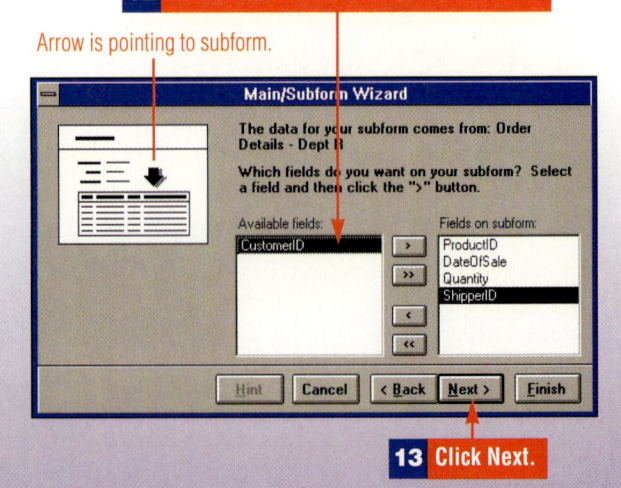

Arrow is pointing to main form.

Main/Subform Wizard

The data for your main form comes from: Customers

Which fields do you want on your main form?
Select a field and then click the ">" button.

Available fields:
- Credit Rating
- Phone Number
- Referral Type

Fields on main form:
- CustomerID
- FirstName
- LastName
- Address
- City
- State
- Zip

[Hint] [Cancel] [< Back] [Next >] [Finish]

11 Click Next.

---

12 Select fields to be used in the subform.

Arrow is pointing to subform.

Main/Subform Wizard

The data for your subform comes from: Order Details - Dept R

Which fields do you want on your subform? Select a field and then click the ">" button.

Available fields:
- CustomerID

Fields on subform:
- ProductID
- DateOfSale
- Quantity
- ShipperID

[Hint] [Cancel] [< Back] [Next >] [Finish]

13 Click Next.

Relationships: Defining, Using in Queries and Subforms

Sample of selected style

14 Select how you want the form to look.

Main/Subform Wizard

What style do you want for your form?

- ○ Standard
- ○ Chiseled
- ○ Shadowed
- ○ Boxed
- ● Embossed

[Hint] [Cancel] [< Back] [Next >] [Finish]

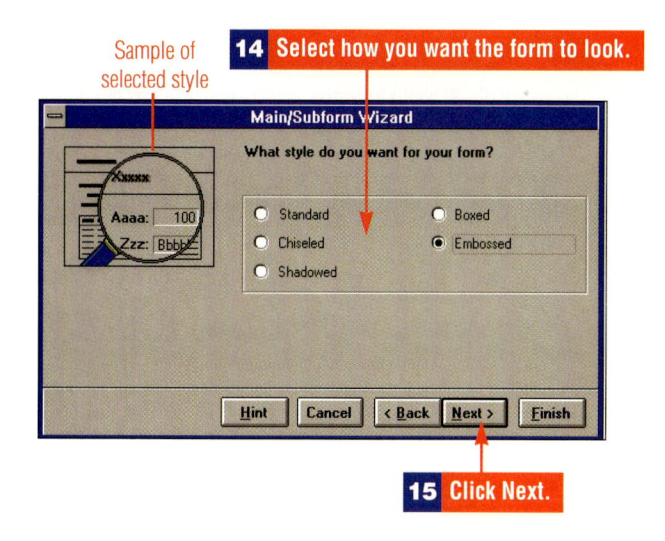

15 Click Next.

16 Type a title for the top of the main form.

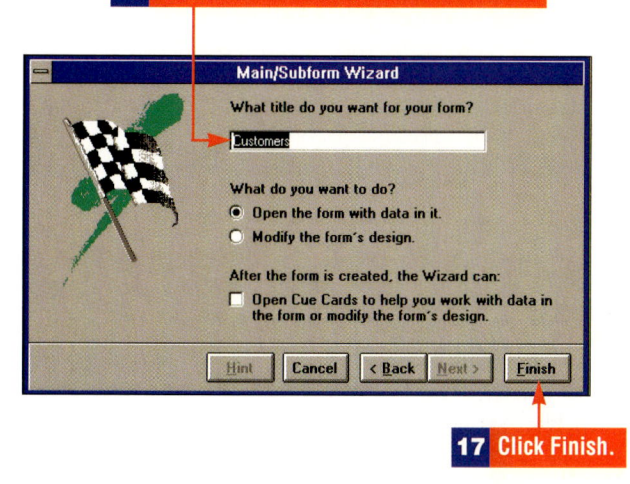

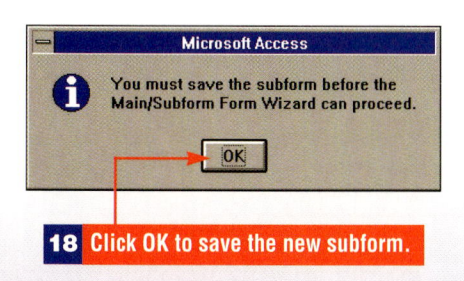

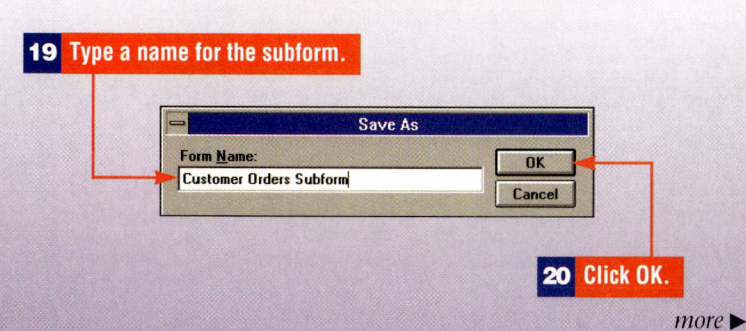

Main/Subform Wizard

What title do you want for your form?

Customers

What do you want to do?
- ● Open the form with data in it.
- ○ Modify the form's design.

After the form is created, the Wizard can:
- ☐ Open Cue Cards to help you work with data in the form or modify the form's design.

[Hint] [Cancel] [< Back] [Next >] [Finish]

17 Click Finish.

Microsoft Access

ⓘ You must save the subform before the Main/Subform Form Wizard can proceed.

[OK]

18 Click OK to save the new subform.

19 Type a name for the subform.

Save As

Form Name:
Customer Orders Subform

[OK] [Cancel]

20 Click OK.

more ▶

117

Relationships: Defining, Using in Queries and Subforms

This is the main form.

This is the subform.

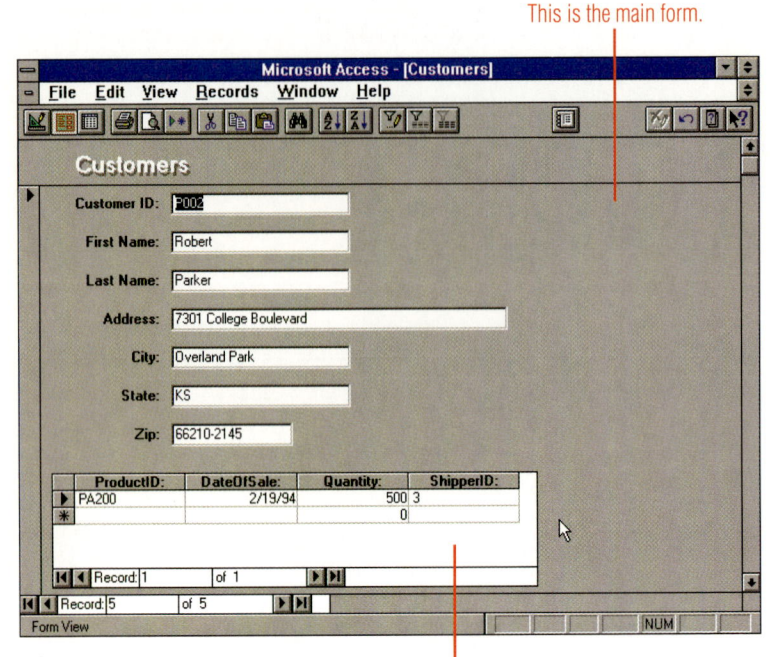

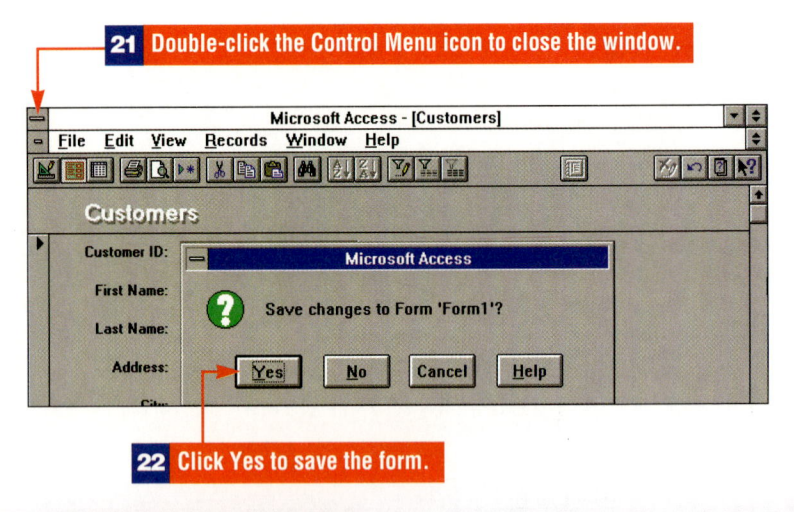

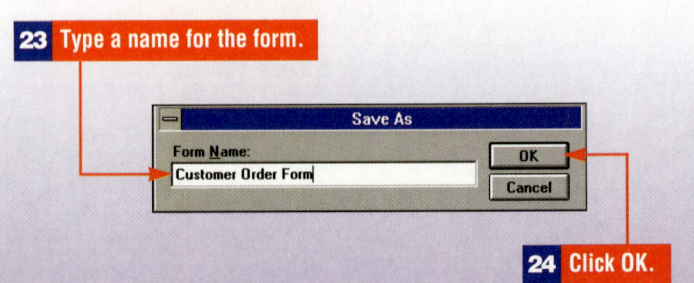

Fields updated in either form will be saved to their respective tables.

21 Double-click the Control Menu icon to close the window.

22 Click Yes to save the form.

23 Type a name for the form.

Form Name: Customer Order Form

24 Click OK.

118

Reports—Creating: Editing, Previewing, and Printing

Creating a Report

While you can easily print out the datasheet from a table or the dynaset from a query, you may want to create a nicer looking printout with titles and page numbers. For more control over how the printout will look, you should create a report. The easiest way to create a report is to use one of the built-in Report Wizards.

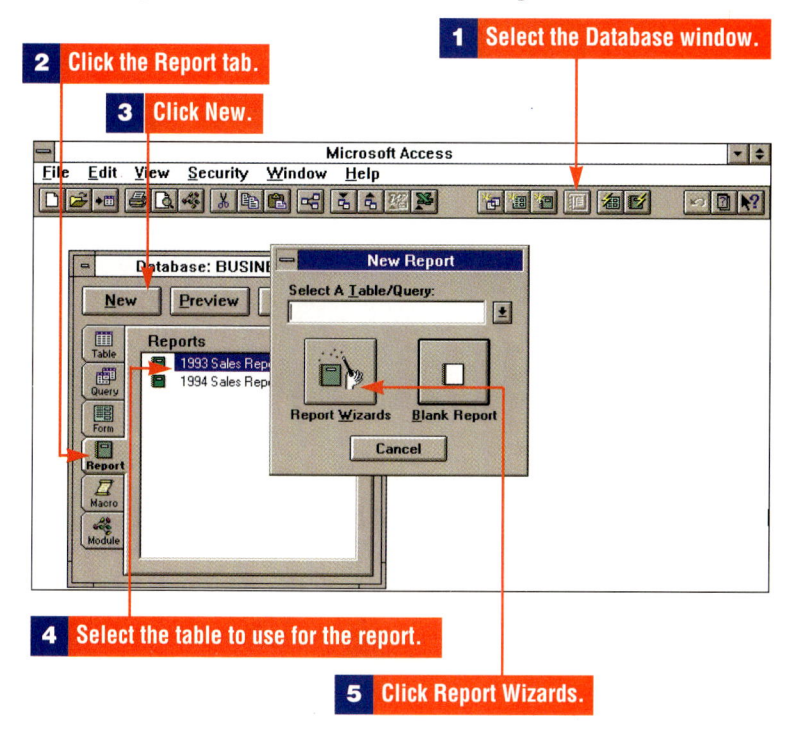

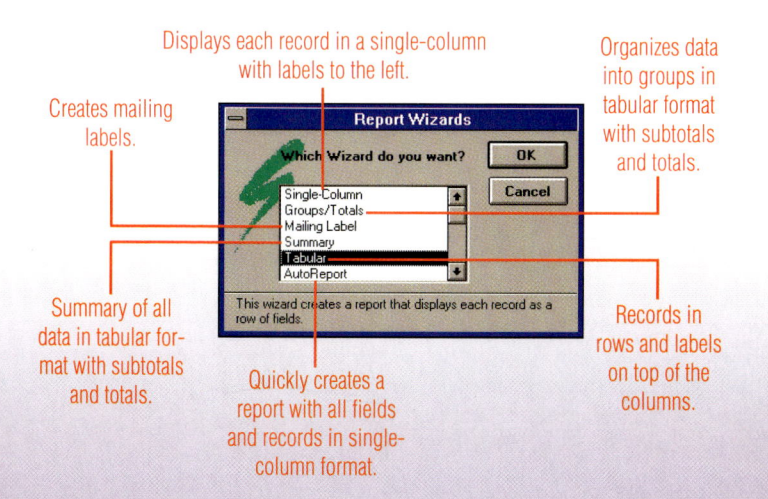

1 Select the Database window.

2 Click the Report tab.

3 Click New.

4 Select the table to use for the report.

5 Click Report Wizards.

Creates mailing labels.

Displays each record in a single-column with labels to the left.

Organizes data into groups in tabular format with subtotals and totals.

Summary of all data in tabular format with subtotals and totals.

Quickly creates a report with all fields and records in single-column format.

Records in rows and labels on top of the columns.

more ▶

119

Reports—Creating: Editing, Previewing, and Printing

6 Select the Tabular report.

Report Wizards

Which Wizard do you want?

- Single-Column
- Groups/Totals
- Mailing Label
- Summary
- Tabular
- AutoReport

This wizard creates a report that displays fields in a single column.

7 Click OK.

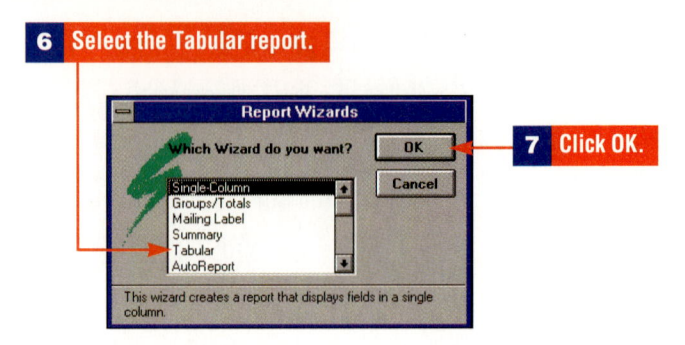

8 Choose fields to show in report.

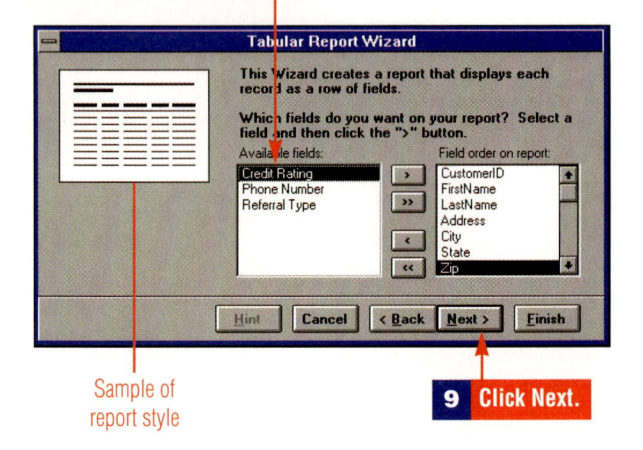

Tabular Report Wizard

This Wizard creates a report that displays each record as a row of fields.

Which fields do you want on your report? Select a field and then click the ">" button.

Available fields:
- Credit Rating
- Phone Number
- Referral Type

Field order on report:
- CustomerID
- FirstName
- LastName
- Address
- City
- State
- Zip

Sample of report style

9 Click Next.

---

10 Choose fields on which to sort the report.

Tabular Report Wizard

Which fields do you want to sort by?

Available fields:
- CustomerID
- Address
- City
- State
- Zip

Sort order of records:
- LastName
- FirstName

11 Click Next.

120

Reports—Creating: Editing, Previewing, and Printing

Sample of report style

12 Select a style.

Taller than it is wide

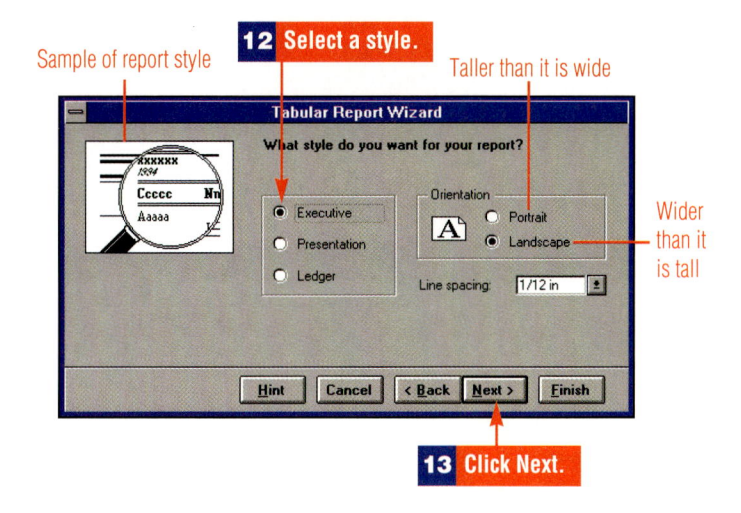

Tabular Report Wizard

What style do you want for your report?

- ● Executive
- ○ Presentation
- ○ Ledger

Orientation
- ○ Portrait
- ● Landscape

Line spacing: 1/12 in

Wider than it is tall

Hint | Cancel | < Back | Next > | Finish

13 Click Next.

14 Type title for the top of the report.

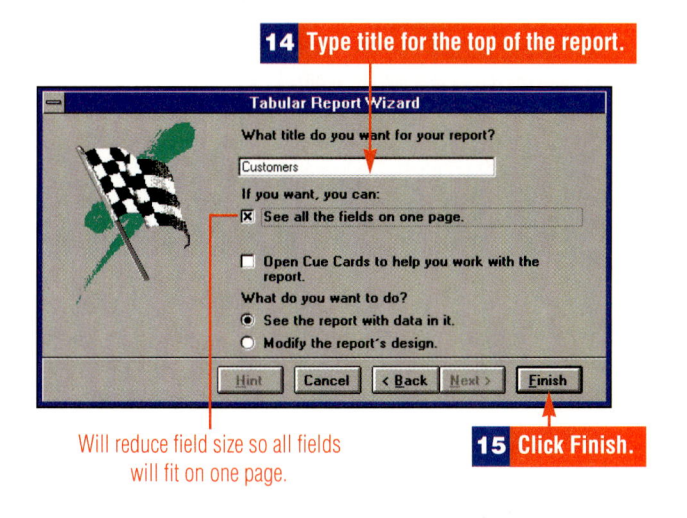

Tabular Report Wizard

What title do you want for your report?

Customers

If you want, you can:
- ☒ See all the fields on one page.
- ☐ Open Cue Cards to help you work with the report.

What do you want to do?
- ● See the report with data in it.
- ○ Modify the report's design.

Hint | Cancel | < Back | Next > | Finish

Will reduce field size so all fields will fit on one page.

15 Click Finish.

Print Date put in Report Header automatically.

Print preview of report

16 Maximize the window.

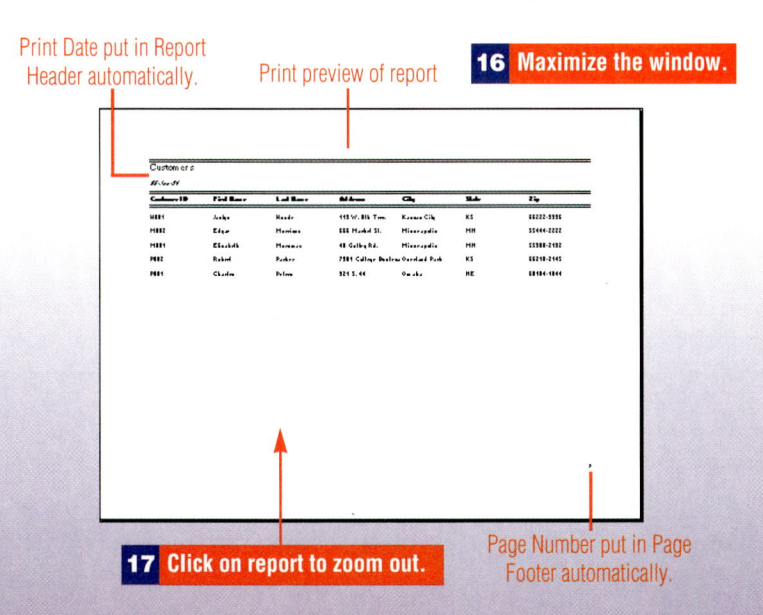

17 Click on report to zoom out.

Page Number put in Page Footer automatically.

more ▶

121

Reports—Creating: Editing, Previewing, and Printing

Click to change print setup.

18 Click in middle of report to zoom in.

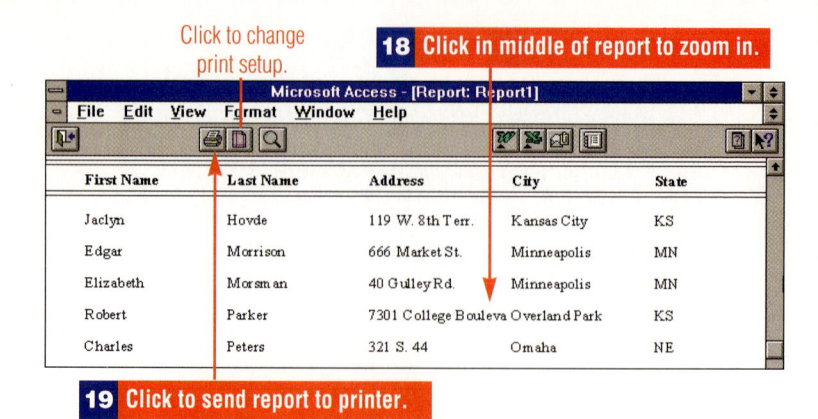

Microsoft Access - [Report: Report1]
File Edit View Format Window Help

First Name	Last Name	Address	City	State
Jaclyn	Hovde	119 W. 8th Terr.	Kansas City	KS
Edgar	Morrison	666 Market St.	Minneapolis	MN
Elizabeth	Morsman	40 Gulley Rd.	Minneapolis	MN
Robert	Parker	7301 College Bouleva	Overland Park	KS
Charles	Peters	321 S. 44	Omaha	NE

19 Click to send report to printer.

20 Click OK after making selections to send report to printer.

Print

Printer: Default Printer (HP LaserJet IIP Plus on LPT1:)

Print Range
- All
- Selection
- Pages
  From: To:

Print Quality: 300 dpi
☐ Print to File
Copies: 1
☒ Collate Copies

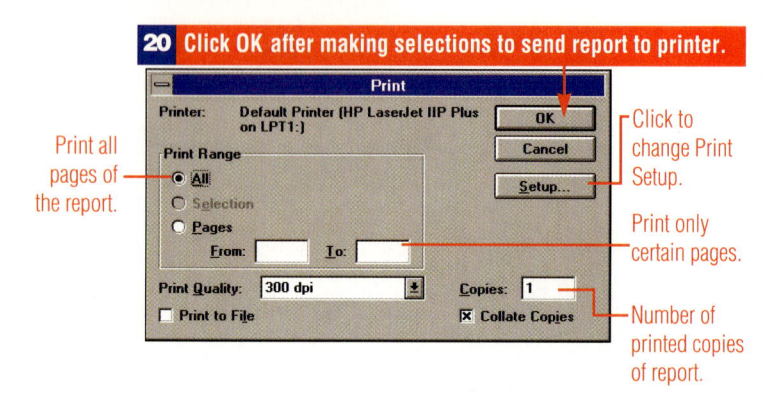

- Print all pages of the report.
- Click to change Print Setup.
- Print only certain pages.
- Number of printed copies of report.

21 If you choose Setup, click OK after making selections.

Print Setup

Printer
- Default Printer (currently HP LaserJet IIP Plus on LPT1:)
- Specific Printer: HP LaserJet IIP Plus on LPT1:

Orientation
- Portrait
- Landscape

Paper
Size: Letter 8 1/2 x 11 in
Source: Upper Tray
☐ Data Only

Margins
Left: 1.000 in Right: 1.000 in Top: 1.000 in Bottom: 1.000 in

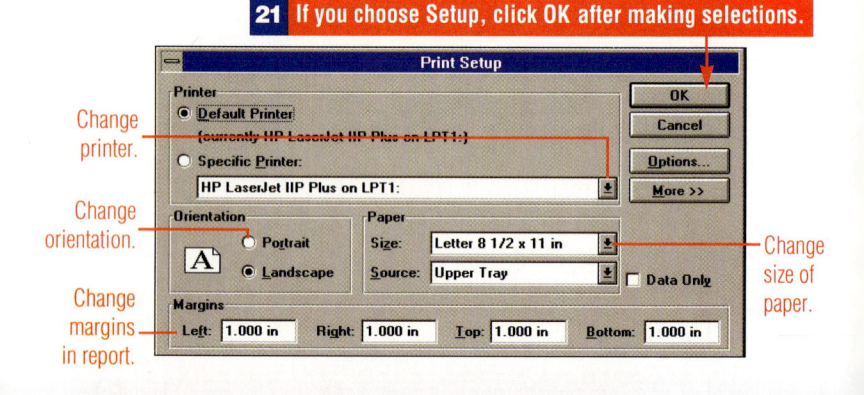

- Change printer.
- Change orientation.
- Change margins in report.
- Change size of paper.

22 Double-click the Control Menu icon to close report.

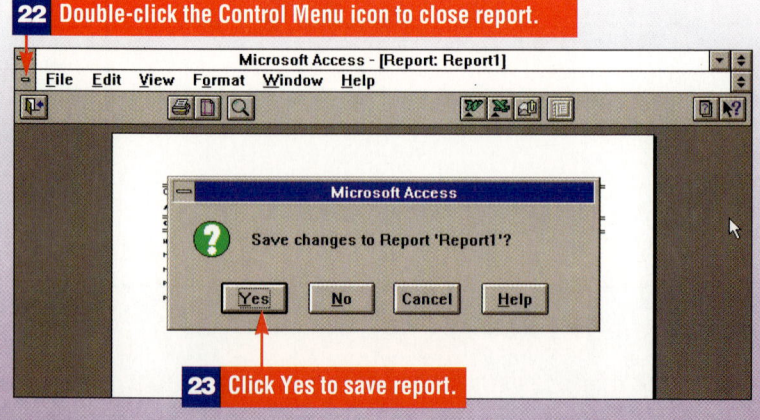

Microsoft Access - [Report: Report1]
File Edit View Format Window Help

Microsoft Access

? Save changes to Report 'Report1'?

Yes No Cancel Help

23 Click Yes to save report.

122

Reports—Creating: Editing, Previewing, and Printing

24 Give the report a name.

Save As
Report Name: Customer List

25 Click OK.

Printing a Report

Once a report has been created and saved, it can be previewed and printed at any time with the most current data.

To preview a report

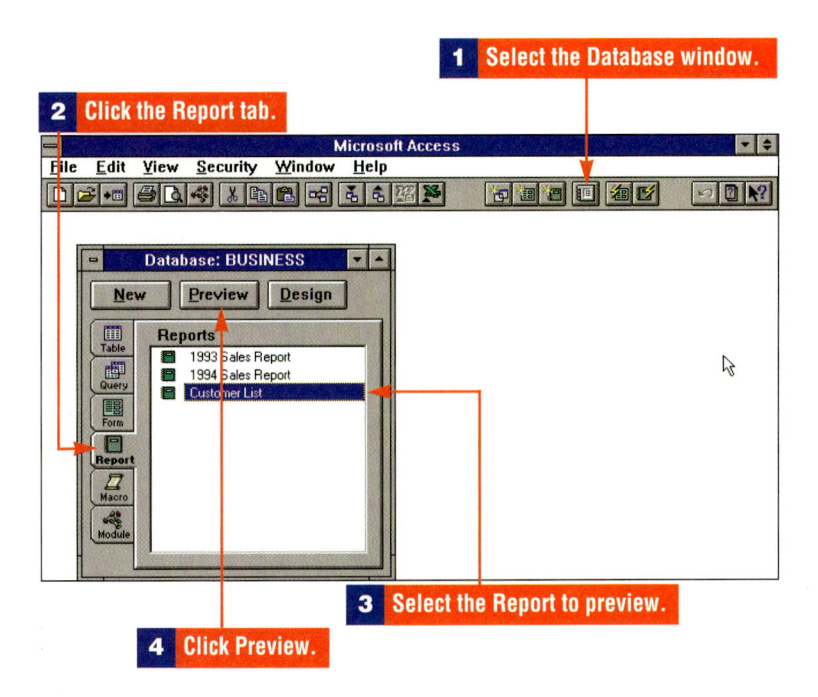

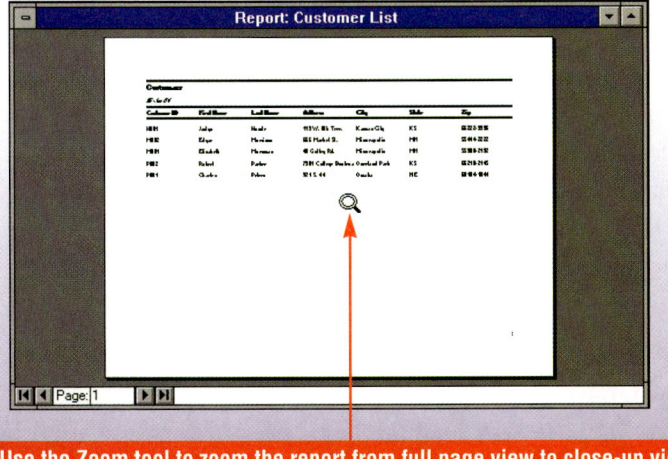

1 Select the Database window.

2 Click the Report tab.

3 Select the Report to preview.

4 Click Preview.

5 Use the Zoom tool to zoom the report from full page view to close-up view.

123

Reports—Creating: Editing, Previewing, and Printing

To print a report

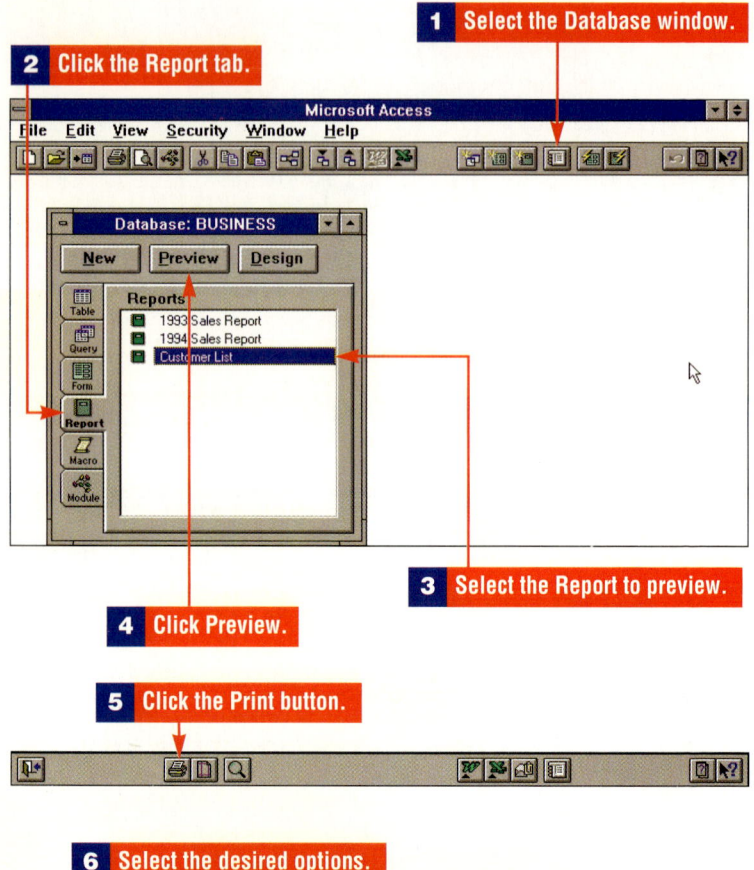

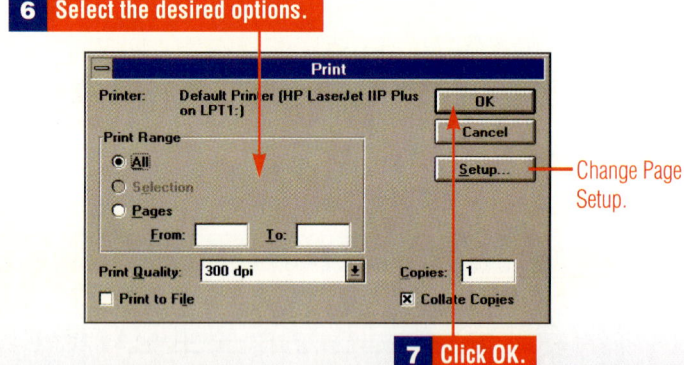

1 Select the Database window.

2 Click the Report tab.

3 Select the Report to preview.

4 Click Preview.

5 Click the Print button.

6 Select the desired options.

Change Page Setup.

7 Click OK.

Editing a Report

Using a Report Wizard is an easy way to create a report, but you may want to change the report manually. If you have many changes to make, it may be easier to create an additional report using the Report Wizard. Use one of the methods below to select portions of a report so that you can change them.

Reports—Creating: Editing, Previewing, and Printing

To select parts of a report

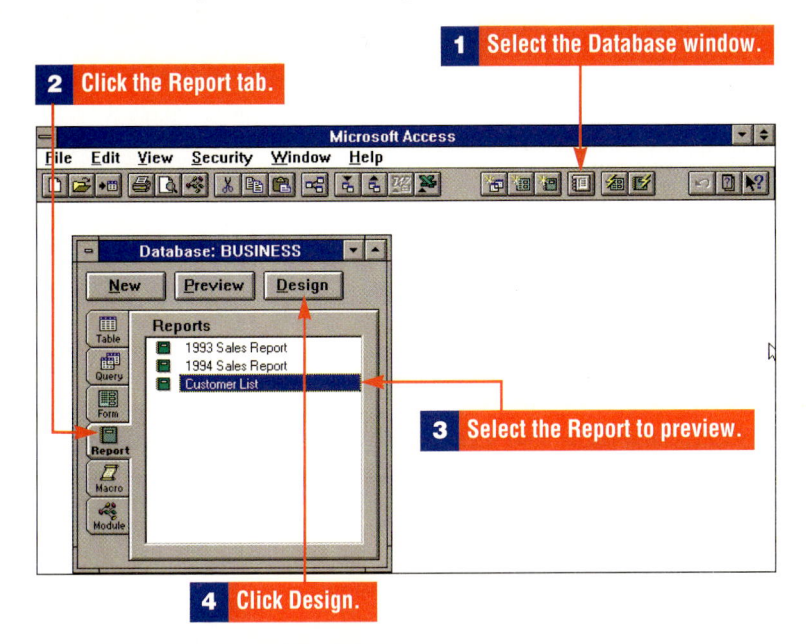

1 Select the Database window.

2 Click the Report tab.

3 Select the Report to preview.

4 Click Design.

5 Click on the part of the report to be edited.

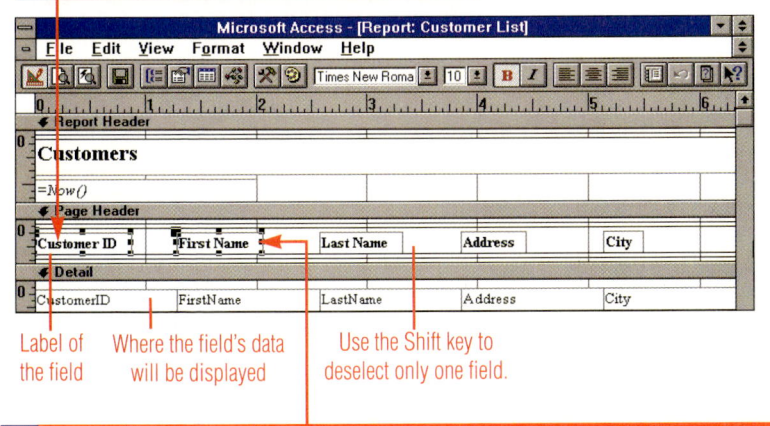

- Label of the field
- Where the field's data will be displayed
- Use the Shift key to deselect only one field.

6 To select more than one part, hold down the Shift key and click on another one.

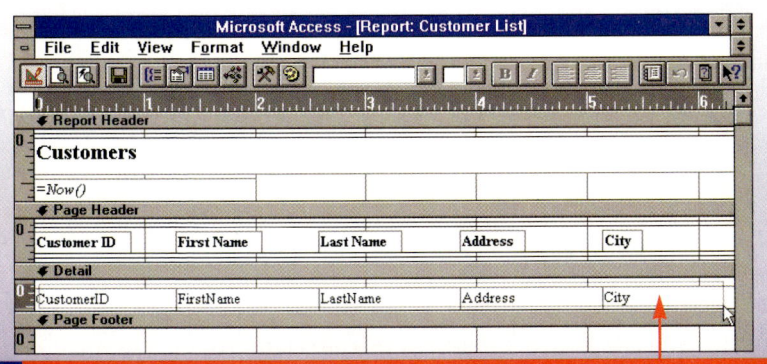

7 To select several parts in the same area of the report, click and drag over them.

more ▶

125

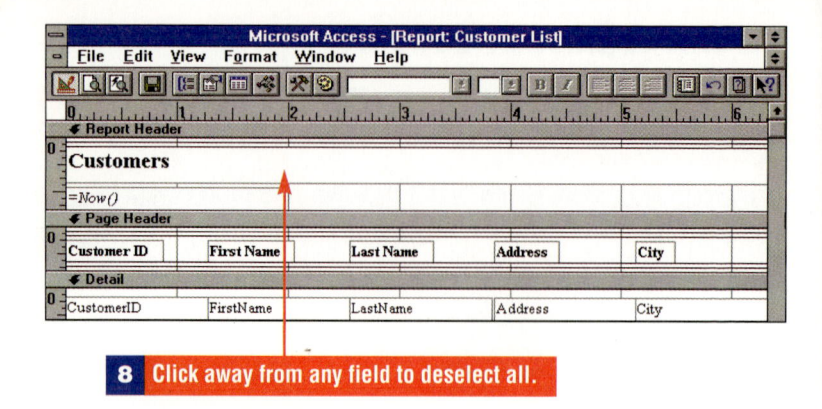

Reports—Creating: Editing, Previewing, and Printing

8 Click away from any field to deselect all.

To move a field

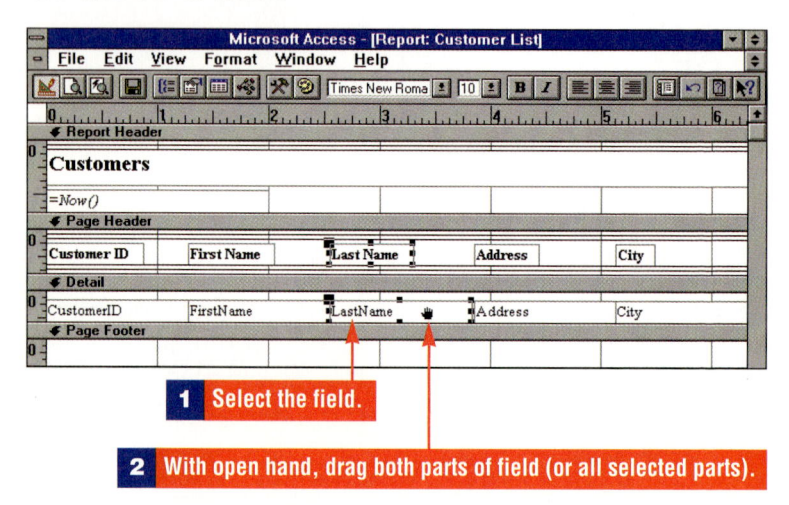

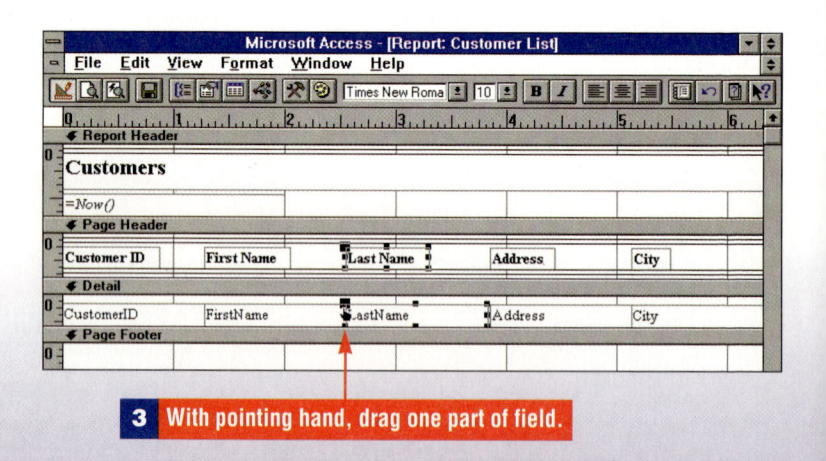

1 Select the field.

2 With open hand, drag both parts of field (or all selected parts).

3 With pointing hand, drag one part of field.

Reports—Creating: Editing, Previewing, and Printing

To adjust the size of a field

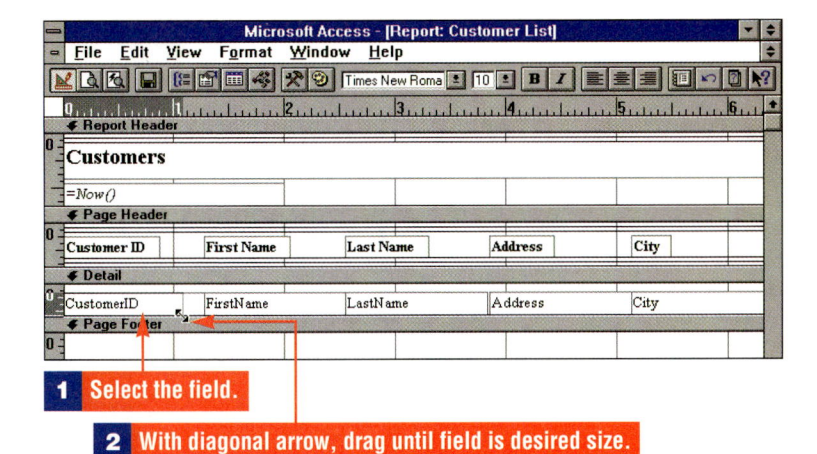

1 Select the field.

2 With diagonal arrow, drag until field is desired size.

To change a label

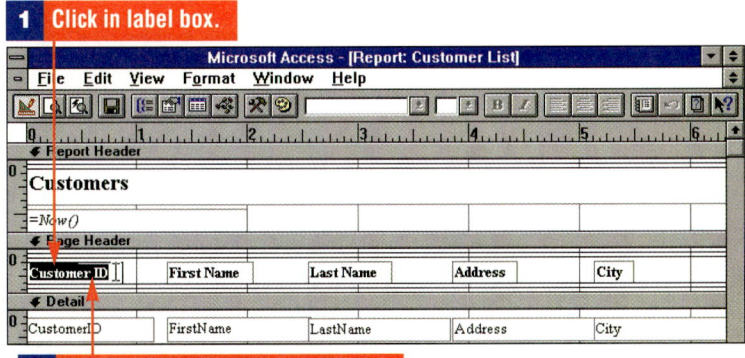

1 Click in label box.

2 With I-beam, drag over text in box.

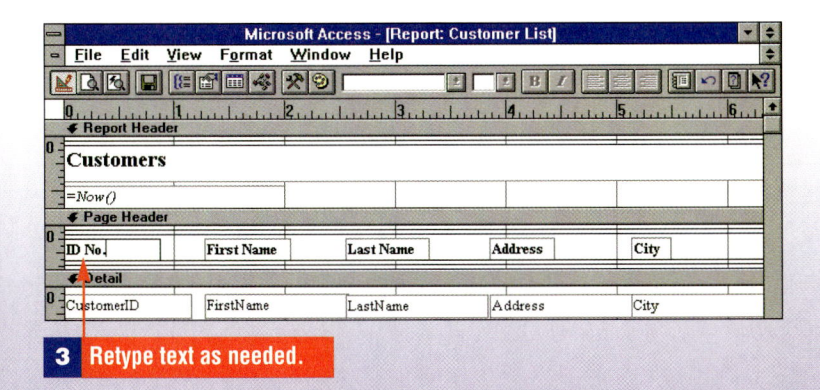

3 Retype text as needed.

127

Reports—Creating: Editing, Previewing, and Printing

To change the look of labels and fields

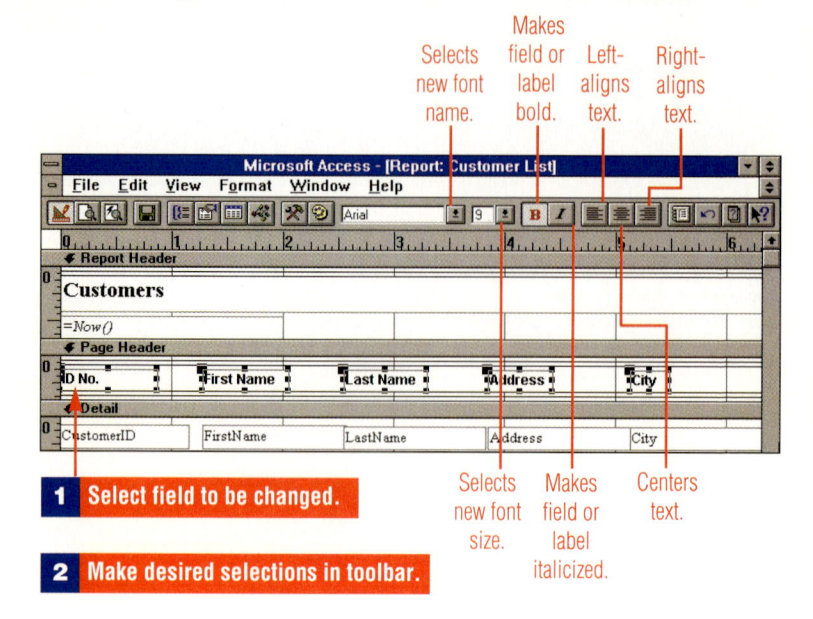

Selects new font name.
Makes field or label bold.
Left-aligns text.
Right-aligns text.

Selects new font size.
Makes field or label italicized.
Centers text.

1 Select field to be changed.

2 Make desired selections in toolbar.

To add borders and other special effects to a field

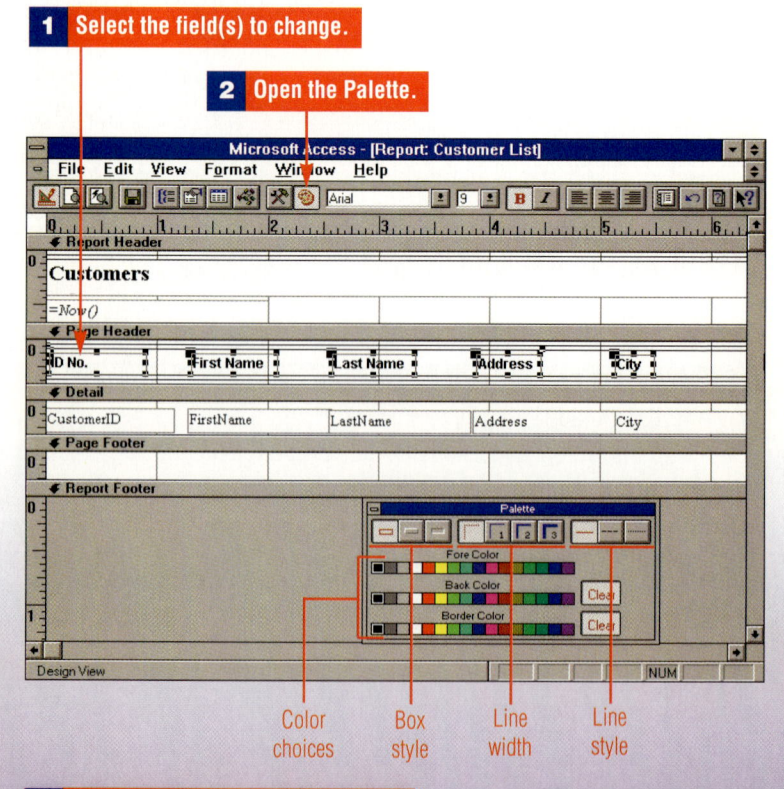

1 Select the field(s) to change.

2 Open the Palette.

Color choices
Box style
Line width
Line style

3 Make desired selections in Palette.

128

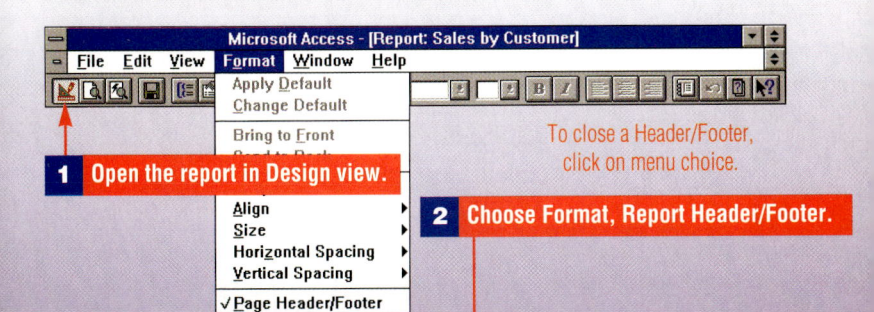

Reports—Enhancing: Graphics and Mailing Labels

Enhancing a Report

The Report Wizards help you create great looking reports, but are limiting in design features. Your report is only useful when it displays your data the way you intend. There are many settings that can be changed to enhance the look of a report. All of these changes are done in Design view of the report.

To add a page break to a report

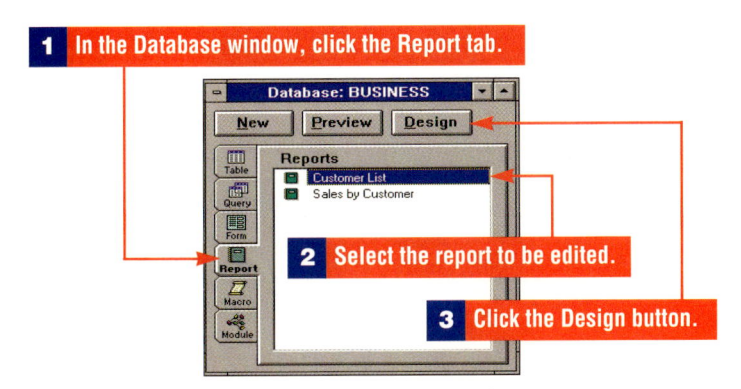

1 In the Database window, click the Report tab.

2 Select the report to be edited.

3 Click the Design button.

4 Click the Toolbox button, if the Toolbox is not showing.

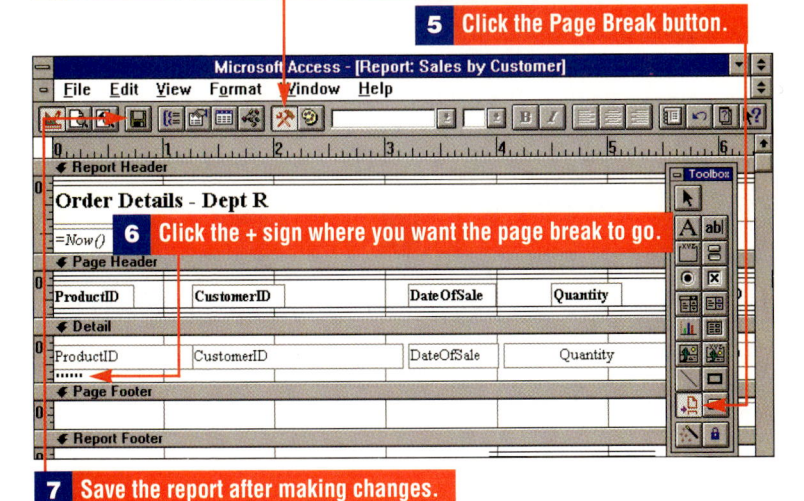

5 Click the Page Break button.

6 Click the + sign where you want the page break to go.

7 Save the report after making changes.

To add a header or footer

1 Open the report in Design view.

2 Choose Format, Report Header/Footer.

To close a Header/Footer, click on menu choice.

129

Reports—Enhancing: Graphics and Mailing Labels

To add a label to a report

1. Open the report in Design view.
2. Click the Toolbox button, if the Toolbox is not showing. 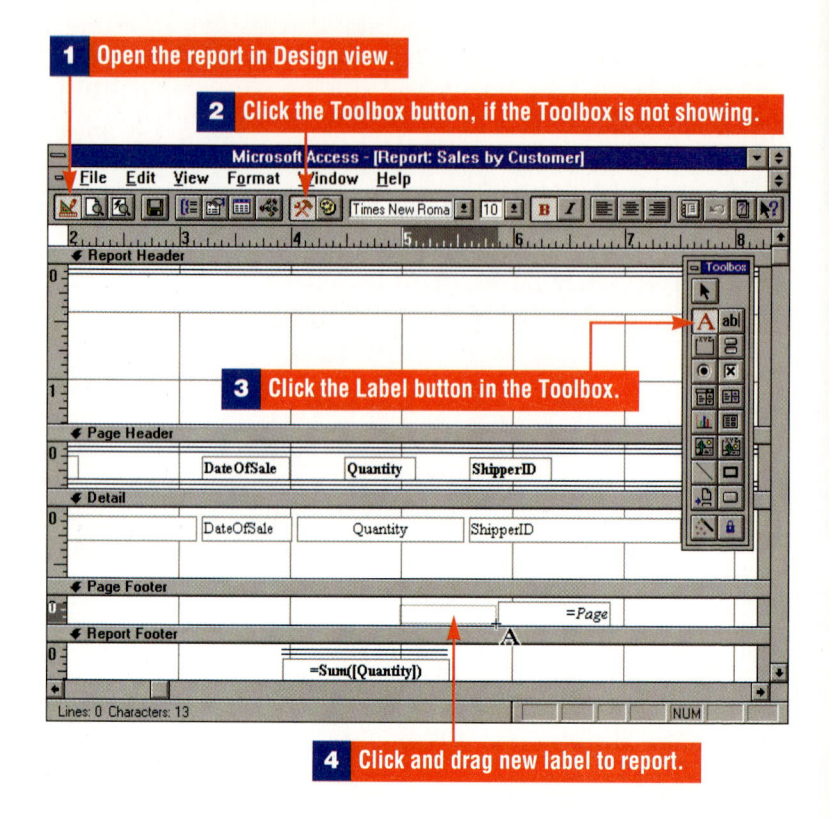
3. Click the Label button in the Toolbox.
4. Click and drag new label to report.
5. Select and type in new label.
6. Change desired attributes.

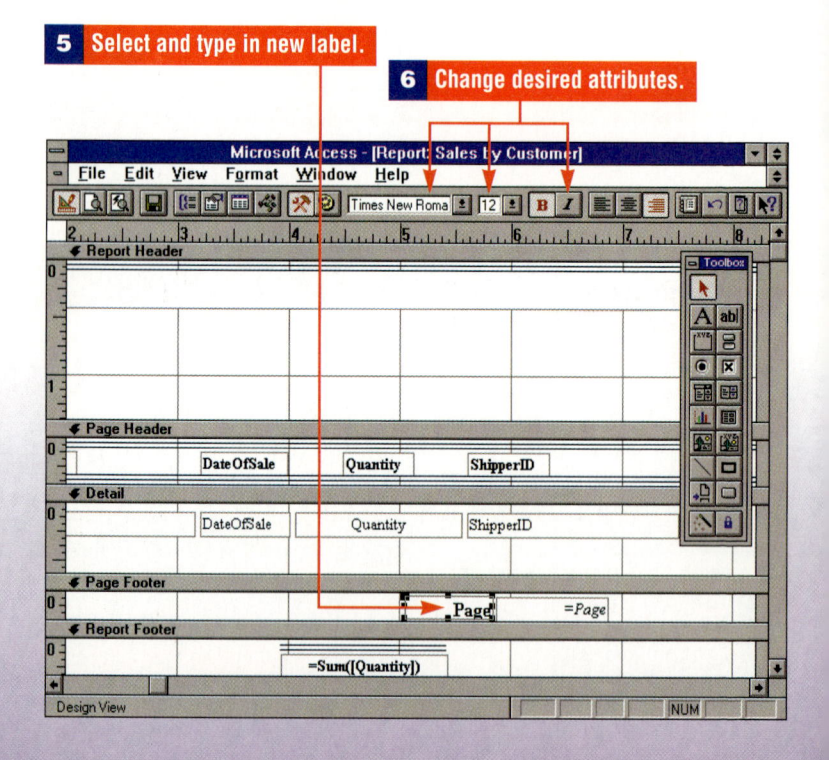

Reports—Enhancing: Graphics and Mailing Labels

Using Graphics in a Report

A bound object is one that is already stored in a table field in your database. An unbound graphic object is not stored in a table. We will add an unbound, embedded object as a logo for a report.

1 Open the report in Design view.

2 Open the Toolbox.

Hold down button and drag if you want the frame to be bigger than the default size.

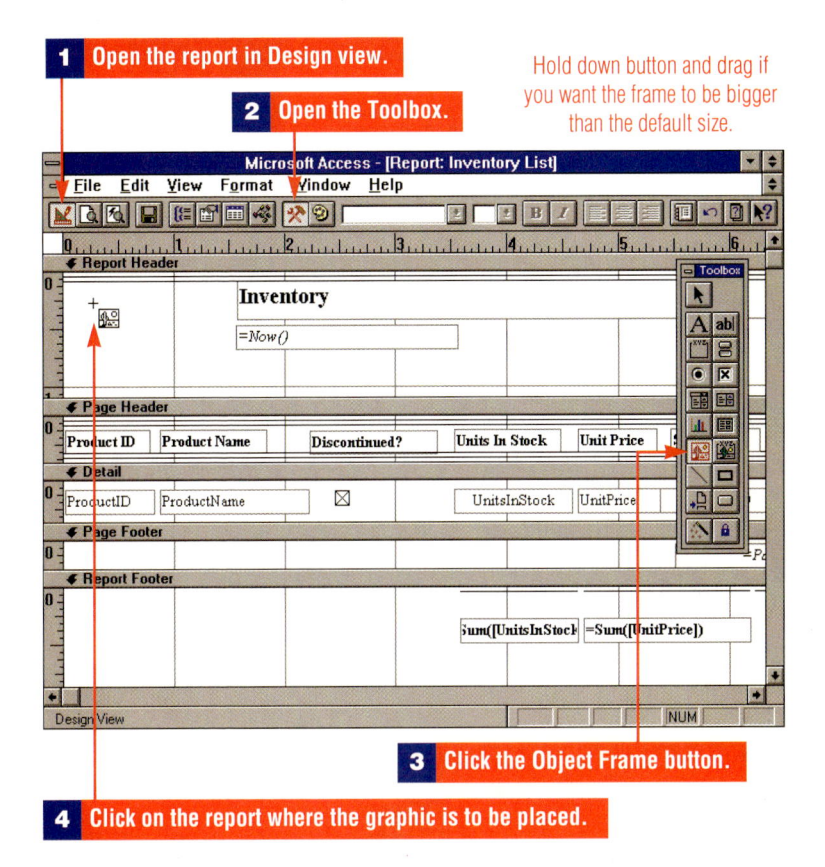

3 Click the Object Frame button.

4 Click on the report where the graphic is to be placed.

5 Choose Create From File.

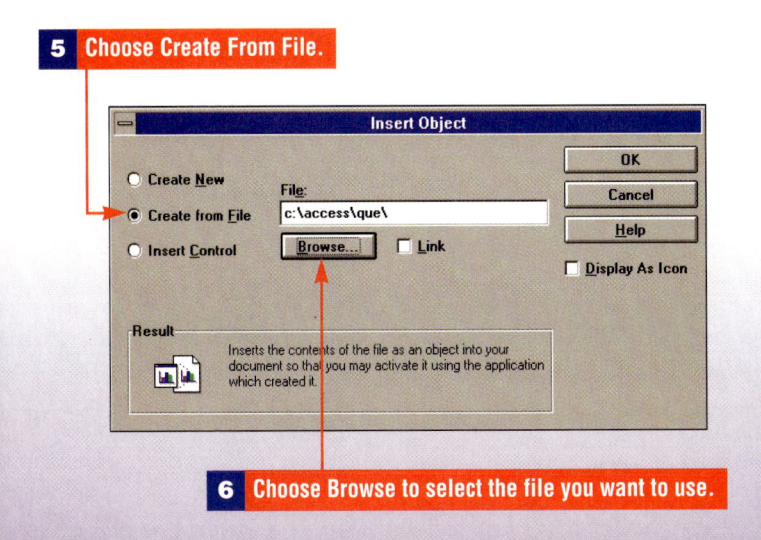

6 Choose Browse to select the file you want to use.

more ▶

131

Reports—Enhancing: Graphics and Mailing Labels

7 Choose the desired file.

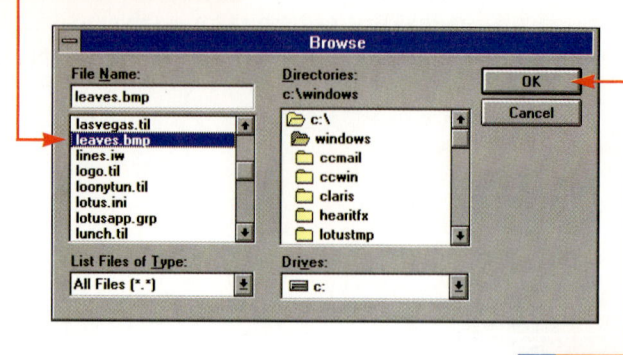

8 Click OK.

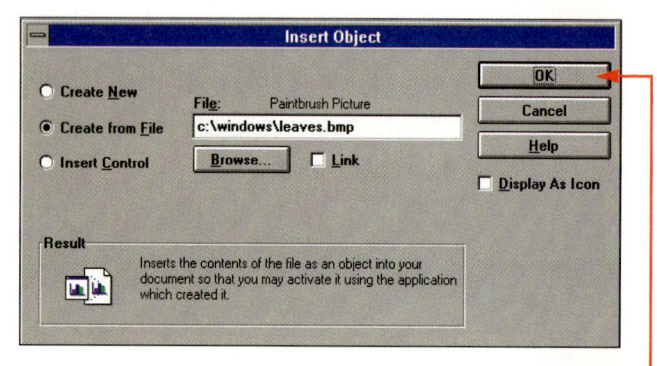

9 Click OK.

10 If object doesn't fill frame, click the Properties button.

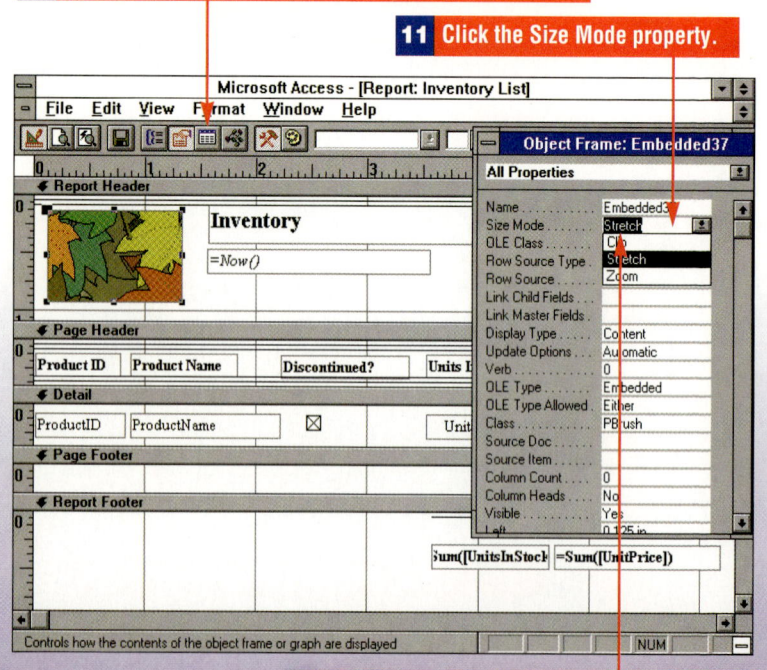

11 Click the Size Mode property.

12 Choose Stretch to make object fit the frame.

132

Reports—Enhancing: Graphics and Mailing Labels

Creating Mailing Labels

One of the most useful types of reports in Access is the Mailing Label report. You also can create file folder labels, diskette labels, and inventory labels. As long as the information is in a database table or query, you can create a label for it.

1 In the Database window, click the Report tab.

2 Click the New button.

3 Choose the table or query to use for the report.

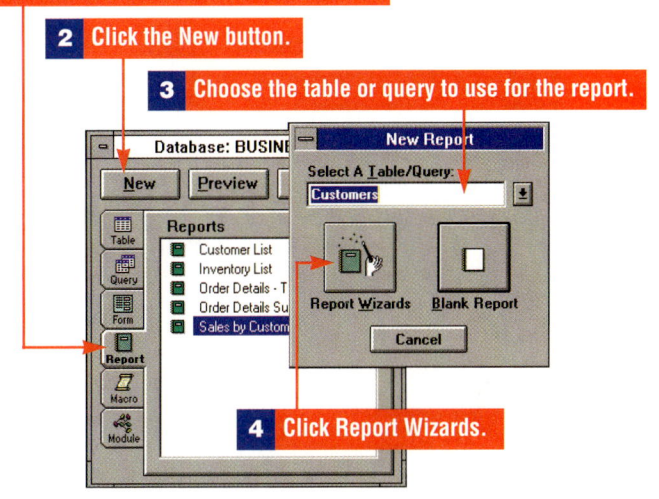

4 Click Report Wizards.

5 Choose the Mailing Label Report Wizard.

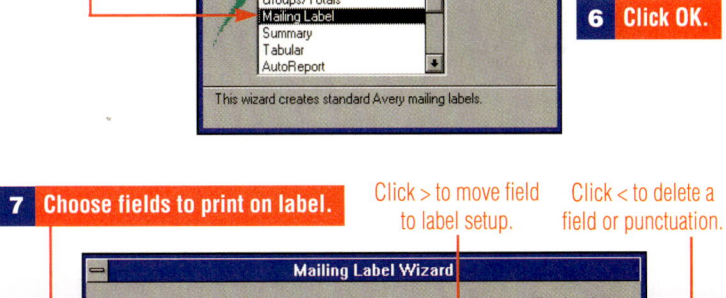

6 Click OK.

7 Choose fields to print on label.

Click > to move field to label setup.

Click < to delete a field or punctuation.

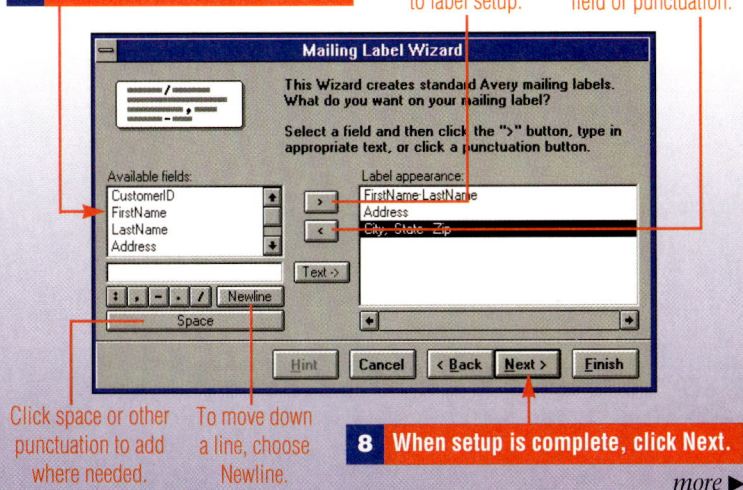

Click space or other punctuation to add where needed.

To move down a line, choose Newline.

8 When setup is complete, click Next.

more ▶

133

Reports—Enhancing: Graphics and Mailing Labels

9 If you need to have the printed labels sorted, choose field to sort by.

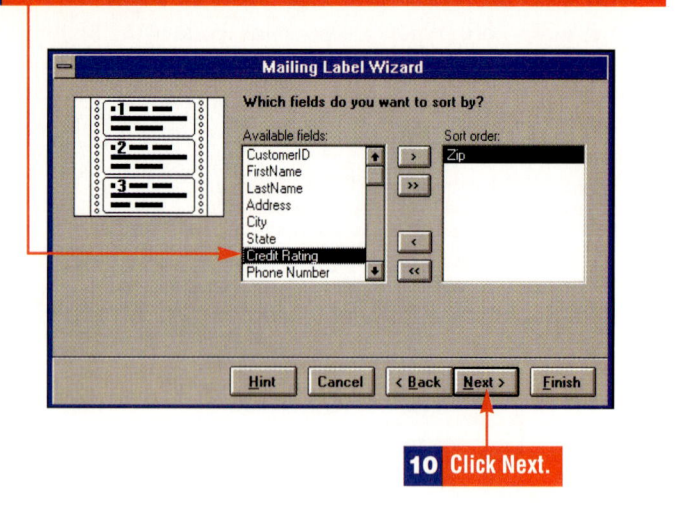

Mailing Label Wizard — Which fields do you want to sort by?
Available fields: CustomerID, FirstName, LastName, Address, City, State, Credit Rating, Phone Number
Sort order: Zip

10 Click Next.

11 Choose the Avery label number.

Number is found on Avery label box.

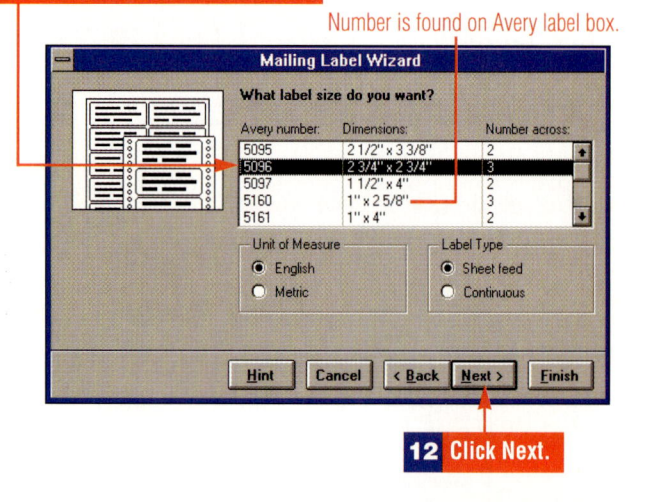

Mailing Label Wizard — What label size do you want?

Avery number:	Dimensions:	Number across:
5095	2 1/2" x 3 3/8"	2
5096	2 3/4" x 2 3/4"	3
5097	1 1/2" x 4"	2
5160	1" x 2 5/8"	3
5161	1" x 4"	2

Unit of Measure: ● English ○ Metric
Label Type: ● Sheet feed ○ Continuous

12 Click Next.

13 Choose desired options for text appearance

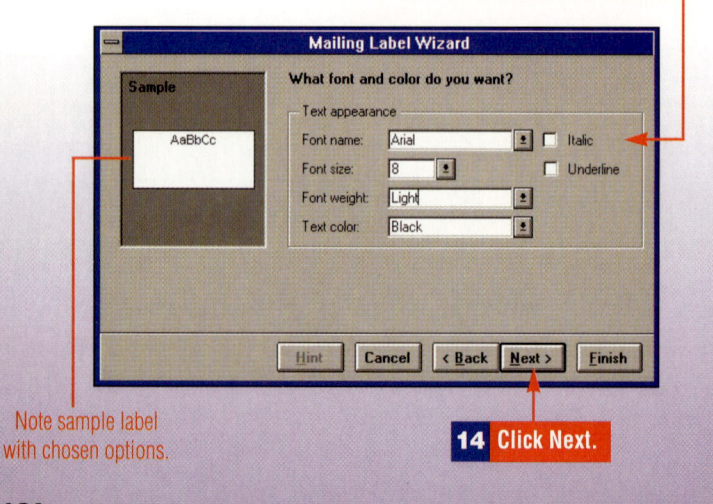

Mailing Label Wizard — What font and color do you want?

Text appearance:
- Font name: Arial
- Font size: 8
- Font weight: Light
- Text color: Black
- ☐ Italic
- ☐ Underline

Sample: AaBbCc

Note sample label with chosen options.

14 Click Next.

Reports—Enhancing: Graphics and Mailing Labels

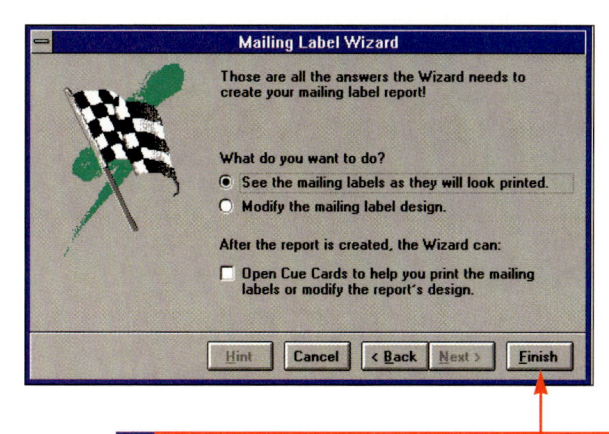

Mailing Label Wizard

Those are all the answers the Wizard needs to create your mailing label report!

What do you want to do?
- ● See the mailing labels as they will look printed.
- ○ Modify the mailing label design.

After the report is created, the Wizard can:

☐ Open Cue Cards to help you print the mailing labels or modify the report's design.

[Hint] [Cancel] [< Back] [Next >] [**Finish**]

15 Click Finish to see Print Preview of labels on-screen.

16 Click Print button to print labels.

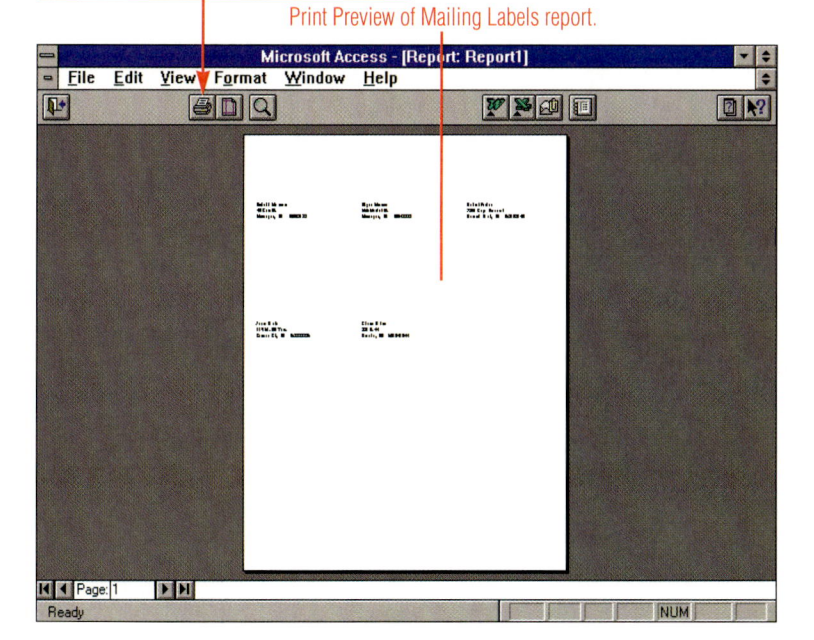

Print Preview of Mailing Labels report.

135

Tables—Basics: Creating, Maintaining, and Printing

Understanding Table Basics

Tables will hold only one specific kind of data, such as: customer information, inventory information, or sales order information. The smallest piece of data in a table is called a *field* (a customer's first name). A group of fields is called a *record* (all the information about one customer). A group of records is saved in a *table* (all the information about all the customers). In Access you can have multiple tables that are linked by common fields.

To create a table using the Table Wizard

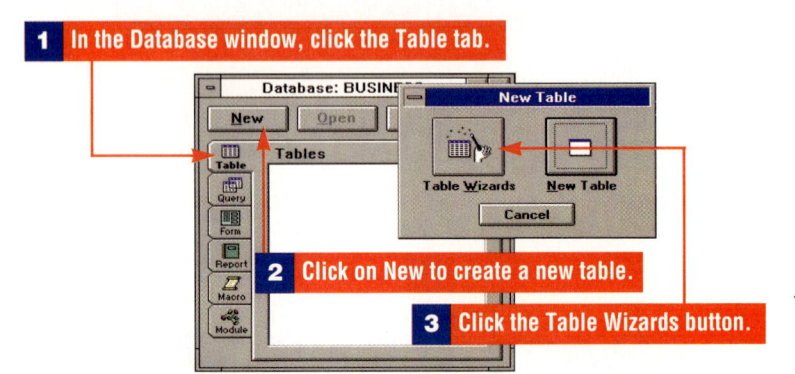

1 In the Database window, click the Table tab.

2 Click on New to create a new table.

3 Click the Table Wizards button.

4 Choose the Business or Personal button to show the appropriate sample tables.

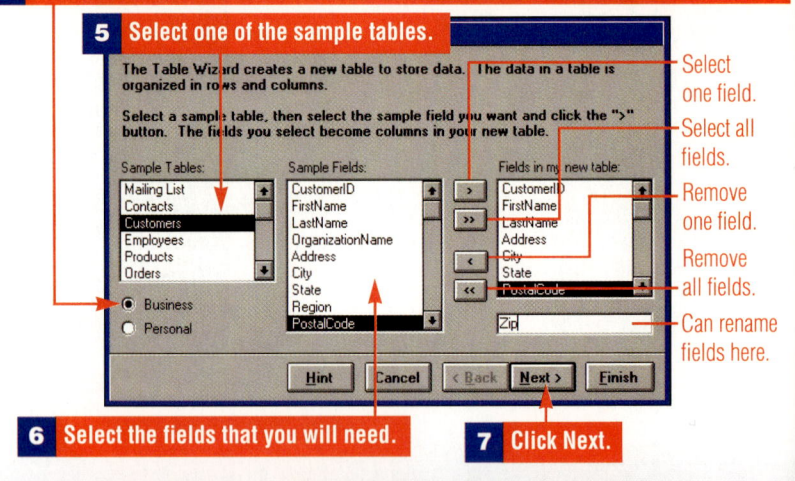

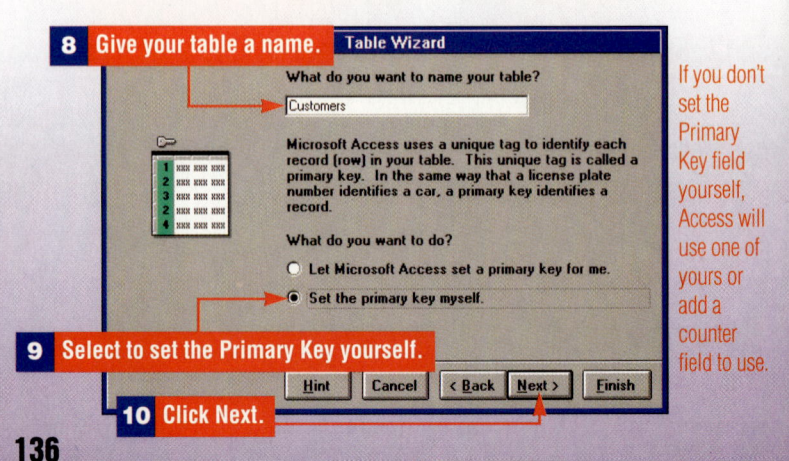

5 Select one of the sample tables.

- Select one field.
- Select all fields.
- Remove one field.
- Remove all fields.
- Can rename fields here.

6 Select the fields that you will need.

7 Click Next.

8 Give your table a name.

9 Select to set the Primary Key yourself.

10 Click Next.

If you don't set the Primary Key field yourself, Access will use one of yours or add a counter field to use.

Tables—Basics: Creating, Maintaining, and Printing

11 Choose which field to use as the Primary Key field.

This will be the field which is unique for each record.

Symbol for the Primary Key field

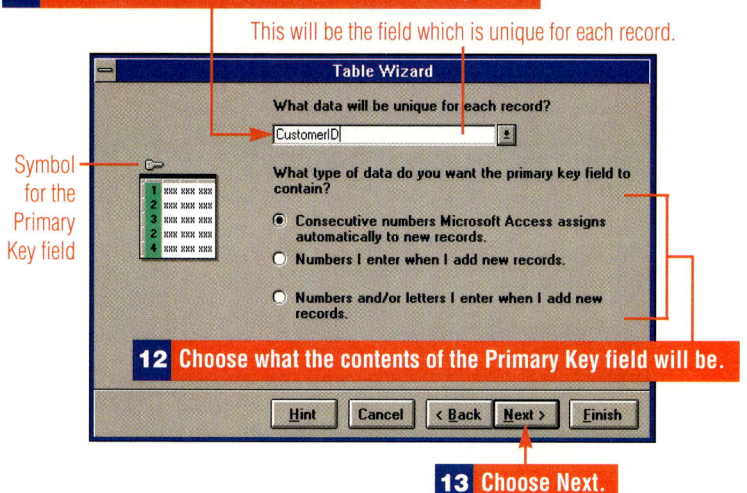

[Table Wizard dialog]
What data will be unique for each record?
CustomerID

What type of data do you want the primary key field to contain?
- Consecutive numbers Microsoft Access assigns automatically to new records.
- Numbers I enter when I add new records.
- Numbers and/or letters I enter when I add new records.

12 Choose what the contents of the Primary Key field will be.

13 Choose Next.

14 Choose Modify the Table Design to see the design of the table.

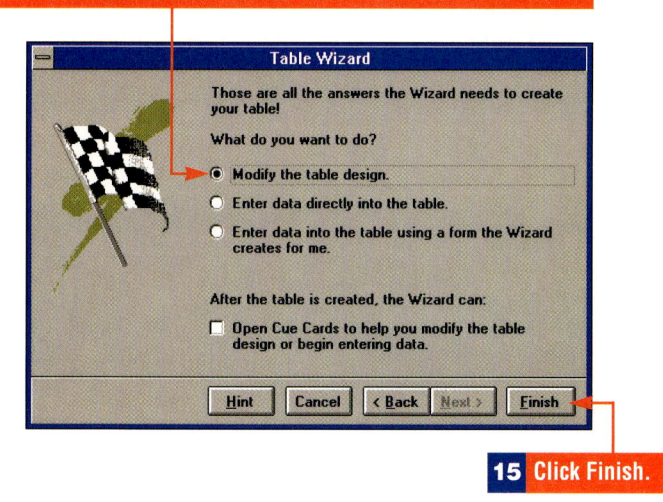

[Table Wizard dialog]
Those are all the answers the Wizard needs to create your table!
What do you want to do?
- Modify the table design.
- Enter data directly into the table.
- Enter data into the table using a form the Wizard creates for me.

After the table is created, the Wizard can:
- Open Cue Cards to help you modify the table design or begin entering data.

15 Click Finish.

To open a table

1 In the Database window, click the Table tab.

Click the Design button if you want to redesign a table.

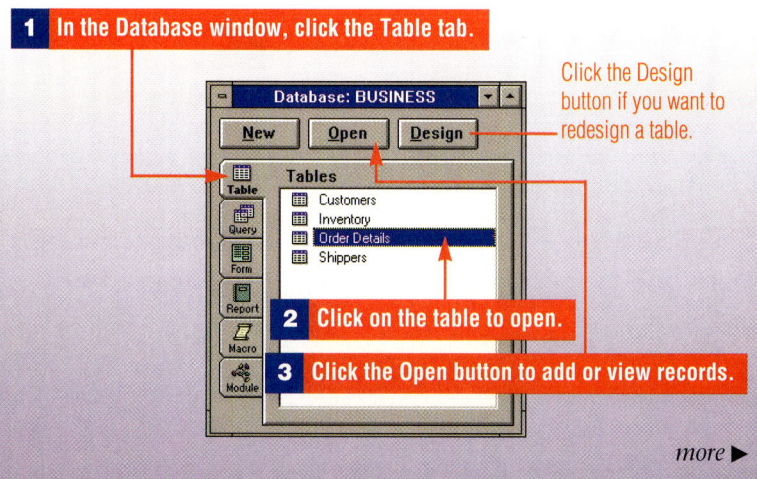

[Database: BUSINESS]
Tables
- Customers
- Inventory
- Order Details
- Shippers

2 Click on the table to open.

3 Click the Open button to add or view records.

more ▶

137

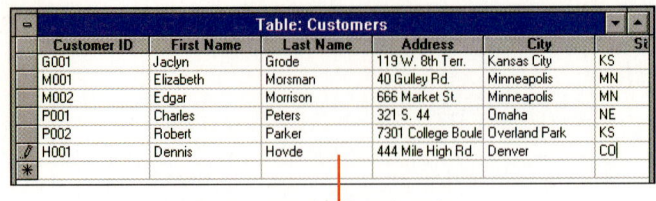

Tables—Basics: Creating, Maintaining, and Printing

Table is opened in Datasheet view.

To close and save a table

1 Double-click the Control Menu icon to close.

Access automatically saves data entry and will only prompt to save a design change.

To delete a table from the database

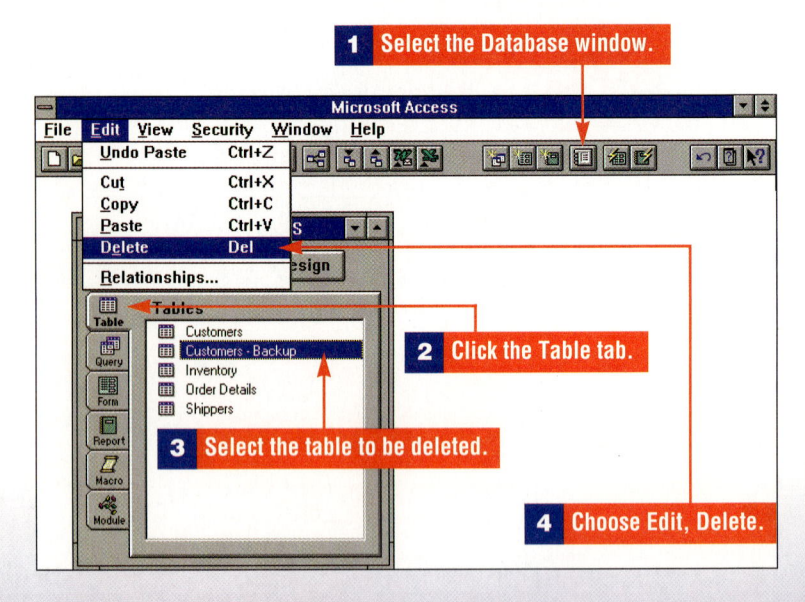

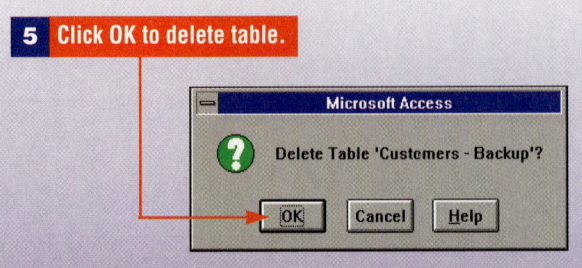

1 Select the Database window.

2 Click the Table tab.

3 Select the table to be deleted.

4 Choose Edit, Delete.

5 Click OK to delete table.

This will delete all information in the table.
Make certain that this is what you want to do.

Tables—Basics: Creating, Maintaining, and Printing

To create additional tables using the Table Wizard

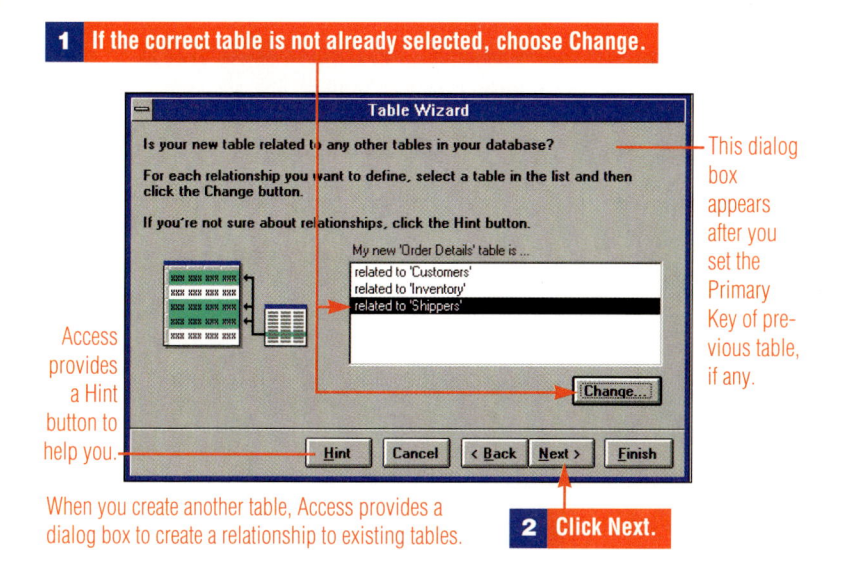

1 If the correct table is not already selected, choose Change.

Access provides a Hint button to help you.

This dialog box appears after you set the Primary Key of previous table, if any.

When you create another table, Access provides a dialog box to create a relationship to existing tables.

2 Click Next.

Maintaining Records

Once the table has been created, the next step is to put your data into the tables. There are two ways to add information to a table: by using Datasheet view of a table or by using a form. In the Datasheet window, the names of the fields are at the top of each column.

To add records to a table

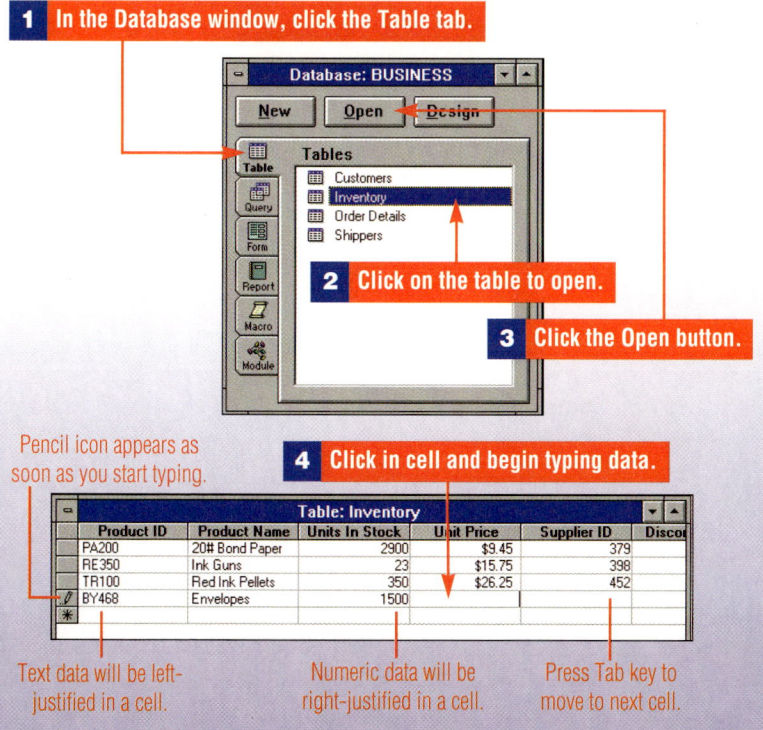

1 In the Database window, click the Table tab.

2 Click on the table to open.

3 Click the Open button.

Pencil icon appears as soon as you start typing.

4 Click in cell and begin typing data.

Product ID	Product Name	Units In Stock	Unit Price	Supplier ID	Disco
PA200	20# Bond Paper	2900	$9.45	379	
RE350	Ink Guns	23	$15.75	398	
TR100	Red Ink Pellets	350	$26.25	452	
BY468	Envelopes	1500			

Text data will be left-justified in a cell.

Numeric data will be right-justified in a cell.

Press Tab key to move to next cell.

139

Tables—Basics: Creating, Maintaining, and Printing

To edit data in a table

1 Select cell or part of cell data to retype.

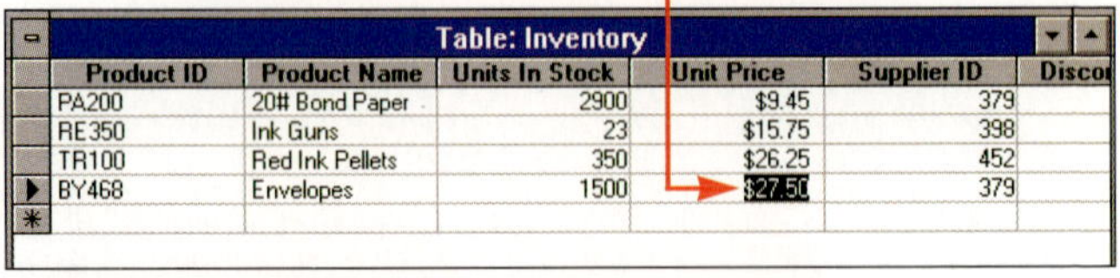

Table: Inventory					
Product ID	Product Name	Units In Stock	Unit Price	Supplier ID	Disco
PA200	20# Bond Paper	2900	$9.45	379	
RE350	Ink Guns	23	$15.75	398	
TR100	Red Ink Pellets	350	$26.25	452	
BY468	Envelopes	1500	$27.50	379	

2 Use Backspace or Del to remove characters.

3 Retype information.

To delete a record from a table

1 Click on the row selector for record to be deleted.

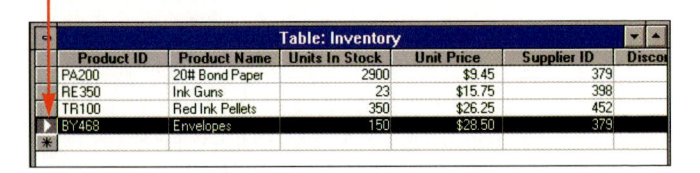

Table: Inventory					
Product ID	Product Name	Units In Stock	Unit Price	Supplier ID	Disco
PA200	20# Bond Paper	2900	$9.45	379	
RE350	Ink Guns	23	$15.75	398	
TR100	Red Ink Pellets	350	$26.25	452	
BY468	Envelopes	150	$28.50	379	

2 Press Del.

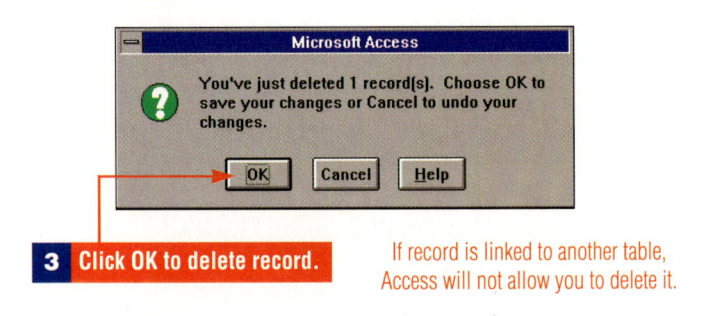

> **Microsoft Access**
>
> You've just deleted 1 record(s). Choose OK to save your changes or Cancel to undo your changes.
>
> [OK] [Cancel] [Help]

3 Click OK to delete record.

If record is linked to another table, Access will not allow you to delete it.

Tables—Basics: Creating, Maintaining, and Printing

To copy data from one cell to another

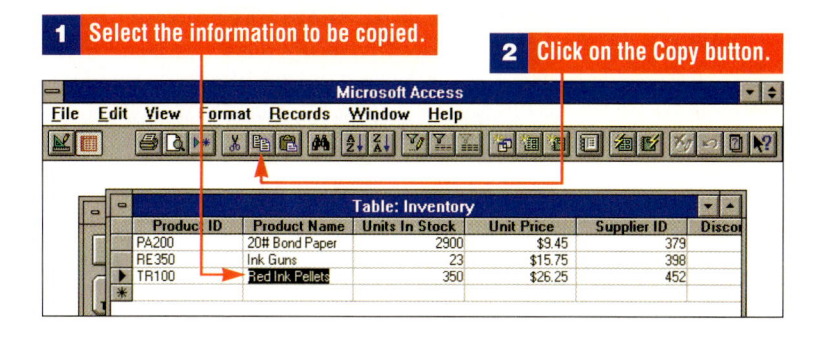

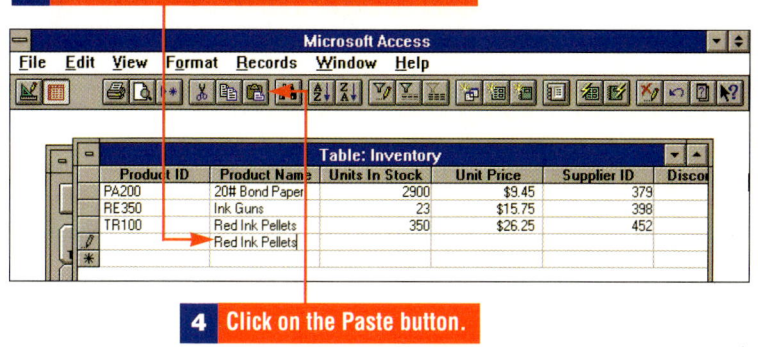

1 Select the information to be copied.

2 Click on the Copy button.

3 Click in the cell where data is to be placed.

4 Click on the Paste button.

To copy an entire record

1 Click on the row selector for the record to be copied.

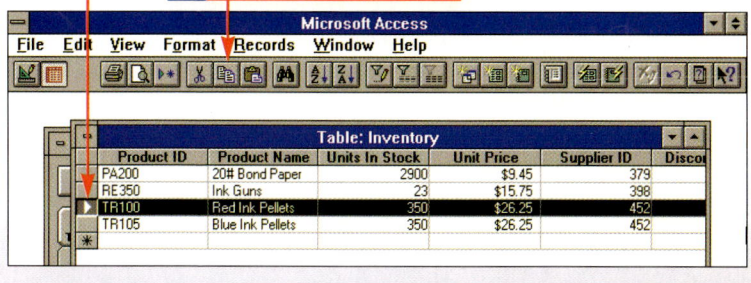

2 Click on the Copy button.

more ▶

Tables—Basics: Creating, Maintaining, and Printing

3 Choose Edit, Paste Append.

New record will be placed at the bottom of the table.

[Microsoft Access Edit menu showing: Can't Undo Ctrl+Z, Undo Current Record Esc, Cut Ctrl+X, Copy Ctrl+C, Paste Ctrl+V, Paste Special..., Paste Append, Delete Del, Select Record, Select All Records Ctrl+A]

Table: Inventory

Product ID	Product Name	Units In Stock	Unit Price	Supplier ID	Disco
PA200	20# Bond Paper	2900	$9.45	379	
RE350	Ink Guns	23	$15.75	398	
TR100	Red Ink Pellets	350	$26.25	452	
TR105	Blue Ink Pellets	350	$26.25	452	
TR110	Green Ink Pellets	350	$26.25	452	

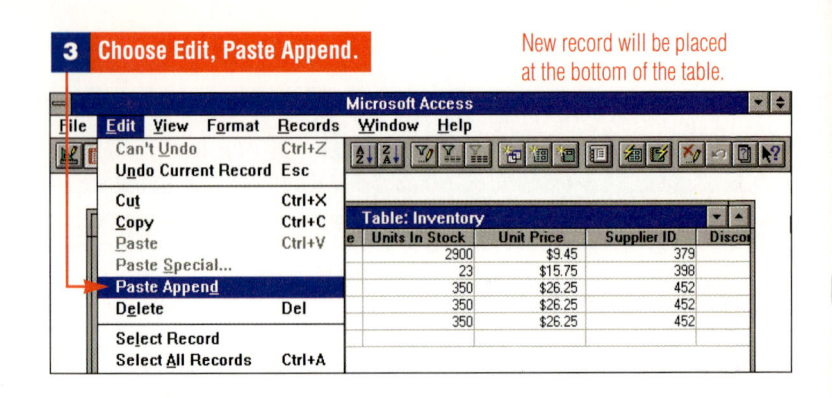

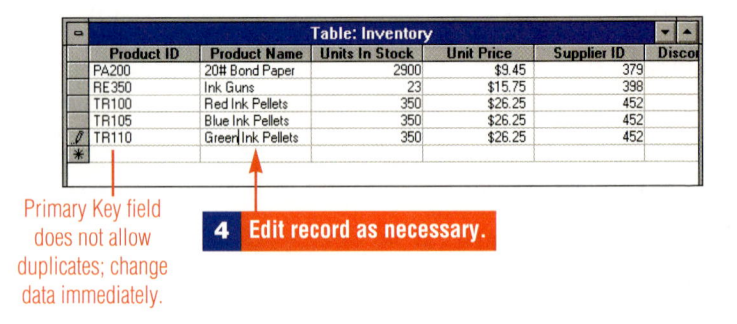

Primary Key field does not allow duplicates; change data immediately.

4 Edit record as necessary.

To use Undo to cancel changes

To undo most recent change to an entire record, click the Undo Current Field/Record button.

To undo most recent change to a cell, click the Undo button.

Printing a Table

When you need a quick printout of a table, and you don't care if the printout appears as it does on-screen, you can print the Datasheet view of a table. If you need to print the data from two tables, need calculations, want only certain records, or want other choices in appearance, you will need to use the report function.

To print an entire table

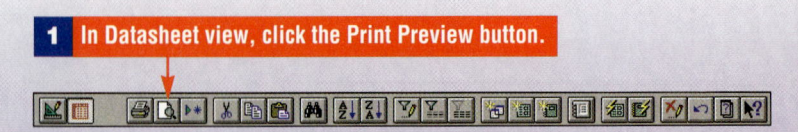

1 In Datasheet view, click the Print Preview button.

Tables—Basics: Creating, Maintaining, and Printing

2 Maximize the window, if necesary.

Table name and print date placed in Header automatically.

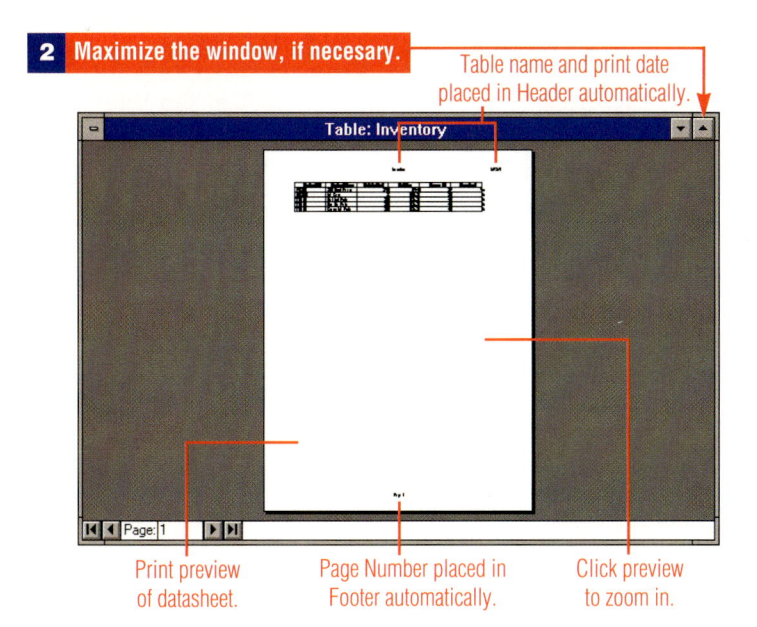

Print preview of datasheet.

Page Number placed in Footer automatically.

Click preview to zoom in.

3 If ready to print, click the Print button.

If you need to change margins or orientation, click Page Setup button.

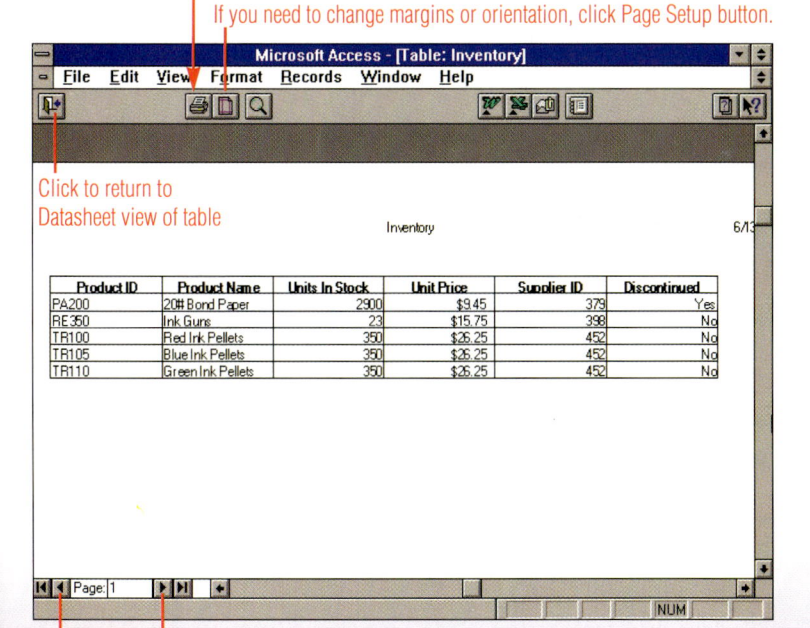

Click to return to Datasheet view of table

Product ID	Product Name	Units In Stock	Unit Price	Supplier ID	Discontinued
PA200	20# Bond Paper	2900	$9.45	379	Yes
RE350	Ink Guns	23	$15.75	398	No
TR100	Red Ink Pellets	350	$26.25	452	No
TR105	Blue Ink Pellets	350	$26.25	452	No
TR110	Green Ink Pellets	350	$26.25	452	No

Move forward or backwards through the pages by clicking on these buttons.

more ▶

143

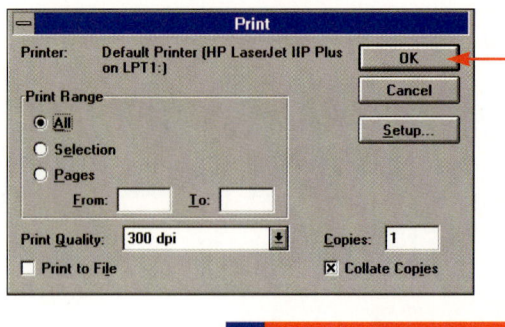

Tables—Basics: Creating, Maintaining, and Printing

4 Click OK after making selections.

To print selected records from a table

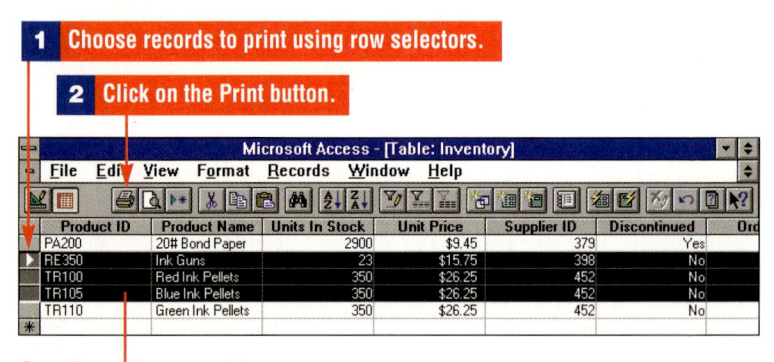

1 Choose records to print using row selectors.

2 Click on the Print button.

Records must be sequential.

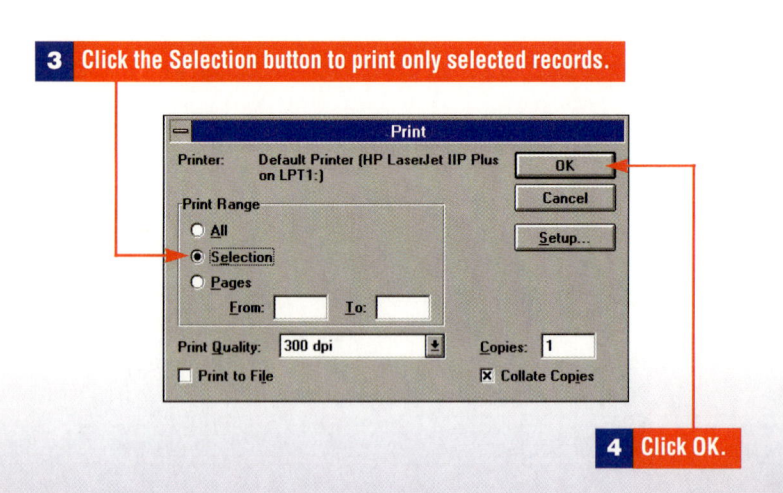

3 Click the Selection button to print only selected records.

4 Click OK.

Tables—Designing: Adding Fields and Data Types

Adding Fields to a Table

Even with the best laid plans, sometimes things need to be changed. Fortunately, Access makes changing the table design easy. You may need to add a field later that you hadn't anticipated. Or maybe some field of data is no longer needed and is just taking up storage space on the computer. You can use Design view of a table to redesign the existing table.

To add fields to a table

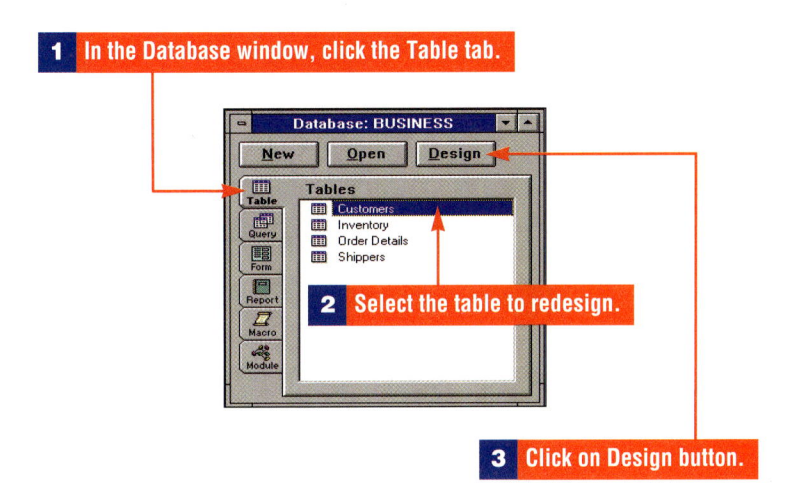

1 In the Database window, click the Table tab.

2 Select the table to redesign.

3 Click on Design button.

4 Click on row selector for new row.

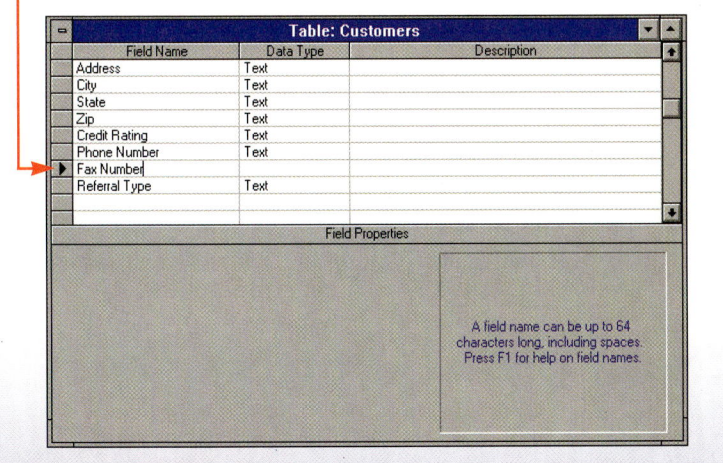

5 Choose Edit, Insert Row.

6 Click in the Field Name cell of the new field row.

7 Press Enter to continue.

more ▶

145

Tables—Designing: Adding Fields and Data Types

8 Click in the Data Type cell.

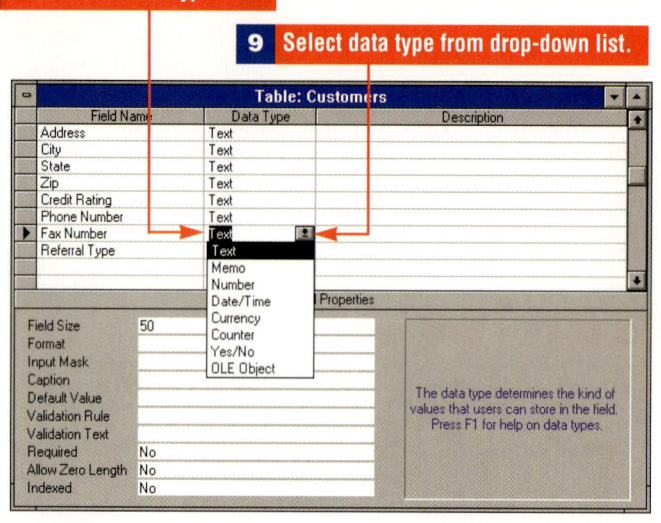

9 Select data type from drop-down list.

10 If desired, click Description field and type description of data in that field.

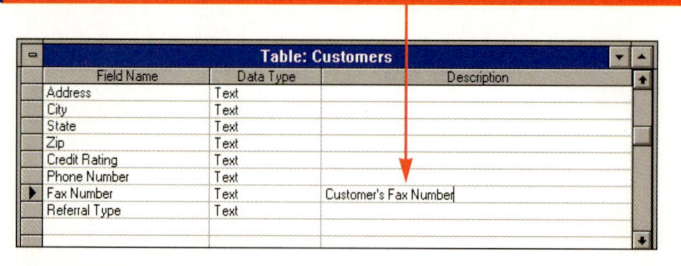

11 Click in the Field Size cell and change to number of characters needed.

12 Click on the Save button to save the design changes.

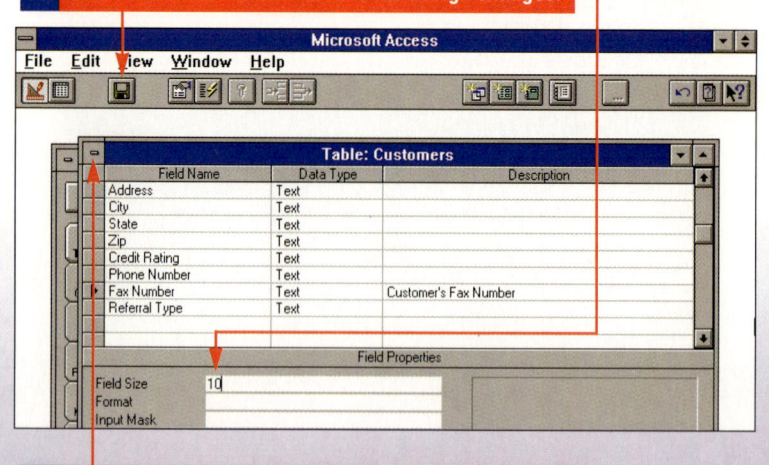

13 Double-click the Control Menu icon to close the table.

Tables—Designing: Adding Fields and Data Types

To delete fields in a table

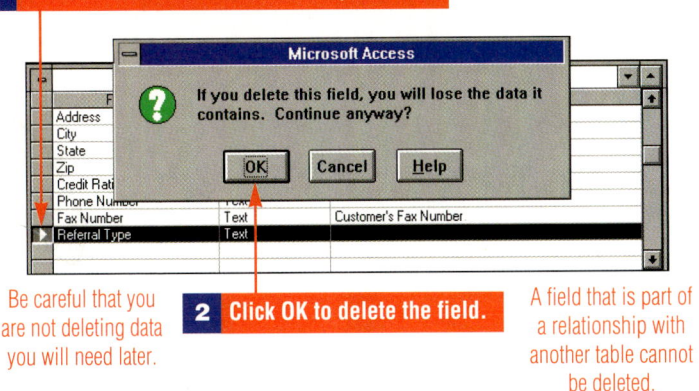

1 Click on row selector of field and press Del.

Be careful that you are not deleting data you will need later.

2 Click OK to delete the field.

A field that is part of a relationship with another table cannot be deleted.

Dialog: "If you delete this field, you will lose the data it contains. Continue anyway?" [OK] [Cancel] [Help]

To rearrange field sequence in a table

1 Click on row selector of field you need to move.

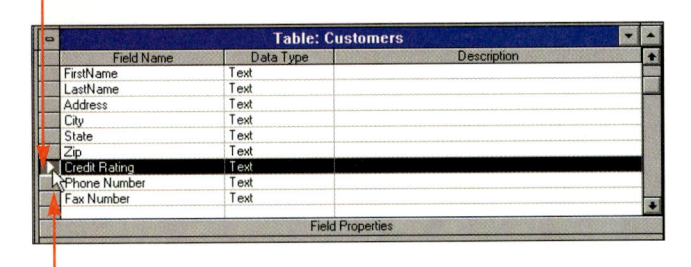

2 Move back to row selector and drag field to new position.

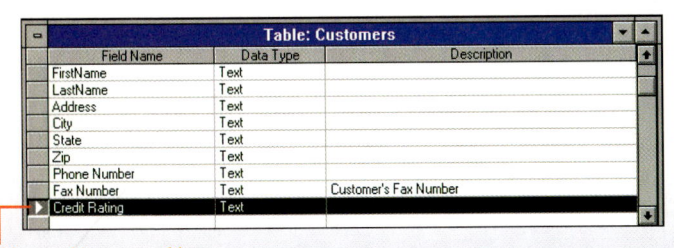

Field moved to new position

Tables—Designing: Adding Fields and Data Types

Setting Data Types

One of the most important pieces of information that you can provide in the design phase of your database is what type of data will go into each field. Data type information is used to help prevent you from entering the wrong information into a field.

1 Click in the Data Type cell.

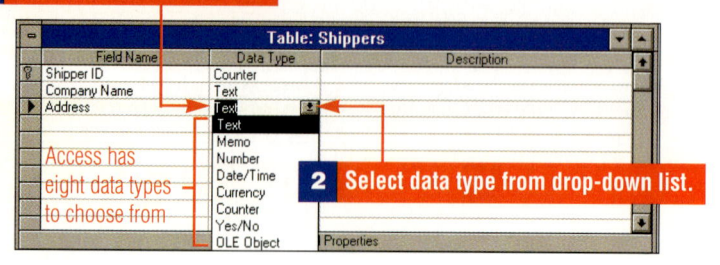

Access has eight data types to choose from

2 Select data type from drop-down list.

Data Types

Text: for any kind of data up to 255 characters

Memo: for larger blocks of data like comments.

Number: set if field is to be used for calculations.

Date/Time: only for dates or time values.

Currency: a number field for money calculations.

Counter: a unique number which can't be changed.

Yes/No: data which is Yes or No, True or False, On or Off.

OLE Object: used to store a picture or sound in the database.

Changing Row and Column Setup

Access makes each column the same width and each row the same height. You may need to change these to make the data easier to view. You might also want to hide a row so that it cannot be viewed. Or you may want to freeze an identifying column so that it does not scroll off the screen as you move through a record.

To change the column width

1 Click the Datasheet View button.

2 Click the right edge of the column heading with the two-way arrow.

3 Drag to the width desired.

This does not affect the size property of the field, just the column in which you are viewing it.

Tables—Designing: Adding Fields and Data Types

To change the widths of multiple columns

1 Select multiple columns by dragging across the column heading.

All selected columns will be the same width.   Columns must be adjacent.

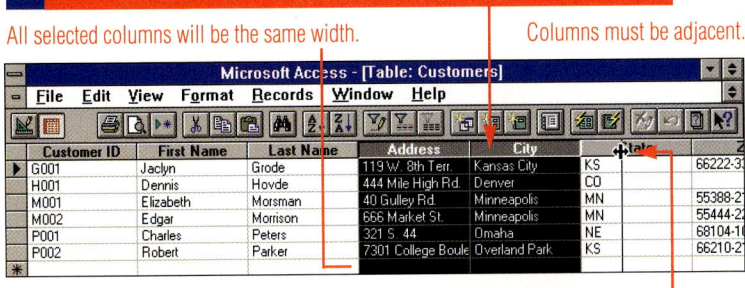

2 Select the right edge of any column heading with the two-way arrow.

3 Drag to the width desired.

To change the row heights

1 Select the bottom edge of any row heading with the two-way arrow.

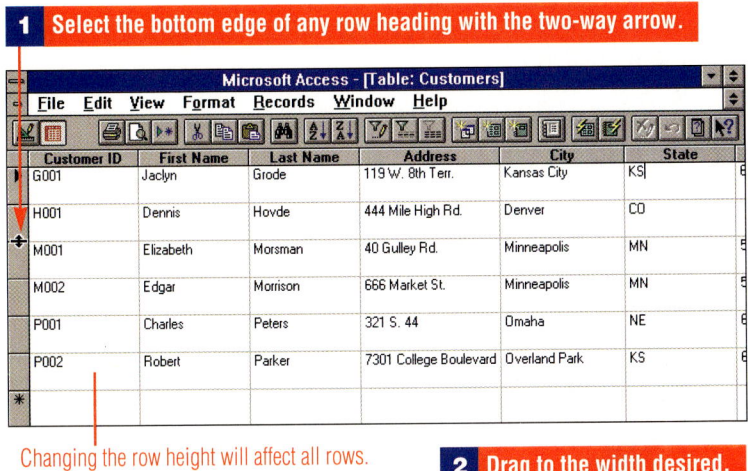

Changing the row height will affect all rows.

2 Drag to the width desired.

To freeze a column

1 Select the columns to be frozen by dragging across the column headings.

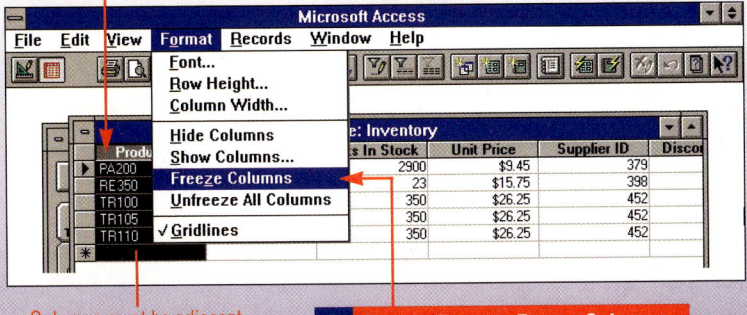

Columns must be adjacent.

2 Choose Format, Freeze Columns.

more ▶

149

Tables—Designing: Adding Fields and Data Types

As you scroll to the right, frozen columns will remain on the screen.

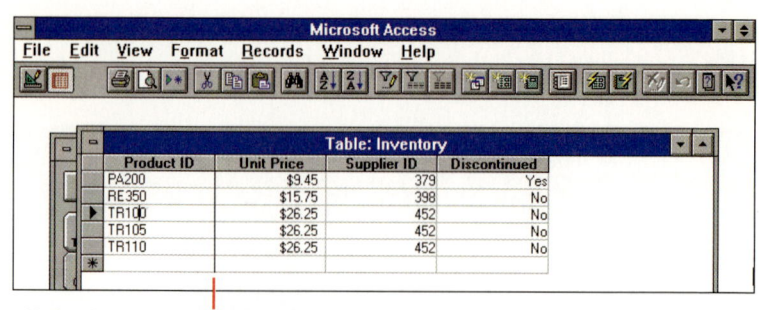

Notice darker line to the right of the frozen columns.

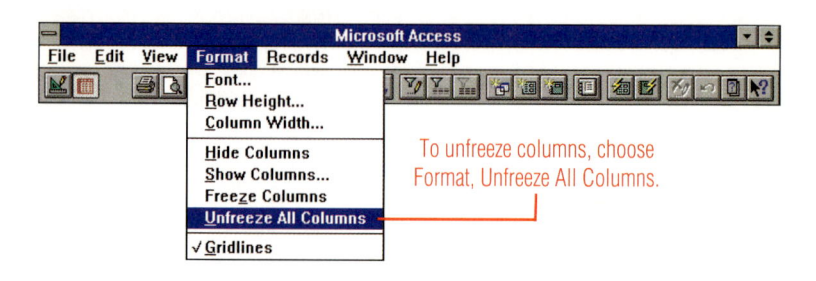

To unfreeze columns, choose Format, Unfreeze All Columns.

To hide a column from view

1 Select the columns to be hidden by clicking the column headings.

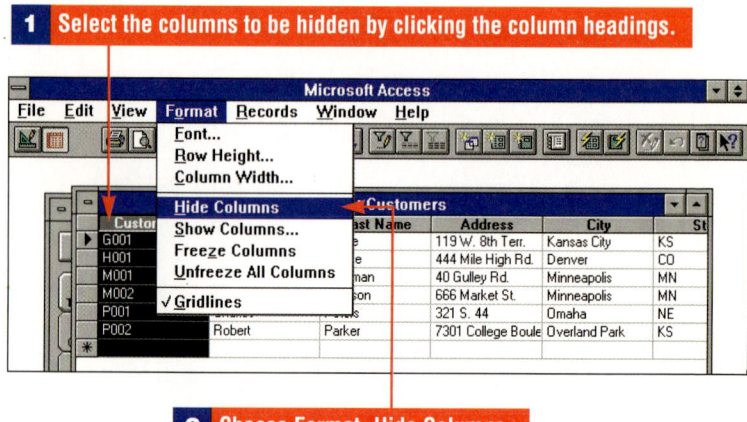

2 Choose Format, Hide Columns.

150

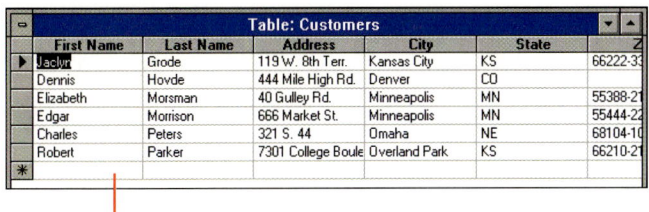

Tables—Designing: Adding Fields and Data Types

	Table: Customers					
	First Name	Last Name	Address	City	State	Z
▶	Jaclyn	Grode	119 W. 8th Terr.	Kansas City	KS	66222-33
	Dennis	Hovde	444 Mile High Rd.	Denver	CO	
	Elizabeth	Morsman	40 Gulley Rd.	Minneapolis	MN	55388-21
	Edgar	Morrison	666 Market St.	Minneapolis	MN	55444-22
	Charles	Peters	321 S. 44	Omaha	NE	68104-10
	Robert	Parker	7301 College Boule	Overland Park	KS	66210-21
*						

Column is not visible on the screen or on printout.

3 To unhide columns, choose Format, Show Columns.

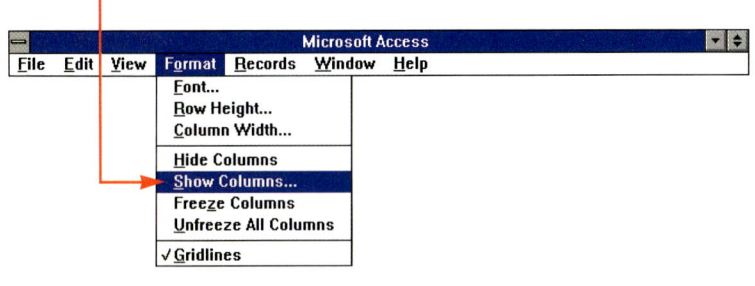

Microsoft Access — File Edit View Format Records Window Help

- Font...
- Row Height...
- Column Width...
- Hide Columns
- Show Columns...
- Freeze Columns
- Unfreeze All Columns
- √ Gridlines

4 Select the field from the Column list box.

Show Columns

Column:
- √ Address
- √ City
- √ Credit Rating
- **Customer ID**
- √ Fax Number
- √ First Name

Hide / Show / Close

5 Click Show.

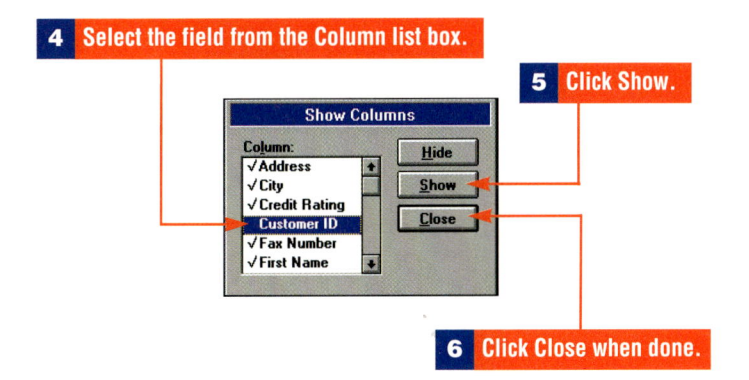

6 Click Close when done.

151

Tables—Field Properties: Sizes, Formats, and Keys

Setting Field Properties

Setting the field properties can help you prevent data entry errors, control how the data is shown, specify default values, and speed up searches. The properties for each field are shown when the cursor is in that field.

To choose field size for text field

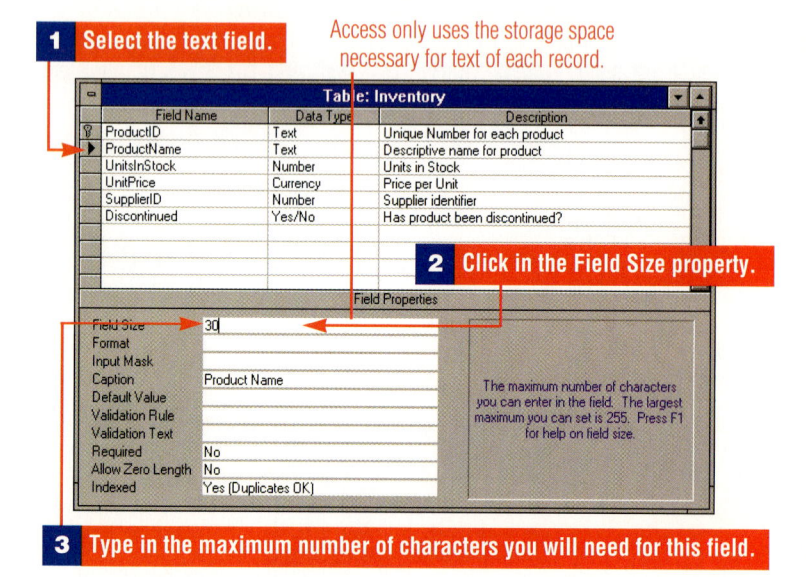

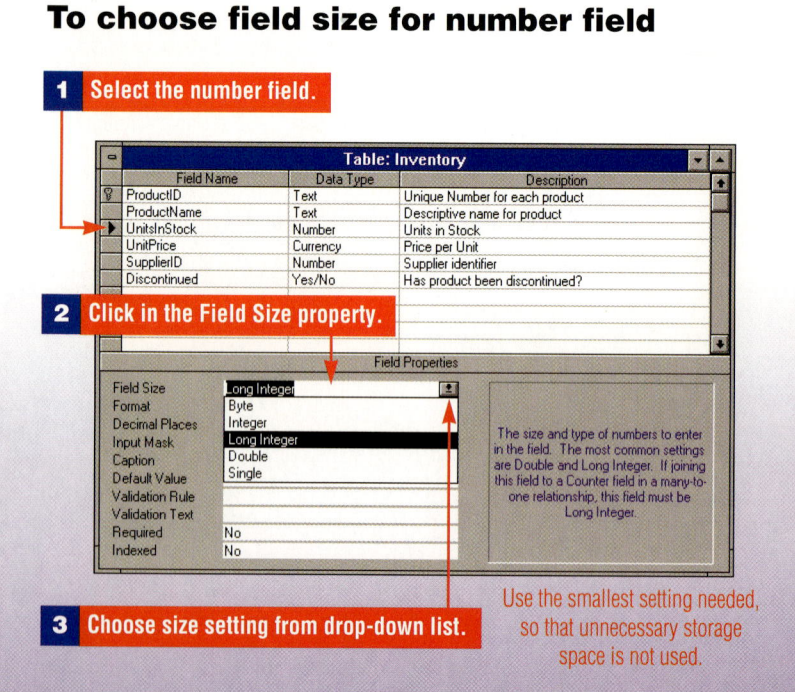

1 Select the text field.

Access only uses the storage space necessary for text of each record.

Table: Inventory

Field Name	Data Type	Description
ProductID	Text	Unique Number for each product
ProductName	Text	Descriptive name for product
UnitsInStock	Number	Units in Stock
UnitPrice	Currency	Price per Unit
SupplierID	Number	Supplier identifier
Discontinued	Yes/No	Has product been discontinued?

2 Click in the Field Size property.

Field Properties

Field Size	30
Format	
Input Mask	
Caption	Product Name
Default Value	
Validation Rule	
Validation Text	
Required	No
Allow Zero Length	No
Indexed	Yes (Duplicates OK)

The maximum number of characters you can enter in the field. The largest maximum you can set is 255. Press F1 for help on field size.

3 Type in the maximum number of characters you will need for this field.

To choose field size for number field

1 Select the number field.

Table: Inventory

Field Name	Data Type	Description
ProductID	Text	Unique Number for each product
ProductName	Text	Descriptive name for product
UnitsInStock	Number	Units in Stock
UnitPrice	Currency	Price per Unit
SupplierID	Number	Supplier identifier
Discontinued	Yes/No	Has product been discontinued?

2 Click in the Field Size property.

Field Properties

Field Size	Long Integer
Format	Byte
Decimal Places	Integer
Input Mask	Long Integer
Caption	Double
Default Value	Single
Validation Rule	
Validation Text	
Required	No
Indexed	No

The size and type of numbers to enter in the field. The most common settings are Double and Long Integer. If joining this field to a Counter field in a many-to-one relationship, this field must be Long Integer.

3 Choose size setting from drop-down list.

Use the smallest setting needed, so that unnecessary storage space is not used.

Tables—Field Properties: Sizes, Formats, and Keys

To set display format for number field

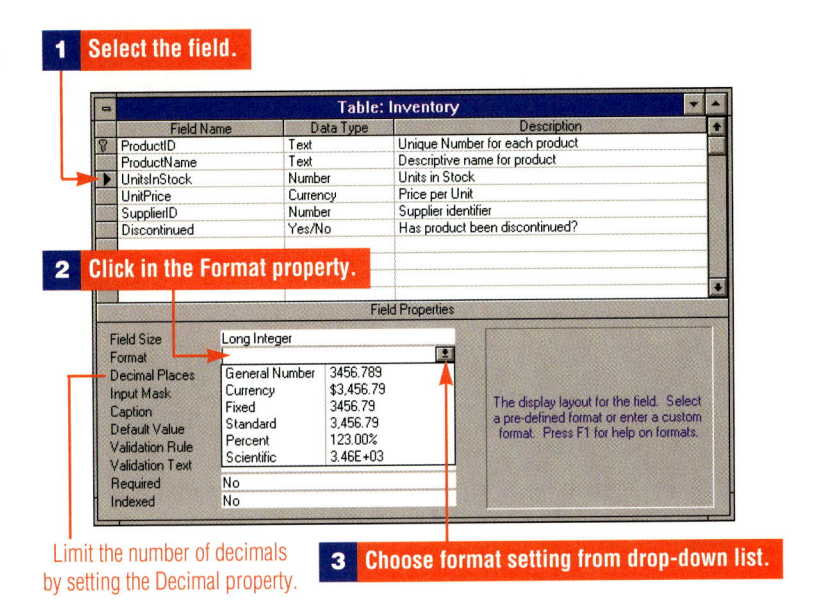

1 Select the field.

2 Click in the Format property.

3 Choose format setting from drop-down list.

Limit the number of decimals by setting the Decimal property.

To create indexed fields for faster sorting

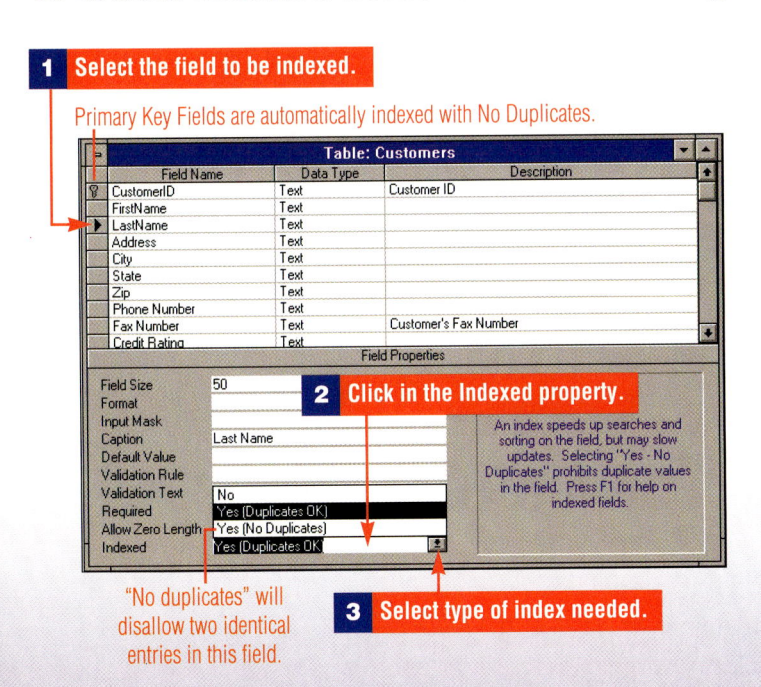

1 Select the field to be indexed.

Primary Key Fields are automatically indexed with No Duplicates.

2 Click in the Indexed property.

3 Select type of index needed.

"No duplicates" will disallow two identical entries in this field.

153

Tables—Field Properties: Sizes, Formats, and Keys

To validate data entry

1 Select the field to have validation rule.

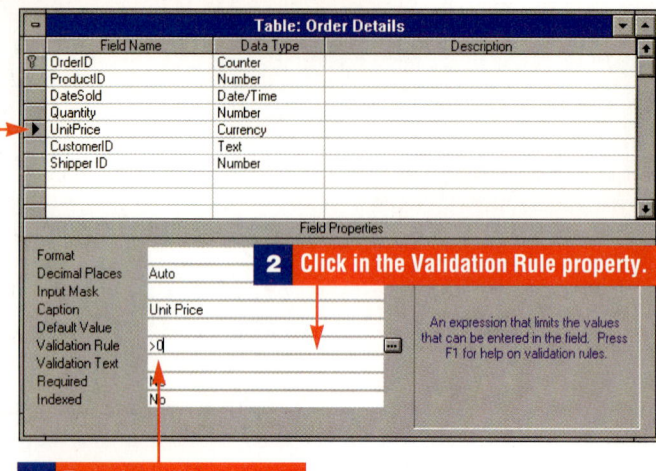

Table: Order Details

Field Name	Data Type	Description
OrderID	Counter	
ProductID	Number	
DateSold	Date/Time	
Quantity	Number	
▶ UnitPrice	Currency	
CustomerID	Text	
Shipper ID	Number	

Field Properties

Format	
Decimal Places	Auto
Input Mask	
Caption	Unit Price
Default Value	
Validation Rule	>0
Validation Text	
Required	No
Indexed	No

2 Click in the Validation Rule property.

An expression that limits the values that can be entered in the field. Press F1 for help on validation rules.

3 Type the validation rule.

4 Click in the Validation Text property.

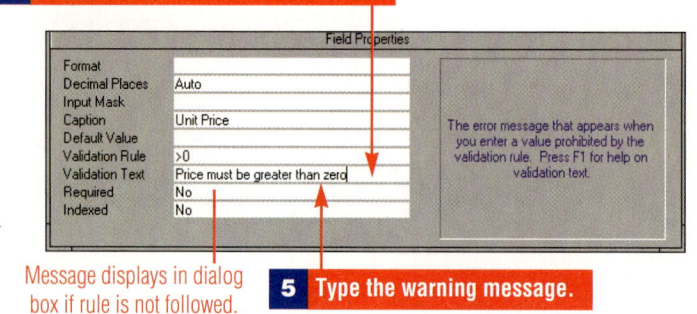

Field Properties

Format	
Decimal Places	Auto
Input Mask	
Caption	Unit Price
Default Value	
Validation Rule	>0
Validation Text	Price must be greater than zero
Required	No
Indexed	No

The error message that appears when you enter a value prohibited by the validation rule. Press F1 for help on validation text.

Message displays in dialog box if rule is not followed.

5 Type the warning message.

To set default values

1 Select the field to have the default value.

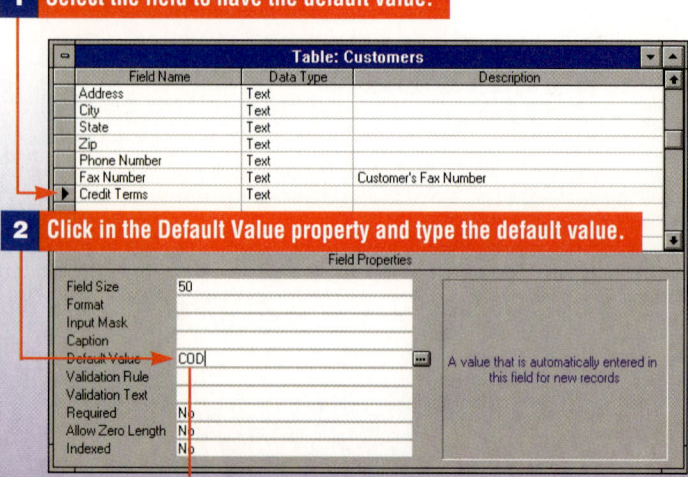

Table: Customers

Field Name	Data Type	Description
Address	Text	
City	Text	
State	Text	
Zip	Text	
Phone Number	Text	
Fax Number	Text	Customer's Fax Number
▶ Credit Terms	Text	

2 Click in the Default Value property and type the default value.

Field Properties

Field Size	50
Format	
Input Mask	
Caption	
Default Value	COD
Validation Rule	
Validation Text	
Required	No
Allow Zero Length	No
Indexed	No

A value that is automatically entered in this field for new records

Value will be automatically entered in this field in each new record.

154

Tables—Field Properties: Sizes, Formats, and Keys

Setting the Primary Key

The primary key in a table uniquely identifies each record to Access. Access then uses the primary key to speed up searching and sorting of records and also for linking two tables in a relationship.

To set a primary key field

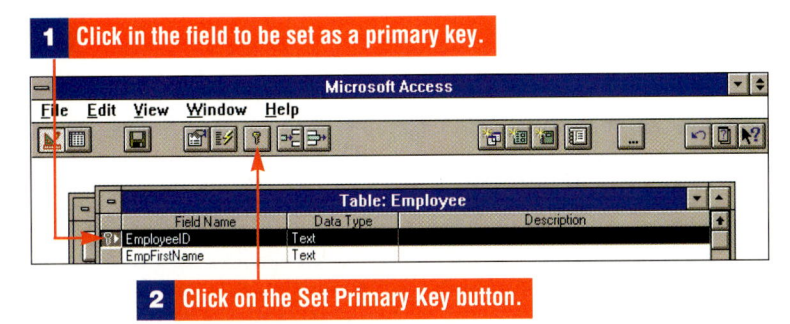

1 Click in the field to be set as a primary key.

2 Click on the Set Primary Key button.

To set multiple primary key fields

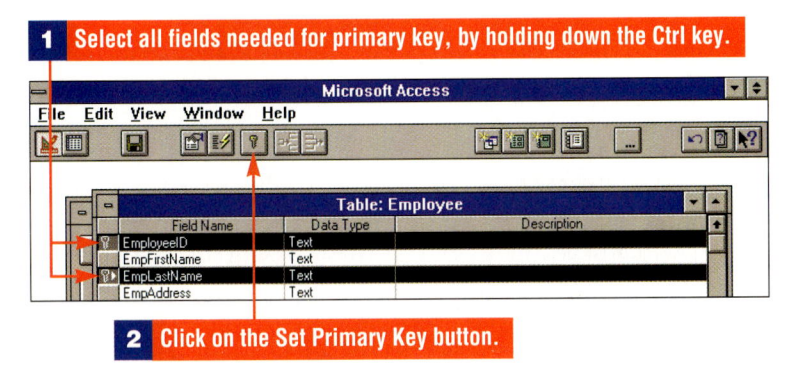

1 Select all fields needed for primary key, by holding down the Ctrl key.

2 Click on the Set Primary Key button.

To remove a primary key

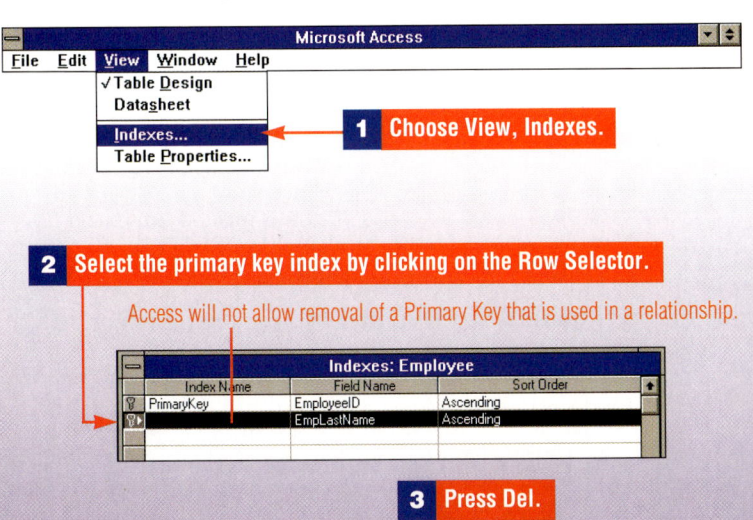

1 Choose View, Indexes.

2 Select the primary key index by clicking on the Row Selector.

Access will not allow removal of a Primary Key that is used in a relationship.

3 Press Del.

155

Index

A
aligning controls to grids, 47
And criteria (queries), 109
Append queries, 81-82
appending
    fields to tables, 145-146
    records, 25
    records to tables, 139
    tables to queries, 105
Archive queries, 78-80
attaching
    external tables, 60-61
    macros to forms, 64-68

B-C
bound fields (forms), 48-49

calculated fields, 39
calculations (queries), 91-92
cell copying, 141
check boxes, 33-34
Close Database command (File menu), 12
closing
    databases, 1-3
    reports, 122
    select queries, 99
colors (text), 44
columns
    changing width in queries, 106
    freezing, 149-150
    hiding, 150-151
    table setup, 148-151
combining fields, 89-90
combo boxes, 31-33
commands
    Edit menu
        Delete, 26
        Paste Append, 141
        Relationships, 110
        Tab Order, 50
    File menu
        Close Database, 12
        Compact Database, 12
        Rename, 15
        Repair Database, 13
    Format menu
        Hide Columns, 150
    Help menu
        Contents, 51
    View menu
        Grid, 47
Compact Database command (File menu), 12
compacting databases, 12
Contents command (Help menu), 51
context-sensitive help, 52
Control Wizards tool, 29
controls
    aligning to grid, 47
    editing, 40-41
    special effects, 45
copying
    cells, 141
    records, 141-142
Counter data type, 148
crosstab queries, 8-11
Cue Cards, 53
Currency data type, 148

D
data types, 148
databases
    attaching external tables, 60-61
    closing, 1-3
    compacting, 12
    creating, 1-3
    importing data, 54-56
    opening, 1-3
    repairing, 13
Date/Time data type, 148
Default Value property, 154
defining query criteria, 107-109
Delete command (Edit menu), 26
Delete queries, 75-77
deleting
    fields from tables, 147
    query fields, 102
    records, 26, 140
    relationships (tables), 112-113
    tables, 138
    tables from queries, 105
Design view, 4
designing forms, 21-24
duplicate records, 87-88

Index

E

Edit menu commands
    Delete, 26
    Paste Append, 141
    Relationships, 110
    Tab Order, 50
editing
    form controls, 40-41
    records, 25-27
    records from tables, 140
    reports, 124-128
    select queries, 102-106
empty fields, 83-84
exporting data, 58-59
expressions, 39, 91-92

F

field properties, 152-154
Field Size property, 152
fields
    appending to tables, 145-146
    combining, 89-90
    custom names in queries, 106
    data types, 148
    deleting from tables, 147
    empty, 83-84
    hiding in queries, 107
    moving in queries, 103
    reports, 126-128
    sequence changes, 147
    see also calculated fields
File menu commands
    Close Database, 12
    Compact Database, 12
    Rename, 15
    Repair Database, 13
filtering records, 18-19
finding
    duplicate records, 87-88
    records, 16-17
footers, 28, 129
Format menu commands
    Hide Columns, 150
Format property, 153
formatting values, 38
forms
    attaching macros, 64-68
    bound fields, 48-49
    boxes, 46
    designing, 21-24
    editing controls, 40-41
    editing records, 25-27
    expressions, 39
    finding records, 17
    footers, 28
    graphics, 49
    graphs, 4-7
    headers, 28
    lines, 45
    opening, 24
    printing, 24-25
    saving, 23
    sizing, 47
    special controls, 29-37
    special effects, 42-47
    subforms, 115-118
    tab entry order, 50
freezing columns, 149-150

G

graphics
    embedding, 49
    in reports, 131-132
graphs, 4-7
Grid command (View menu), 47
grids (aligning controls), 47

H

headers, 28, 129
Help
    Contents command, 51
    context-sensitive, 52
    Cue Cards, 53
    on-line, 51
Hide Columns (Format menu), 150
hiding
    columns, 150-151
    fields in queries, 107

I-J

importing data
    from databases, 54-56
    spreadsheet data, 56-58
Indexed property, 153
inserting query fields, 102

K-L

keyboard shortcuts (macros), 67-68

labels (reports), 127-130
Line tool, 45
list boxes, 29-31

M-N

macros
    attaching to forms, 64-68
    creating, 62
    keyboard shortcuts, 67-68
    running, 64
    saving, 63
mailing labels, 133-135
Make Table queries, 71-74
Memo data type, 148
moving
    controls, 41
    fields in queries, 103
multiple table queries, 113-114

Number data type, 148

Index

O

objects
    renaming, 14-15
    switching, 3
OLE Object data type, 148
on-line help, 51
opening
    databases, 1-3
    forms, 24
    selected queries, 100
    tables, 137
option buttons, 35-37
Or searches, 107-108

P

Palette, 45
parameters (queries), 93-94
Paste Append command
  (Edit menu), 141
primary key, 155
Print dialog box, 24
printing
    forms, 24-25
    records, 144
    reports, 123-124
    selected query results, 101
    tables, 142-144

Q

QBE grid, 100
queries
    Append type, 81-82
    Archive type, 78-80
    crosstab queries, 8-11
    Delete type, 75-77
    duplicate records, 87-88
    empty fields, 83-84
    expressions, 91-92
    Make Table type, 71-74
    multiple table queries,
      113-114
    parameters, 93-94
    select queries, 97-101
    sorting records, 98-99
    summarizing data, 95-96
    Update type, 69-71
    wildcards, 85-86

R

records
    appending, 25, 139
    combining fields, 89-90
    copying, 141-142
    deleting, 26
    deleting from tables, 140
    duplicates, 87-88
    editing, 25-27
    editing from tables, 140
    filtering, 18-19
    finding, 16-17
    primary key, 155
    printing, 144
    sorting, 19-20
Rectangle tool, 46
relationships (tables)
    defining, 110-111
    deleting, 112-113
Relationships command
  (Edit menu), 110
removing primary keys, 155
Rename command (File menu), 15
renaming objects, 14-15
Repair Database command
  (File menu), 13
repairing databases, 13
reports
    closing, 122
    creating, 119-122
    editing, 124-128
    enhancing, 129-130
    graphics, 131-132
    headers/footers, 129
    labels, 130
    Mailing Label Report Wizard,
      133-135
    printing, 123-124
rows (tables), 148-151
running macros, 64

S

saving
    forms, 23
    macros, 62-63
    select queries, 99
    tables, 138
searching data
    empty fields, 83-84
    wildcards, 85-86
select queries
    creating, 97
    defining criteria, 107-109
    dynasets, 104
    editing, 102-106
    hiding fields, 107
    opening, 100
    printing results, 101
    saving, 99
    select query dynasets, 104
    selecting multiple fields, 100
    sorting records, 98
setting field properties, 152-154
sizing
    controls, 41
    forms, 47
sorting records, 19-20, 98-99
special controls (forms)
    check boxes, 33-34
    combo boxes, 31-32
    list boxes, 29-30
    option buttons, 35-37
special effects
    controls, 45
    forms, 42-47

Index

subforms, 115-118
summarizing data (queries), 95-96
switching
    objects, 3
    views, 3

T

tab entry order (forms), 50
Tab Order command (Edit menu), 50
tables
    appending fields, 145-146
    appending to queries, 105
    attaching external tables, 60-61
    column/row setup, 148-151
    deleting, 138
    deleting fields, 147
    deleting from queries, 105
    field sequence, 147
    finding records, 16
    opening, 137
    printing, 142-144
    records
        appending, 139
        copying, 141-142
        deleting, 140
        editing, 140
    relationships
        defining, 110-111
        deleting, 112-113
    saving, 138
    Table Wizard, 136-139
text colors, 44
Text data type, 148

U-V

Update queries, 69-71

Validation Rule property, 154
value formatting, 38
View menu commands
    Grid, 47
views (switching), 3

W-Z

wildcards, 85-86

Yes/No data type, 148